Your Baby
Skin to Skin

Your Baby Skin to Skin

Learn to trust your baby's
instincts in the first year

Rachel Fitz-Desorgher

white
LADDER

Important note

The information in this book is not intended as a substitute for medical advice. Neither the author nor White Ladder can accept any responsibility for any injury, damages or losses suffered as a result of following the information herein.

This first edition published in Great Britain in 2017 by White Ladder, an imprint of Crimson Publishing Ltd, 19–21c Charles Street, Bath BA1 1HX.

British Library Cataloguing in Publication Data
A catalogue record for this book is available from the British Library.

ISBN 978 1 910336 31 1

Typeset by IDSUK (DataConnection) Ltd
Printed and bound in Malta by Gutenberg Press Ltd

Picture credits:
Pages 63, 65, 68, 74 & 133 © Camilla Preece (www.preecepr.co.uk)
Page 132: Balashova Ekaterina/Shutterstock

This book is dedicated to Tim. Why wouldn't it be?

Contents

About the author

Rachel Fitz-Desorgher is a midwife with over 30 years' experience, specialising as an infant feeding consultant, active birth teacher and parenting consultant. Always more interested in the parent–baby relationship than 'catching' babies, Rachel co-created Henley Birthcare, a unique freelance midwifery and doula service offering bespoke care (www.henleybirthcare.com). She teaches other midwives and lectures on infant feeding and tongue-tie. Her approach to feeding, soothing and parenting babies is unique, practical and hugely successful.

Testimonials

'Rachel is an inspirational midwife. The help, advice and support she offered to women at the clinic during pregnancy and beyond helped so many prepare for motherhood and cope well in those early weeks. This book will be essential reading for all new mothers.'

Zita West

'*Your Baby Skin to Skin* is fantastic, like having Rachel round for a cup of tea and a reassuring chat. It gave me confidence as a mother to trust and follow my instincts, feel safe, feel that I could do this and that everything would be alright; that it was normal to just listen to my baby and work together as a little team. Rachel's like the best mother, doula, midwife and best friend all rolled into one.'

Joanna Page

Acknowledgements

That this book ever made it to print is down to the efforts and support of people to whom I am eternally indebted. My wonderful sister, Charlotte, who straightforwardly talked me through my initial anxieties and got me started. My daughter-in-law, Gemma, who took time out from beautifully and instinctively mothering her first baby to read the emerging book, and Hilary, my oldest friend, who read chapters while tearfully waving goodbye to her son as he left home. My gorgeous grandson, Arthur, who arrived just before I started writing. Watching him grow and develop as I wrote kept me focused on the subject and reminded me of so many little things that I had forgotten since my own sons grew up. Milla for her lovely photos of real-life suckling scenarios, and the generous subjects of the photos, Megan and her beautiful baby, Albie. 'The Mitzies': Becky, Jennie, Jules, Linda and Sharon. Inspirational midwives and my treasured friends. Karen, the Henley Birthcare doula, for helping me see things from a different perspective and for being a little voice of calm.

My agent, Jane, who steadfastly helped me get to grips with the reality of writing a book and to navigate around this new world in which I found myself. My editor, Beth, who arduously picked through my writing while leaving my voice untouched and the meaning intact, listened to me ramble for hours and helped me clarify those ramblings into something useful. My publicist, Lyndsey, who took confident control of ensuring that this work reaches its audience and lifted a weight off my shoulders.

Finally, my men! My four sons, Ted, Alasdair, Laurence and Connor. Vibrant, articulate, thoughtful, warm and funny, you inspire me and your stories and energy shine through in this book. And my husband and soulmate, Tim. Without you there would be no book. Quite simply, you help me to believe in myself when my confidence sags. Thank you from the bottom of my heart for walking by my side, day after day.

Introduction

It has taken me 30 years to write this book. Hardly a working day goes by without a couple telling me: 'Everything you say makes perfect sense. Why doesn't anyone else tell us this? You need to write a book!' Then I come home from work and worry to my poor husband about yet another mother and her partner telling me that their baby just doesn't behave as they were led to expect. And HE tells me to write a book.

Why have I held off? I have spent my working life encouraging women to put down the book and look at their baby. To accept that this new bundle is perfectly adapted, through millions of years of evolution, to be perfect at being a baby. That babies have evolved to do all the things that keep them safe. Every day I gently suggest that a woman take notice of her own natural behaviour in response to her baby's cries and stop fighting the urge to suckle, again. To stop ignoring their visceral need to pick up and cuddle – for hours – this baby who simply refuses to go down in the beautiful Moses basket that was chosen with such care.

How can I spend my time telling women to ditch the book and then write one myself? Ultimately, I realised that I was rather a lone voice. Shockingly, although we have all been brought up to understand the theory of evolution, to accept that most innate behaviours serve a purpose and that those behaviours have settled into our DNA over the millennia so that they are at the very heart of being human, I rarely, if ever, hear professionals explaining to parents that their baby is on a survival mission and not set to self-destruct.

Well-meaning carers and family continue to tell exhausted mums that their baby needs to learn night from day, that if a baby is 'well fed' he should settle down to sleep in his crib. That parents should somehow work to mould their little one into the correct shape and that this is 'common sense'. Endless books line the shelves promising to hold the secret to helping babies sleep and I am told, repeatedly, that babies need to get into a routine! Yet the actual experience of parents is that their baby has other ideas. Of course.

To me it has always seemed so obvious that if a certain baby behaviour is universal, there must be a good protective evolutionary reason for its existence. Fighting this evolutionary driver will therefore be fundamentally at odds with the drive to survive. The constant need to suckle, the refusal to be put down from dusk to dawn, the growing stranger anxiety as a baby gets old enough to move are not signs of incompetent parents who need 'how to' lessons from professionals, but inbuilt survival mechanisms with which we interfere at our peril.

As adults we also have reflexes and responses hard-wired into our DNA. We have also evolved to respond in ways that will ensure the survival of our species. So why are parents encouraged to work against these?

By writing this book I hope to reach beyond my own clients. To bring to all parents simple, reassuring messages from across the aeons that what you see in this weird, crazy baby world really is okay.

Taking a primitive story of parenting to explore the evolutionary drivers for why babies and parents behave as they do, I have set about drawing parents' eyes back to our prehistoric beginnings in order to help them see that, instinctively, their baby is right back there in the cave shelter. You may have a twenty-first-century head on your shoulders, but your baby simply does not. In fact, of course, when needs be, your twenty-first-century thinking is forced to take a back seat while your primitive urges and reflexes jump into action and protect you: our natural fear of bumps in the night, for example, makes us sit up, suddenly alert, heart pounding and muscles fired up ready for action. Our modern brain knows that the scuttling, erratic spider can do us no harm, but something deep in our primitive psyche is highly agitated by the random, unpredictable movement and puts us on high alert, ready to run. We may have adapted to a huge degree, but we have barely evolved at all since mankind first stepped onto the world stage.

Of course, we know that evolution is a cruel master. The theory of 'survival of the fittest' allows for a lot of loss along the way of those who are not quite fit enough. But we can have the best of both worlds. Evolution has got us to an astonishing situation. Our branch of the human line is so successful that our numbers have exploded and we can survive in every corner of our planet; and, when glitches do crop up, we have doctors and vaccinations and all manner of great things at our disposal to get things back on track.

A call to parents to keep an eye on their astonishing past in order to understand and work with their baby's instincts and reflexes is not at all at odds with recognising when things have gone awry and there is a need to shout, very loudly, for some lovely twenty-first-century assistance. Modern interventions can help us overcome the problems brought about through our imperfections, but they do not and cannot alter our fundamental drives and urges. They cannot stop us being human.

It is easy to forget in our modern world that, no matter how industrialised our life is now, our survival reflexes and instincts are just the same as when we walked the plains of sub-Saharan Africa, trying to survive through the next 24 hours. After our medicalised births, full of drugs, examinations and interventions, the baby who reaches our arms is no different from the one who reached the waiting arms of our great-great-great-great-grandmothers. Our twenty-first-century baby has exactly the same instinctive, evolutionary drives to survive and takes no account of the modern, noisy world he has entered. He is, fundamentally, back on the plains and in the cave shelter.

So, whatever your circumstances and however your baby entered this world, your baby's instinctive behaviour will be just the same as that of every baby who has come before and every baby who will come after him. Your baby will be just perfect at being a baby and, try as you might, you cannot 'cure' this, no matter how hard you try.

Learn to trust your baby

Your Baby Skin to Skin offers a reassuring and practical journey through parenting in the first year of your baby's life. You are invited to contemplate your baby from a different perspective from the usual – a perspective that can bring calm and solace along with, I hope, many 'light bulb moments' of recognition.

Your Baby Skin to Skin has at its heart the delightful truth that your baby is a highly evolved human, preset instinctively to survive. You can simply step back and let your baby show you how to parent by understanding the inbuilt reflexes and instinctive cues. Instincts are not learned, need no practice and can never be wrong. After all, no one taught us to sneeze, we can't get better at sneezing through practice, and we can't sneeze 'wrong'! Likewise, a newborn baby comes primed to feed, sleep and learn perfectly well and cannot get these things wrong. So, turn down your anxiety and learn from your little instinctive expert.

Inspired by conversations with thousands of parents over 30 years, *Your Baby Skin to Skin* speaks about the real baby before your eyes, not some mythical creature I have yet to meet. It reflects you as a real human parent and releases you from the need to wrestle with your baby's nature and instead allows you to sink naturally together into parenthood.

By stepping back, and accepting that your baby really can't get the business of being a baby wrong, you can finally rid yourself of the need to teach your newborn the basics of life. Parenting can be about watching evolution unfold before your eyes, safe in the knowledge that there are millions of years of natural selection wrapped up in your child and you, ensuring that both of you will respond to each other naturally and correctly.

So don't panic. All is as it should be. Millions of years of evolution have got us here safely and now you can relax and get to know your baby.

A word on breastfeeding, suckling and bottle-feeding

You will notice that a very different language around feeding pervades this book. I have specialised in infant feeding for over 30 years and know just how much words can change our perceptions. I believe it is time that we ditched the word 'breastfeeding' wherever possible and I have done just that, using it as rarely as I can possibly get away with. It is a deeply unhelpful and awkward word.

When it comes to nurturing our babies, women quickly discover that their babies spend hours every day on the breast when they are not hungry. Rather, they are suckling for comfort, or simply enjoying a cuddle. The constant focus on 'feeding' is therefore really very misleading and causes endless worry and confusion as we try to guess how much our baby has 'taken', leading to mums resorting to 'topping up' when there's no need.

Interestingly, other languages do not harp on about 'feeding' but have words that reflect the reality of having our babies on our boobs: the German word is 'Stillen', which means 'to calm', and many other languages have a word that is something like 'to suckle'. How much more reassuring, liberating and accurate. In this book, I'll most commonly refer to 'suckling' your baby.

Rarely do I hear women refer to their breasts as 'breasts', and mothers simply do not speak to their babies about 'breastfeeding': I have yet to hear a mother, gazing down at her sweet open-mouthed baby, saying, 'Hey, sweetheart! Do you want to breastfeed?' I hear, 'Hey, sweetheart! Do you want a bit of booby/booby-milk?' Or, 'Do you want to suckle/snuzzle/smooch/snuggle/soothe/cuddle/cwtch?' Cwtch is a Welsh word with no literal translation into English but is something like 'safe place' or 'cuddle'. Perfect!

In Your Baby Skin to Skin, we learn about the evolutionary behaviour of babies and how, as parents, we can best adapt to our babies' needs and follow their instincts. Inevitably, the evolutionary norm for human nurturing is through suckling, and this is reflected throughout this book. However, I feel passionately that women who choose to, or find that they must, formula-feed their babies reap all the benefits of behaving in an instinctive way, and I hope that the distinct lack of the 'breastfeeding' word (except where no other word seems to fit) will help welcome you to this calmer, more instinctive world. Turn to Chapter 5 to read how I believe you can bottle-feed instinctively, and then, as you read the rest of the book, know that when I use the word 'suckling' I mean you too, snuggled down, baby in arms, bottle of milk in hand, revelling in those warm cuddles ...

Author's note

This book starts with birth and goes right through to the first birthday. Although the chapters can be read out of order, it makes more sense to read from beginning to end, or at least to read all the chapters at some point. Even if you have bought this book some months into your parenting life, it is well worth reading the early chapters to begin with to help you make sense of what has been going on so far and to give you an idea of the overall philosophy of the book. Throughout this book, chapter by chapter, the baby gender switches from girl to boy.

1 Coming into the world: your highly evolved baby

Reaching back ...

Some days ago, in the dark of the late evening, not long after the sun dropped suddenly below the horizon, a young woman, hidden with her group in the protection of some fallen trees, felt the first cramps of her impending labour. Deep in her belly and back, sporadic waves of tension grew and eased. She rested and fidgeted through the night and walked through the days, stopping occasionally to eat, drink and rest. Her companions stayed close but un-interfering, busy as they were with surviving and finding a suitable shelter for the safe birth of their newest member.

Now, a few days later, the cramps gradually strengthen and lengthen, grabbing her attention and driving this primitive woman into herself on waves of endorphins. As bright as the midday sun is, inside the labouring woman's head the lights gently dim as she becomes quieter and more settled. Her companions help her into a cave shelter where she creeps into a hidden corner and hunkers down, moaning with the waves of intense power that flow through her. As the day wears on, her moans grow louder and more urgent. She is up now, swinging her aching hips, pressing her hot brow against the cold stone wall of her shelter and hanging on the shoulders of her strong companion. Oblivious to the world, she is wrapped entirely in her own experience as the hours slip by. And then, just before dusk, the cramps stop and she sleeps for a few delicious moments, listening to the reassuring hum of gentle activity around her.

So, here we are, at the very dawn of time, watching in wonder, and waiting for the moment ...

Suddenly she wakes; urgent, adrenaline-filled eyes; frantically trying to get up on her haunches. Her animation alerts her companions, who now gather around her, supporting her weight and watching as she starts to gasp, grunt and urge. Throwing her head backwards, arching her back and heaving again. And now, the wave gone, she is quiet again, but attentive. And another, bigger urge, greeted with deep, throaty groans and gasps. And another, and another. It seems like forever, and just when she thinks she is nearly ready to birth, another great wave hits and the groans deepen and intensify. A sudden gasp and yelp, and now she is panting quickly with the shock of her baby's head stretching her open with a hot burn that takes the breath out of her body. The woman, numb from the stretch, breathes silently, eyes focused steadily ahead as the moment lingers. Now the urge builds again, the stretching starts and then, emerging slowly, glistening and dark amid the wolf-like howling, a head! The baby faces away from its mother and she looks straight ahead, searching for reassurance, almost oblivious now to the nature of her work and suddenly freed for a moment or two from the stretch that made white stars dance in her eyes.

Perfectly still, silent, the baby stays, head out, aware of the cool air around its face; its body held tight inside the mother for a minute before gently turning slightly to bring it around ready to emerge. As the baby's body turns inside, the head turns too, bringing the tiny, scrunched-up face into view. Dark skin, bubbles of fluid popping at the mouth, eyes clenched tightly shut. The mother, wondering what is emerging from her body, reaches down between her legs and the baby, in response to its mother's touch, wiggles its head ever so slightly. Shocked, the mother draws her hands away, holding sticky fingers star-like in the air as the urgent, irresistible force of another wave rocks her body one last time.

On a wave of shiny fluid, accompanied by one long, low hum, like a grateful hymn, the baby finally slips out onto the dusty floor. The baby, lying like a landed fish between its stunned mother's legs, takes a minute to respond. Its mother, likewise, does not grab her new baby but looks lost, unaware momentarily of quite what has happened ...

... and now she moves. Hands between her legs, searching, finding her baby and drawing it up into her hot arms, close to her, where she can just see in the dim light of her cave shelter that she has a girl! The thick cord hanging warmly from her daughter's belly to her own vagina, swollen and numb from the birth, still pulses with blood from the placenta, giving her baby enough time to adjust to her new surroundings. Even now, as she starts to cough and cry little bubbly cries, her heart is adjusting to the outside world: her circulation changing as some valves snap shut for good, no longer needed now the baby is starting to breathe for herself and her once-blue body gradually infuses to pink.

Now the new baby smells her mother, like a small, snuffly hedgehog in the dark. Her own amniotic fluid, still warm and slippery, mingling with her mother's salty sweat. Her tongue creeps out and licks around, catching the sea tang of her mother that seals her forever-knowledge of who she must cling to now. And at the same time another sound, another sniff but this one long and deep, like the drawing in of the first sweet air of morning. The newly birthed mother, sticky hands steadying her slippery eel-child on her chest, is smelling her too! She doesn't even know she is doing it. As the mother–baby dance begins, the new cries build and the mother, high on a sea of adrenaline, learns it by heart in that moment. From now on this cry will touch her in a way that no other baby cry has before. It is part of her own experience, a reminder of the struggle she endured to bring this baby into the world. While others may be able to turn away from this noise, it will reach straight into her heart and wrench at it until she responds. Even now, that first cry is working its purpose: mother shushes gently into her daughter's ear, muttering and gently calling to her. No words are needed; the gentle sounds, mixed with the warm smells and touch, signal that this is sanctuary.

Before the cord has even broken, or the afterbirth pushed out, the baby bobs her head about. Her hands opening and shutting, grasping at flesh, legs pushing over and over against her mother's damp, warm skin, gradually moving her just-landed body, heavy in the air, over her mother's chest. She snuffles and bobs, cries and then falls quietly asleep for a moment before moving again. Creeping around, more sniffing, more bobbing. Slowly, so slowly, she searches for something of which she has no knowledge, no understanding: a nipple. Her eyes opening in the easy natural just-light, she is drawn to an area of contrast, where the flesh of her mother's chest meets the darker flesh of her areola. No smudged line here but a sharp edge between light and dark, with an oily aroma that tickles her nose. Irresistible. She reaches her destination and then falls asleep, again! Her tired but alert mother wraps her close, beginning to feel cramping again, softer now than the sweeping torrents an hour ago but intense all the same and accompanied by a deep fullness in her vagina. Moaning and grasping at her baby, she lurches upright and the warm afterbirth falls heavily out. Another second of surprise before she turns back to her baby, who has, while her mother's attention was away, drawn herself onto the dark nipple, pulling it deep into her mouth.

Adrenaline seeps slowly away as endorphins start to flood mother and her newborn. Eyes glazing over, the mother starts to shiver and her companions, having broken the cord and hidden the placenta from the attention of hunting animals, cover the pair and snuggle up nearby for added safety and warmth. The mother and baby, the two who have had the hardest of days, are wide awake, staring at each other in the dark, eyes just inches apart.

We will leave our primitive family now and check back over the next few days and months. They remind us of where we came from and can help us find our own way back to a calmer, more settled experience of parenting in the modern world.

Highly evolved beings

Modern life can look so very different from that of the earliest humans, but some things bind us together in our experience. Birthing our babies, bringing a new human being into the world, discovering our child for the first time – none of this has changed in thousands of years. Whatever our birth story, we are linked, down through generations as far back as you care to go, to our mothers, grandmothers, great-grandmothers, to our friends and to strangers. All highly evolved to carry, birth and protect the next generation. This simple knowledge is at the heart of this book: you and your baby are the highly evolved survivors carrying, silently and without realising it, the knowledge and ability to do just fine.

Of course, life is complex and noisy and we can't get away from that – the house must be cleaned, the car must be serviced, the shopping must be done, not to mention the emails that must be answered! But mothering our baby does not need to be scary or fraught with impractical rules. If we can relax and watch evolution at play, just as we did at the start of this book, we will realise that, far from needing to learn how to wrestle our newborn into some book-invented, regulated creature to save us from creating 'a rod for our own back', our babies will show us perfectly well what it is to be a new human and we can find ourselves just simply responding. So scary to think that we should know what to do and how to teach this tiny being; how much more fascinating and creative to watch and learn from evolution itself.

The newborn baby comes with its very own set of reflexes and instincts. These have evolved over many millions of years for one purpose: to ensure survival. The process has been long and messy: in order to achieve the survival of the fittest, a lot of weaker babies have been lost along the way. This is how evolution works, whether we like it or not. Other branches of early human-like creatures became extinct while our own branch strengthened and evolved, gradually getting better and better at adapting and surviving. We developed language and social structures, discovered fire and cooking, and learned to control our environment. The rate of the explosion of knowledge and learning has been staggering and we now feel so sophisticated and smart in comparison to our early ancestors that we forget that they had to survive against the odds.

But our babies are not sophisticated like us. They are not able in their earliest weeks to make choices and conscious efforts to control their environment. They are little bundles of instinct, without critical thinking, and this is what keeps them safe.

Birthing instincts

Think about a modern birthing scene. Mentally strip away the buzzers, lights and machines, and you will see the same things happening as in our primitive birth scenario – even in assisted births, many of these things still happen, and are noticed by the midwife, although the mother may not be aware of them. Here we'll examine what the mother may experience while birthing her baby naturally, and what she may feel without any epidural. If you had an assisted delivery or Caesarean, you may feel robbed of some of the emotions and experiences described above and grieve for them even though your baby was born safe and healthy. Turn to the Q&A section of this chapter for more on how you can capture some moments of wonder, whatever your birth story.

The importance of healthy bacteria

The baby comes into the world, generally speaking, facing downwards towards the mother's bottom, the mother's pelvis perfectly shaped to help this happen. This may seem odd – why wouldn't the baby want to see the mother looking down at her? But in our ancient scenario the gloom would make seeing a face difficult, and babies cannot clearly see that far (they have no need to). There is something more important right now to the baby's long-term survival: this baby is just about to exit a bug-free environment and enter a very dirty world! Facing the mother's bottom as she emerges into the world allows the baby's face to pick up some of the mother's gut bacteria, which contain, among the bad bugs, millions of helpful bacteria that will get into the baby and help her to fight infection during the early days. What a brilliant adaptation!

But when I first trained as a midwife, and we knew a baby was about to be born, we swabbed the mother's thighs, perineum and vulva enthusiastically with cleaning solutions. Apart from the horrible sensation of having cold water sloshed onto your delicate vulva during maximum stretch and concentration, it prevented the baby from naturally obtaining protection from the very bugs we were swilling away. Somehow we thought that babies should be born into a sterile environment because they lack the ability to fight off bugs, when all the while, had we looked back, we would have seen that evolution had taken care of things for us. Happily, we stopped doing this many years ago, but women still worry about being dirty when they give birth. Of course, the very first labour contractions usually cause the bowels to empty well before birth and, in any case, once the baby's head is in the pelvis there really isn't room for anything else, so pooing is not an issue. The vagina and perineum, uncleansed with chemicals, provide just the right number, type and mix of bugs to ensure that the infant skin and gut become quickly inhabited and protected.

How the 'ouch' of crowning protects us and baby

The birth of the head takes a few contractions, giving the vagina time to stretch gently and the baby to adjust to the different pressures in the outside world compared with those in the tightest parts of the pelvis. A very fast birth of the head can cause your baby to have quite a headache, so evolution has sorted that out for us and slowed it all down just enough. Women have huge, irresistible reflexes and urges and, in most cases, need absolutely no guidance as to how to birth their babies. Over millions of years we have evolved to do just the right things to keep us and our little ones safe. So, as the head crowns, the intense heat of the stretch causes women to gasp and pant, which, in turn, slows down the speed at which the head slides out, thereby adding protection. Women will often instinctively bring their thighs together a little as they gasp and pant away the burning and stretching and this adds further protection by steadying the pace and taking a little of the stretch off the perineum, protecting against tearing. We may wish the head could pop out double-quick, but this wouldn't serve us or our baby at all well. And then, at the exact second the head finally births, as women we know for absolute certain exactly how a champagne bottle feels when the cork has been popped! The relief is instant, the contraction has ended, there are a couple of minutes before the next contraction comes, and, awash with adrenaline, women often start to talk animatedly, telling the midwife about their latest shopping trip while seemingly unaware that there is a baby's head just outside their vagina! A midwife's job is often a surreal one.

With the next contraction the baby's body slithers out with a sudden rush, which can leave us feeling as if 'someone has just walked over our grave'. More often than not, the midwife either quickly puts the warm newborn on the mother's chest or suggests that the mother 'takes' the baby herself. Sometimes a midwife will let the baby lie, just as in primitive times, between the newly birthed mother's thighs. In any event, the same thing happens if you watch closely: there is a brief moment during which the mother is not quite ready or aware. She doesn't immediately engage with her baby but time stops for a tiny moment, a brief suspension in the clatter and noise. And then she shakes back to reality, takes her baby onto her chest and the sniffing begins!

The first moments

Hello, little one

Mothers with their still-damp babies inhale deeply, instinctively drinking in the musky aroma of their own and their baby's body scents mingled together like some heady cocktail. The high adrenaline level in both mother and baby heightens their awareness and ensures that these aromas fix themselves deep in the memory for good. Even months (and, indeed, years) after birth, a lot of time is spent burying their noses into each other. As sweet and cosy as this is, it is simply evolution's solution to ensuring that a mother and baby know each other in the dark of the night and that we protect our own genetic inheritors first. Remembering this with the birth of my first son, I now find myself sniffing my grandson in a way I have never felt moved to do with the thousands of babies I have held as a midwife. I already know his unique smell and can sometimes catch it on myself days after seeing him.

Much the same happens with our baby's first cries: they move us so deeply to respond. Even if we have never held a baby before, we hear those first tiny gasps and mewls and immediately our hands begin to hold, stroke, soothe and reassure. We slide our baby up closer to our face so we can whisper in the tiny ear and kiss the top of the warm head. The higher female voice being particularly 'keyed into' the baby brain, and the mother being particularly triggered by her new baby's cries, further two-way bonding and imprinting takes place. Our baby will take a little while to learn the unique look of our face but she already recognises the particular pattern and timbre of our voice from those months listening to the bath-like echoes inside the womb. During the early hours and days, the imprinting deepens and mothers find that they are completely unable to relax until they have responded to their baby's cry and feel anxious when separated for even a very short time. Seeing someone else holding their crying newborn will make them twitchy and want to grab her back – this complete stranger already a permanent resident in their heart.

Skin to skin

In the modern birthing environment, irrespective of how the baby made her entrance, women are encouraged to enjoy prolonged 'skin to skin' time. While this automatically happened before the times of mass hospitalisation, during the 1970s and early 1980s increased medicalisation led to babies being bathed, dressed and wrapped before their exhausted mothers got to hold them after birth. By the mid-1980s 'bonding' was all the rage, and women today still ask me if the purpose of skin to skin is to help them 'bond'. In fact, those early hours when we hold our peach-soft, damp, warm bundles of wiggliness on our chests do very much more than give us sniffing time. This is where our baby picks up more friendly bacteria – the ones that we have bred to protect us from the harmful bacteria we always carry on our bodies. So our babies gain protection from the bugs in our homes that we have as our companions.

More than that, skin to skin time calms the baby's autonomic nervous system (ANS) right down. We will look at the ANS in great detail in Chapter 6 as it tells us so much about why our babies behave in the seemingly random way that they do, but, for now, you just need to know that skin to skin helps the newly birthed baby to stay soothed, warm and safe while you get to know each other.

Falling asleep during skin to skin

The first in-bed snuggles after birth are often wide-awake ones as the adrenaline that has permeated labour hasn't quite left yet. Women describe staring at their newborn baby for hours; right through the first night together. However, you might fall asleep on a sea of endorphins and oxytocin and you need to keep yourself and baby safe. The safest way to share a bed in these early hours is skin to skin together under light covers (a hospital sheet and light blanket or, if you are at home, your summer duvet tucked under your elbow); don't swaddle your baby in your bed and don't try to limit her movement with pillows or tucked-in sheets; if she is tucked up with you like this, she really doesn't need a hat!

If you are bottle-feeding formula milk or are still under the influence of labour drugs, sleeping with your baby is not safe: set an alarm on your phone to buzz after about 20–30 minutes so that, if you do nod off despite your best efforts to stay awake, you will wake pretty soon and can put your baby in a crib. If you are at home, make sure that, if your partner is in bed with you, he or she is not drunk or been smoking.

Your baby, after the first post-birth suckling, may sleep for many hours and, as long as she is kept skin to skin, she will wake when she is ready to suck again.

The first suckling

Even more soothing and calming for both the baby and her mother is suckling. As we saw with our primitive baby, soon after birth, the newborn, lying seemingly helpless on the mother's chest, starts to instinctively search out the breast. She isn't thinking 'I must feed. I must get just the right amount of calories and nutrients inside me and I know just the restaurant!' She is driven by primitive reflexes and instincts, just like every other mammal on the planet, to search out a nipple. Smells, sensations and sounds guide her and, to begin with, her journey can seem pretty random. But as she gets closer to the breast, that enticing contrast line of the paler flesh against the dark edge of the areola catches her eye, and off she heads to explore. Women often tell me when I ask about the first feed that 'It just happened. I don't really remember doing anything. She just knew what to do!' Of course. It would be a bit of a disaster if our primitive mother, having just given birth in the dark shadows of a cave shelter and still needing to urge out the afterbirth, had to know how to get a baby onto her breast to suckle. This baby can't wait around for her mother to practise and learn! In any case, in the low light, the mother wouldn't be able to see much of what she is doing. The baby can do this solo.

We are really not very far away from this early setting, and evolutionary adaptation ensures that the newborn baby, driven by a rooting reflex, hunts and snuffles around until eventually she finds the nipple and, after prolonged head-bobbing and faffing, draws it in and sucks. Endorphins and oxytocin flood the bloodstream of baby and mother, taking away the pain of birth and replacing it with a deep relaxation and sense of calm, at the same time causing contractions in the womb to push out the placenta and stop bleeding. With the surge of the placenta contraction, the mother pulls her baby in even closer to her chest and the baby suckles more deeply. There is no need to help or direct the baby and, in fact, she will manage better without you doing very much except what comes instinctively. She has a reflex and, just like with a sneeze, if you try to help it might get a bit messy!

Love at first sight?

You may believe you should feel an immediate thunderbolt of love hit you when you first hold your baby or, at the very least, soon afterwards.

And if you don't, you feel there's something wrong with you. In my experience, although many women do indeed feel an almighty rush of instant love at first sight when they first hold their baby, for just as many it isn't like that at all. So, whereas for some new mothers it feels like an instant recognition of a loved one – 'Oh my word, it's YOU! I know you and I love you so much!' – it may feel more like 'Oh! Hello. Not quite sure what you mean to me. I'm pretty puzzled right now because I really don't know you at all. Who ARE you?' or 'Hmm, you're a funny-looking thing! Not at all what I expected and I'm not sure quite how much I care about you at the moment. We will have to muddle this one through ...'

Sometimes relationships simply take a while to grow, settle and cement. Don't worry. Your baby doesn't have any of these worries and doesn't care about your musings (she doesn't know that you feel somewhat ambivalent right now). She will show you how to mother her. As you feed her and change her over the days and weeks, her smells and her cries and her searching eyes will gradually, bit by bit, get inside you if you just relax into what it is rather than try to wrestle it into what you think it should be.

Partner ponderings

Although much of this book inevitably looks at mothering, there is plenty here for partners. Reading through the whole of the chapters will help you understand things from your child's mother's perspective. It may help you make sense of her hormonal swaying, explaining why it can seem at times as if the woman you love has left the building and been replaced by a stranger! At the end of each chapter is a bit just for you, to help you discover your unique and essential role, different as it is from that of the mother. Your baby needs you and your partner to be different; this helps build flexibility of thinking and, in time, your baby will grow into a child who understands how to respond differently to different people and how to understand emotional needs.

Labour

During the labour, birth and first minutes and hours, the birthing woman is completely awash with hormones, driven by instinct and reflexes to bring your child into the world safely. It can be tough to watch. Many partners feel a huge need to rescue their birthing woman, but there is no need. She needs your strong emotional and physical support right now. She is quite safe with the midwives and doctors, who are expertly trained to do the checking and rescuing (if necessary) so that you can be the support coach to the marathon runner. There is nothing to be scared of – this is simply what we look like and sound like when we are pushing another human being into the universe. It's fine to ask the midwife if you can watch your baby's head emerging if you like (and if your partner doesn't need you to hold her while she pushes) and even to ask if you can help hold the baby as she is finally born. If all is going well, most midwives are only too happy to guide your hands. Or simply watch in awe ...

The first moments after birth

The moments immediately after the birth can be very emotionally mixed. Exhaustion and adrenaline mix with shock and delight. Watch now as your partner and baby, driven by deep, deep instinct, discover each other. This is millions of years of evolution laid out in front of you. Your baby may take some time to splutter and cry. Don't worry: the cord is still pulsing with oxygen and nutrients and she will breathe for herself in good time. Stay close to your partner and just be. It's fine to join in the gentle touching and see if you can smell those musky tones too. Your partner's senses are massively heightened to ensure that she knows her baby's scent from the very beginning. It won't be so strong for you – you have a different role to play – but you may still be surprised by how powerful and good your baby's smell seems.

Refreshments all round

When your baby starts to nuzzle and move around, searching for a nipple, don't feel moved to help: the baby needs to take her own journey in her own time and her mother will ease her up without even thinking. Instead, while your baby sets about foraging, you can ensure that your partner is warm and nourished. Pop a warm blanket or towel over the snuggling couple first and then sort out refreshments. If she needs stitches, you will need to wait until these are done before sorting out food. You and your partner will need plenty to eat and drink, but keep it light. Tea and toast is the usual order of the day. A very newly birthed woman will tell you that the first cup of tea after birth is the best cup of tea in her life, EVER. If you make it, rather than leaving the job to the care assistant, you will get the kudos!

Skin to skin

Eventually, after much nuzzling and eating and chatter, most women want a shower and you can finally enjoy some skin to skin time with your baby. Simply put a hat on her head, pop a nappy on her bottom and then carefully pass her down your T-shirt until just the top of her head is sticking out. That's it! Talk to your baby, kiss her, smell her, or just grin and enjoy this moment in silence.

Questions and answers

At the end of each chapter you will find some answers to common questions. Tempting though it is to turn straight to this bit, do read the full chapter as it will help you make sense of the answers.

Caesarean

I am expecting to give birth/have given birth by Caesarean. How can I ensure that my baby gets the friendly bugs?

Evolution has done a brilliant job of getting us here, but there are still inevitable glitches (that kind of defines how evolution works), and medical interventions give us a means to survive these glitches. Caesarean-section (C-section) births, forceps births, ventouse births, epidurals: these things have dramatically improved the lives of thousands of mothers and babies. For our part, we need to look at the bits that science can't yet replicate and add those in as best we can. Compared with vaginally born babies, those born by C-section are more likely to develop asthma, allergies, eczema, type 1 diabetes and coeliac disease. They are more likely to be hospitalised with tummy bugs. While some of this may be attributable to the greater likelihood of these babies having formula milk in the early days, there is growing interest in the notion that babies born by C-section just don't get the good bacteria from the mum's vagina and perineum. Some maternity units now encourage mothers expecting to birth by C-section to collect friendly bugs from their vagina before the operation. If your unit does not suggest this to you, just put it in your birth plan and do this:

1. Take a piece of gauze soaked in normal sterile saline.

2. Fold it up like a tampon with lots of surface area and insert it into your vagina.

3. Leave for one hour, remove just prior to surgery, and keep it in a sterile container (the sort of pot you collected your pee in during pregnancy is ideal).

4. Immediately after birth, simply wipe the swab around the baby's mouth, face, then the rest of the body.

Note: It is really important that you only do this if you are free from HIV, thrush, group B strep and any STDs or other infections. If you are in any doubt, talk to your midwife.

Also, as soon as possible, get skin to skin and stay that way with your baby for as long as possible (hours rather than minutes and days rather than hours). There is no reason not to have skin to skin while the post-op stitching is completed unless you are too poorly to hold your baby. If this is the case, your partner could, if possible, hold your baby skin to skin on you or on themselves. Let your baby suckle freely and don't feel the need to bathe her for at least 24 hours. If possible, take your own linen into hospital and don't be obsessive about you or your partner forever cleaning yourselves! Just normal daily hygiene is enough.

Special care

My baby is in special care! What now?

It is incredibly stressful for everyone when a baby is too poorly or too little to be with her parents and needs the care of a neonatal unit. The newly birthed mother can feel split between gratitude that her baby is in safe hands and misery that her arms ache to cuddle her newborn. This upset can be made even worse when a baby has to stay in hospital after the mother has been discharged. There is clear evidence of the benefits of 'comfort holding' and 'kangaroo care' for premature and sick infants. 'Comfort holding' can simply mean touching your baby with your warm hands on her skin while she rests in an incubator and it can also extend to sitting quietly in a chair with her lying on your chest. This can bring rest and comfort to mother (or partner) and baby and is also a simple, effective way of reducing stress for both when a baby has to have unpleasant procedures like blood tests.

'Kangaroo care' is an extension of 'comfort holding' and involves putting the baby, skin to skin, with mum or her partner, either sitting in a chair or while they are getting on with something else. Skin to skin has a profound positive impact on babies and their parents, settling breathing and heart rate, reducing stress and managing temperature as well as helping to protect against infection by increasing the baby's exposure to those essential friendly bugs. As well as getting close to your baby as often as possible, express your milk for her. Even tiny amounts of your milk will protect her from infection and soothe her emotionally. Read Chapter 4 on feeding for tips on expressing.

Skin to skin during stitching

I want to keep my baby skin to skin for a long time after birth, but what if I need stitches?

If we hold and suckle our babies while we are stitched, have blood taken, have 'after pains' or are upset for any reason, we get a rush of endorphins and oxytocin and feel better! Most women simply don't ask or, if a midwife says 'I need to give you a few stitches – maybe your partner would like to hold baby?', they don't say 'Thank you very much for your kind offer, but I'd like to keep her with me and feed her.' If needs be, get your partner to hold your baby against your bare skin. Of course, your partner could hold the baby skin to skin with themselves, but the ideal is for baby to get your friendly bugs first and foremost. There will be ample time ahead for cuddles with others.

No skin to skin

I had a vaginal birth but didn't get any skin to skin time.
Is it too late?

No! Things just don't always go according to plan. We have tougher labours and births than anticipated, we have drugs that make us and our babies sleepy, we are too sore or poorly just after birth to hold our babies ... so don't panic! Just let the dust settle and then catch up. Strip your baby down to her nappy, strip yourself off down to your pants and get snuggling. Don't worry about your baby getting cold: as long as her tummy is skin to skin with yours and her back is snuggled under your blanket, you will share your body heat and smells with her. Explore her with your hands and face or simply relax and read a good book – you will quickly discover that those 'lost' moments just after birth will fade.

2 The first day: a new dawn

Reaching back ...

The night after the birth of her daughter the mother rests, eyes wide open and glinting in the moonlight, which has just crept into the opening of her temporary sanctuary; her quiet murmurings are barely audible over the rustling in the trees; her downy soft baby is nuzzled in and sleeping. Once or twice the baby stirs and turns in the darkness towards the ever-present nipple to suckle. There's no crying.

The new mother barely understands what happened just a few hours earlier, a dream-like memory already replacing the visceral experience. The smell and feel of her newborn are already settling into her bones, her adrenaline draining out of her and oxytocin oozing into her like warm syrup. The only reminder of her feat is a dragging pull in the pit of her stomach, accompanied by an occasional warm flow of blood with each deep suckle of her child.

In the first few days the mother drifts between sleep and tending, rousing every few hours to eat and to leave her bed to stretch her legs and pee. During the bright, warm sunshine hours, the baby sleeps for a few minutes in her mother's bed, initially unaware of her absence, but, before long, a slight wiggling and gentle wailing start and the mother quickly returns to her baby. In the gloomier hours of the late afternoon the baby, seemingly aware of the impending cold and night danger, wiggles and wails the minute her mother strays and so this still-learning mother simply bundles her daughter onto her breast, wrapped in the warmth of her hands, and keeps her there wherever she goes. Her companions busy themselves gathering food to share and keep her company in the *evenings with stories of the outside world. In a day or two this primitive, nomadic family must be rested and strong enough to journey.*

The first night together

The first night with your new baby can feel quite surreal. Your tender, aching body feels empty and winded, and the hormone soup in which you find yourself spins you about from shock and disbelief to wonder and elation. Somewhere in there you also manage to squeeze a wide-eyed buzziness alongside utter exhaustion. Gazing at your baby, you are not yet sure quite who he looks like, or how you feel about him, and what, together, you will become.

In our modern world, surrounded by images of how mothering should look, we read endless stories about how it feels to be a new mum. We have our own idea of exactly what we should expect from this moment forward and have simply forgotten how sweet it is to let a relationship just evolve. We forget that our most precious relationships took an age to emerge into their current sense and that they will continue to change and develop over the coming years.

At home on the first post-birth night, mothers can drift in and out of a calm, quiet dozing. In the modern maternity hospital there may be phones ringing, other babies crying, doctors running. Not quite the romantic and languid start to your new relationship that you might have hoped for. Your baby will, of course, be delightfully oblivious to all the night-time shenanigans if he is kept close to you. All he understands right now is you and him, together. He experiences you as himself and vice versa: me–mummy.

When you are next to him he simply feels complete. Any distance will be unsettling for him; if he is sound asleep he won't notice for a little while but, as soon as he stirs, he will quickly start to panic. He will feel incomplete. This is just as it is supposed to be: a deep knotting together to keep you both settled and safe. Your newborn baby may sleep for many hours that first night if kept close to you, and not cry out at all.

Early suckling

Amid the snoozing and the gazing, baby will occasionally nuzzle around and, if he doesn't bang into a nipple as he bobbles about, he will give a cry. If you gently pull him close in to your body, and, with the light being too dim to clearly see what is happening, let your baby muddle around for some time, bobbing, ducking and snuffling, he will eventually find what he craves and snuggle on to suck. He may not even feed but just be reassured that he could if he wanted to. Some newborns get onto the breast at dusk that first night and stay there all night, utterly drunk on the delights of being safely snuggled. He is not thinking about food: he doesn't really think at all in the same way as we do – he just *is* and he just *does* and he is just right. This is your little one, uninhibited, unrefined and utterly, utterly human.

The deep pull of suckling shocks most women the first few times they feel it. A tight, strong tugging that stretches out the flesh amid a glowing sensation like friction burn. In a few more days, hormonal changes will reduce this tight feeling as well as the hot friction feel. The baby suckles with eyes tightly shut, driven as always by a primeval urge. After a few moments the drawing stops and a light fluttering takes over: little butterfly shudders of the lips and tongue before he stops altogether and nods off for a while, still securely on the breast, before rousing and starting the deep draws again. During this drawing, you may well feel a deep dragging in your tummy. This is your womb being drawn down and is called 'after pains'. They can be mild with first babies but pretty hefty with subsequent babies and they show that your body is working normally to recover. You will feel a flow of blood at the same time; if you are at all worried about whether or not it is too much, just ask your midwife and she will check.

Many babies seem to sleep quite deeply on and off during suckling, the endorphin-rich milk washing over their senses and bringing the ultimate sense of safety and soothing. That milk-drunk look caused by the endorphins makes your baby snooze; he stops taking the endorphin-rich milk as he dozes and so, before long, the endorphins wear off and he starts drawing again with those deep pulls massaging your breast and speaking directly to your primitive brain, ensuring that you produce just the right amount of just the right hormones to make just the right amount of milk for him. The very tiniest amounts of thick, ultra-concentrated colostrum (your very own gold dust) trickles slowly into your baby's mouth. Barely more than a few drops are drawn out and this perfectly matches his needs for now. As his needs change, so will your milk. Day by day the amount of colostrum you make will increase if your baby is free to suckle and 'speak' to your sensitive body.

Sleeping together

Rooming in

You may have already noticed that if you and your baby are apart it feels as if your arm is missing. We know that babies who are 'roomed in' (sleep in the same room as their mother) are less prone to sudden infant death syndrome (SIDS – otherwise known as cot death), and infections, and that babies and mums settle better. We also know that babies who are free to suckle human milk as often as they wish through the night in the early months are even better protected against SIDS and infection, gain more weight and cry less.

It shouldn't really surprise us that the more we behave like the young primitive mother, the more settled and the less difficult our highly evolved baby will be.

Sleeping in a cot

When putting your baby down to sleep in a cot, crib, moses basket or co-sleeping crib, pop him on his back and with his feet right down to the bottom of the cot. This is the safest way to place your baby in order to reduce the likelihood of SIDS. He will not choke if he is sick in his sleep, so don't worry. It is not recommended to use sleep nests or to swaddle a baby as these can make baby too warm and limit movement in a way that may put him at risk. Ensure your baby has the right amount of clothing for the room temperature and then cover him in the cot with blankets tucked in loosely and no higher than his shoulders. Do not ever use a duvet or pillows in a baby's cot when the baby under the age of one. Remember that SIDS is very rare so don't over-worry; just be sensible and follow these simple guidelines.

Safe co-sleeping

Mothers have evolved alongside their babies and find that they are more relaxed and better rested when their baby is close, skin to skin, and naturally drop off to sleep when their baby is next to them. We have known about this phenomenon for many, many years.

- In order to stay safe in bed with your baby if you find yourself drifting off, make sure your baby is undressed except for a nappy. Lie on your side facing each other (women do this naturally anyway); bring your baby under your covers (opt for a nice cosy sheet or a lightweight duvet as you will be hormonally hot) and hook it under your elbow so that your baby's head isn't wrapped.
- There's no need to tuck the sheet in around the baby or under the mattress to 'stop baby falling out'; this can inhibit his safe movements. Likewise, he should be just below the level of your nipple so that he isn't sharing your pillow.
- If you are worried about safe co-sleeping with your baby, set an alarm clock to buzz gently in about half an hour and, if your little one is sound asleep when you wake, dress him gently in a warm blanket and put him in a crib pushed right up against your side of the bed. There is every chance that he will wake again and you will need to bring him in for another soothe and suckle. This is not a sign of a problem. That is simply how evolution works to keep your baby safe during the hours of darkness.
- If you had strong labour drugs and are still pretty sleepy from them, ask your midwife for a bassinet to clip onto your bedside so that your baby can be very close to you without the risk of overlying that can be a factor in the presence of drug use.

It is only safe to sleep in this way if you and your baby are well and you are breastfeeding your baby, as the suckling hormones affect our sleep behaviour and keep baby safe. Exclusively expressing is okay too. Do not try this if you are bottle-feeding infant feeding formula.

You will find lots of information and practical tips on feeding and soothing later in the book, but just for now, try to be led by your baby first and foremost while you rest and recover and watch.

Trusting your primitive instincts

Some hours ago you drank in your baby's scent and heard his first cry and from now on, whether you like it or not, your baby's cry will pull you to him with a fierceness that might puzzle you. You will find yourself constantly looking at him, unable to settle to read or watch TV with any degree of concentration. This little baby whom you are not yet sure that you love has a peculiar pull on you that you cannot resist. Those familiar words ringing in your ears – 'You'll make a rod for your own back'; 'He's already winding you around his little finger'; 'He's just trying it on ...' – that permeate our modern society can make you question the reality of your own feelings.

Whenever I talk to new mums, they tell me: 'I know I should be putting him down in his cot but I can't bear to hear him cry!' So I tell them that it is only natural to feel awful when their baby cries. They are always hugely relieved: they have tried to fight something that they were never meant to fight, ignore the un-ignorable, somehow cheat millions of years of evolution. Go ahead and try to ignore your baby – you will fail, thank goodness!

Getting mobile

If all is deemed well with you and baby, you may find yourself encouraged to go home after just six hours. If you or your baby are not well or are not keen to leave the hospital just yet, you will stay a while longer. In any event, there will be an expectation that you get up and get on. Take it very easy: you will be experiencing fairly heavy blood loss and your perineum will feel tender, swollen and quite 'draggy'. You might feel a little breathless after minimal effort and as if you have been in a wrestling match! Take simple painkillers such as paracetamol and ibuprofen if you are happy to do so. Taken in the normal recommended dose, they are safe for you and your milk.

While it is good to get up periodically and potter about a bit – having a shower, stretching your legs, going to the loo and so on – remember that your body has been through nine months of change and is now suddenly and dramatically changing gear physically, hormonally and emotionally. If you do not rest properly now, you might regret it in a few days. Besides which, your baby has only just emerged and needs you close by all the time if he is not to panic. There will be plenty of time for getting out of the house and showing baby off to the neighbours. Now is the time to stay in your pyjamas or, better still, naked and have a few days in bed. This isn't being lazy; but even if it is, does that matter?

It makes good sense to wriggle your feet and legs periodically to prevent clots and to stretch properly when you get up to use the loo, but then get back to the important business of lazing in bed with your baby.

Baby pee and poo

At some point in the first 24 hours your baby will pee and poo. The first pee is often dark orange and almost powdery, like brick dust. This is hyper-concentrated urine and called 'urates'. Your baby is only getting tiny amounts of fluid from you for the first day or two and this is exactly as it should be. Your baby's stomach is the same size as his fist and cannot stretch yet so just a few millilitres of highly concentrated colostrum is what is needed to keep his blood sugar stable. The kidneys respond to this minimal fluid intake by making the urine very strong so that your baby can conserve water.

The poo, on the other hand, is plentiful and black – your baby's nappy can resemble America's first oil strikes in the 1860s. The black tarry poo, called meconium, is made up of stuff that your baby swallowed while inside you: body cells, soft baby hair, mucus, amniotic fluid, bile and water. It sticks like mud to a blanket!

If you want to avoid the first nappy that you or your partner changes being a confidence-busting nightmare and using up a wheelbarrow's worth of cotton wool, smear a good layer of petroleum jelly over your baby's bottom, upper thighs and perineum/vulva/testicles *before* putting on the very first nappy (before the first poo). You will almost certainly know that your baby has pooed by the black ooze appearing at the leg of the nappy. Don't panic. Get a good handful of cotton wool and soak it in warm water; wring it out slightly so that it is still nice and wet and then grab a clean nappy as you head back towards your bed. Sit on your bed comfortably, pop a soft towel on your lap and lie your baby on that so that he feels secure. Now undo the nappy tabs and use the nappy itself to wipe off the worst of the slime. Using the warm, wet cotton wool, you will find that the meconium slides off quite easily, assisted by the petroleum jelly you put on earlier. Meconium doesn't smell, which is just as well because you will need both hands to do this nappy and so you won't have a spare one to hold your nose.

Exploring your new baby

With your baby's nappy off and the squirming bundle lying warm on a towel on your lap, this is the perfect time to enjoy discovering him. If he starts to cry, you can bring his mouth close to your nipple by raising him on your lap and he will nuzzle in, the noise will stop and you can carry on exploring.

Genitals

Before you pop a clean nappy on, take a look at the perineum. Notice how the genitals are swollen. This is entirely normal and due to your hormones crossing the placenta. If you have a little boy, someone will check in the first day or two to ensure that his tiny balls are down in the sack. They will move up and down but, as long as they can come down, all is well. The foreskin is attached by a film of skin underneath and so you can't, and shouldn't, pull it back. When you change a nappy, just clean what you can see with warm water and leave the foreskin where it is. Over the first four or five years, the foreskin will gradually lose its tethering and your son will then be ready to learn how to wash under it himself.

The vulva of a new baby girl is deeply coloured, full, and may exude a thick white mucus. This is normal, healthy and does not need vigorous cleaning. Be very careful when you wash her at nappy changing as the vulva is very sensitive. Remember that, just like yours, a little girl's body is self-cleaning and self-regulating and so her normal vaginal loss will be quite healthy and needs no concern from you at all. As your hormones leave your baby, the genitals will shrink down somewhat. Note that if your baby was born in the breech position, the genitals will be very swollen and possibly quite bruised. This will settle down but it can look quite shocking if you are not expecting it. If there is anything about your baby's genitals that looks 'wrong' to you, tell the midwife or doctor so that they can check with you and explain properly what you are looking at.

Changes in skin colour

All babies are born a somewhat different colour from their parents. White, Asian, Afro-Caribbean and mixed race babies tend to be born very pink and then, over the next week or two, their colour changes to more of a yellowish-pink and then to a slightly paler shade that is closer to what will be their own natural colour.

The deeper colour that you see right now is caused by the extra oxygen-carrying haemoglobin in your baby's blood. When your baby was inside you, he needed lots of extra haemoglobin to make up for the fact that he could only get his oxygen second-hand, from you, across the placenta.

There was also quite a bit of your baby's blood going around the placenta when he was inside you. One of the reasons why professionals are now encouraged, whenever possible, to leave the umbilical cord alone until it stops pulsating naturally is to allow the baby to get most of 'his' blood back from the placenta before the cord is cut.

So the baby whose cord is left to pulsate can be even pinker than a baby whose cord is cut immediately after birth. If your baby was born in water and the umbilical cord was allowed to pulsate freely, your baby may be pinker still because the warmth of the water can slow down the normal process by which blood stops flowing in the cord after birth. A 'water baby' may be the pinkest on the ward! In the next chapter we will look at, and wonder why, the colour in the skin changes during the first week or two.

An African baby has dark skin at birth but may still be paler than his parents. The pink flush of extra haemoglobin may not be visible and the colour changes may not be so easy to see. Any yellow colouring (jaundice) can be seen in the whites of the eyes and your midwife will check for this.

Any baby of colour may have a bluish 'bruise' across his bottom and/or legs. This is called a 'mongolian blue spot' and is an area of pigmentation. As your baby's skin darkens to what will be his genetically inherited colour, the blue spot will fade. It doesn't always disappear completely. Make sure that any mongolian blue spot is recorded in his baby notes to prevent staff thinking that your baby has been hurt.

Vernix

If your baby was born before about 40 weeks, he may have a few blobs of thick, white cream on his skin. If he hasn't, gently lift up his arms and you will see some in his armpits. He will almost certainly have some inside his groin too. This is called vernix and is made up of fatty oils and the same downy baby hair that is found in meconium. It keeps the baby's skin peachy soft, protects against infection and also helped him ease down your birth canal during labour. It doesn't need to be washed off but will absorb naturally over the next day or so. It has a particular smell, which is similar to the amniotic water that surrounded him inside you, and this smell gets a bit stronger over the days that it hangs around. It hasn't gone bad, so don't worry.

Body hair

Run your hands over your baby: can you feel the soft down? If your baby has a lot of dark hair or was born a little early, you might see quite dark hair on the arms and back. The downy baby hair is called lanugo, which means 'wool'. The lanugo helps to keep the vernix stuck to the skin and therefore helps to protect against infection. Also it seems to ease birth, adding another slippery layer like the vernix. Enjoy the feel and look of it while it lasts: it will be gone in a few days.

Belly button

Look at the belly button. Will it be an 'inny' or an 'outy'? Probably an 'inny', but not just yet. Right now you will be able to see the gristly cut end of the umbilical cord. The cord will be dry by tomorrow and turning blacker and shrivelled by the day after that. The blood vessels that carried blood all the way into your baby's body will also shrivel and, in time, become ligaments. Expect the cord stump to become very black and begin to be pretty smelly just before it falls off. This may happen after three or four days or quite a bit longer (more than a week) and the smell is caused by gangrene. As disgusting as this sounds, this is the body's natural way of getting rid of dead tissue. There are no nerve endings in it and, if you leave it alone, it will sort itself out. There is no need to clean it or wipe spirit on it or powder it, no matter what your granny says. It is better left alone. However, it is also fine for it to get wet, so, if you choose to bath your baby, simply dab it dry afterwards in the same way that you dry the rest of his body.

When you put a nappy on, about 50% of people will tell you to tuck the cord stump inside to stop it getting caught on clothes and about 50% of people will tell you to keep the cord stump outside the nappy to stop it getting damp. Do whatever seems right to you as it makes no difference. The plastic clamp that the midwife put on after the cord was cut stays in place until the cord stump falls off and then, if you are of a sentimental nature, you can cut through the clamp, remove the dead tissue, and clean the clamp to save as a keepsake. Otherwise, bin it.

Hands and feet

Look at your baby's hands and feet: so tiny and so cold. The rest of his body may be toasty warm but his fingers and toes will stay really chilly even if you pop mittens on him. His tiny heart, pumping away ten to the dozen, is busy sending as much blood as possible to the brain and vital organs and just enough (but no more) to the hands and feet. There is really no point in trying to get the blood to go to these extremities by heating them up – after all, the brain needs it far more right now – and, in time, this highly evolved body will sort everything out.

His fingernails will be long, soft and almost paper-thin. They often feel ragged and really quite scratchy and you will see the fingers come up to your baby's face again and again, putting little scratches and scrapes across his cheeks.

Before you dash to the drawer to grab a set of scratch mitts, remember that a little more than 24 hours ago this little person was tucked up inside you and those searching hands were batting about his face, pebble-dashing his delicate features with tiny marks as he tried to get his fingers into his mouth for a suck. Those papery nails were there, just as now, but you were blissfully unaware of their potential to wound. Look and you won't find any scratches on your baby's shins or tummy: it is his mouth he wants to reach. Those sore-looking little scratch marks have been coming and disappearing for many weeks, unbeknown to you, so don't cover his hands and deprive your newborn of his finger-sucking delights; simply leave them to flake off in bits by themselves as they have done, without your help, over the last few months.

If they are just too worrisome for you, simply pick a loose edge carefully while your baby is relaxed and settled during a suckle. Some mums nibble them if they get too long, but be careful not to tear the end of the nail or the fingertips can get sore.

Babies who wear scratch mitts can be more unsettled without the opportunity to self-soothe and may also miss out on a needed feed. This is because the finger-sucking that babies love to indulge in helps to stimulate the waking and feeding part of the brain, so being unable to suck the fingers may lead to a hungrier and grumpier baby.

The toenails are another matter; they look ingrown and a bit odd. It is entirely normal for the toenails of a baby to follow the contour of the toe and curl right in at the edges. As the nails thicken and harden, they will start to grow more like yours until, over time, they will look completely normal. Just as with the fingernails, if they get long and scratchy and worry you, just gently peel and pick the edges carefully to break them back.

Moro reflex

If you gently let your lap drop so that your baby falls a tiny way, you will see him throw his arms and hands back in a sudden startle. This is one of his primitive reflexes – the 'Moro reflex'. His arms fling out and the hands splay widely before they are both quickly brought back in again.

This is thought to be an evolutionary survival strategy for ensuring that the baby clings onto the mother if he feels as if he is dropping. Certainly you notice a baby grabbing onto your body quite well when you walk about with him in your arms.

Now that babies sleep on their backs, many mothers notice it happening every time there is a loud noise or a slight knock on the crib. Babies are quite naturally alert to what is going on, even in their sleep, and this helps to keep them safe.

Breathing

Watch your baby breathing. As he breathes, his tummy swells and falls. Babies breathe like this: much more into their tummies than adults. Your little one will also breathe much more quickly than you, between 30 and 60 times in a minute, whereas you will breathe only between 10 and 20 times a minute. You will notice that his breathing can be a bit erratic and that, at times, he will wait for up to five seconds before taking another breath and then breathe quickly for a short while before going back to a few deeper, slower breaths. To add to this seemingly chaotic breathing pattern, he will also treat you to some snuffles, snorts and panting that worry all new parents and keep you on your toes. When you cuddle him closely, this irregular breathing will settle; when he is further away from you, it will be more chaotic. As long as he is a good colour, warm and well, you can rest assured that this is just normal baby breathing. It is good to get used to this normal type of baby breathing so that you can quickly spot if something is unusual.

Mucus and choking

Sometimes in the early days, and especially when you are cuddling your baby close, he will gag and seem to struggle. If you ask your midwife, she may tell you that your baby is 'mucousy'. This simply means that your little one is working at getting rid of the fluids that were naturally taken down during labour and birth. It can be very alarming if you are not expecting it. Because it tends to happen more when you pick your baby up, it is tempting to leave him quiet in his crib. But this is one of those cases when it is 'better out than in', so don't be put off from those snuggles. If your baby starts to gag and cough, lie him on his tummy on your thigh with his head lower than his bottom and rub his back. He will reward your effort with a good splurge of mucus down your thigh, so be ready with a muslin cloth. If this doesn't do the trick, call your midwife over and she will help.

Heartbeat

To hear your baby's tiny heartbeat, simply press your ear to his sternum (breastbone) and listen carefully. Hear how quick it is? Feel your pulse. Your baby's rate will be about twice yours. By the time a baby is born, his heart has already beaten over 50 million times. It started to beat around three weeks after conception and beat faster when it was really new and tiny than at the end of pregnancy. Every time your baby stirs or kicks or cries, the heartbeat will speed up; when he is dozing and snuzzling at your breast, it will settle right down and become steadier. Now listen to the heartbeat through your baby's back, between his shoulder blades – it can sound a little different here. You can even feel it by gently laying a couple of fingers over the bottom of the breastbone. When he is snuggled in close to your breast, your baby can hear your heartbeat just as you can hear his now. The sound of your heartbeat soothes and reassures him, as his does you, so be still and listen to this astonishing sound.

Eyes

Turn the light down or away just enough and your baby may open his eyes at the sound of your voice and the feel of you kissing his soft lips. They may look dark blue, dark grey or even almost black. No matter what colour eyes your baby has inherited from you and your partner, they will not yet be their finished shade. The melanin that pigments the eyes responds to light and your baby has been in relative darkness for nine months. One of the wonders of parenthood is in watching the colour changes, over the first few years, in the eyes of your child.

The eyes are shiny and moist but don't cry 'real tears' yet because the tear glands only produce enough tears to keep the eyes clean and hydrated, not the excessive amounts needed to roll down those sweet cheeks. After a month or so your baby will break your heart with a display of the saddest, droppiest tears you could imagine and, rather ironically, this is about the same age when he will start to melt that same heart with proper smiles. You can't have one without the other in life.

Lips

Kissing the lips of your fresh, warm baby is delicious. One day your child will turn away from your kiss, hell-bent on getting into the garden to dig for dinosaurs instead, so get those kisses in while you can and indulge yourself and him in that very human expression of love.

Ears

The ears are softer around the edges than yours: so pliable that they can be bent right over. Sometimes babies have bent-over ears at birth when they have been a little squished up inside their mum, but they self-correct pretty quickly. Then, as the baby gets older, the soft edges of the ears gain harder cartilage and form into the shape they will be in adulthood: a mix of your and your partner's genetic gift to your child for which he may, or may not, thank you!

At birth, your baby has just the right amount and type of hearing for this time in his life. Today they may still be rather full of fluid from his labour journey, even when this has cleared, the part of his brain that handles hearing will not yet be fully formed, but he can hear the higher pitch of a female voice more easily than deeper tones and will be tuned in to your voice in particular, recognising it from months of hearing it in the echoey warmth of the amniotic fluid. Talk gently to him and you will see him lock onto the sound, studying it and you intensely: 'Listen! Look! This is the most important person in your world.'

Head

Let your hand glide over the top of your baby's head. There may be a lot of hair or barely any at all. Right in the middle, nearer the front than the back, you will feel the 'soft spot'. Whenever a midwife or doctor picks up your baby, one of the first things they do is sneakily sweep across this fontanelle, checking it in a second. They are feeling for that springy bounce that tells them that your baby is fit and well. It is perfectly tough, so don't be afraid to gently explore it. This fontanelle (there is another one at the back of the head but it is tiny and you may need a midwife to help you find it if you're interested) is the space between the head bones.

In order to let your baby through your pelvis, the head needed to squeeze down a little and so the head bones, separated by spaces, were able to slide across each other just enough to let him birth, and then open up again later. Now the slow process of closing the fontanelle, which takes a few years to complete, can begin.

If your baby cries hard, you will see it bulge, and when your baby is asleep, it will settle flat. If your baby is too dry, it will dip in, and this is why the midwife takes a sneaky feel. If you feel for a little while, you may be able to feel a throbbing pulse through the tough skin of the fontanelle and it may be this that gives it the name – a font or fountain that springs up from a small dent in a rock. Many parents panic when they feel this soft throb, but you know it is normal, so you can relax.

So, top to toe, that is your first baby exploration. Let there be others as the days and weeks pass. Ensure you have a warm towel and your skin on his, as well as the ever-present offer of a breast to soothe, and this can be a regular time of quiet reflection and a deepening of awareness and understanding of the underlying rightness of your beautifully evolved baby.

Partner ponderings

You could be forgiven for asking 'What about me? What can I do?' after reading that. We are not used, in our busy interactive world, to simply sitting and watching. We like to dive in and take an active part, getting busy, taking photos – otherwise we may think we are not really having a full experience. When evolution plays out, it does not really consider the emotional sensibilities of those it affects. Of course, it doesn't think at all. It is simply an exquisite process to ensure survival. And, make no mistake about it, you are essential to the survival of your precious bundle, just not necessarily in the way you might have envisaged. You cannot feed your baby and, right now, your baby does need his mother more than you, but your partner needs you, more than anyone else, to help her with the intensity of this new experience of deeply attaching and bonding. It can be a frightening as well as an exciting time, bringing a huge sense of responsibility and vulnerability for you both, but especially for the new mother. You can help to anchor her.

The joy of being a modern human is that you are not out hunting and gathering, so you can join your partner in the simple business of looking and touching, smelling and listening while offering the emotional strength and physical protection from the outside world that she needs.

Without you, your partner may simply be so caught up in the day-to-day hustle and bustle of the busy maternity ward that she doesn't steal the time to explore your new baby. Even after a home birth, the sudden deluge of visitors can rob mums of the precious serenity of just one day alone with you two.

Help her find that time. Protect it; stand outside the hospital curtains if necessary, but remind this new, elated but weary mother that she can discover her baby. Fill a hot water bottle to warm a soft towel, make some food and drink and turn off the phones for a while. That midwife check can wait, the visitors can come tomorrow, photos will be just as special if taken in a few hours. Right now your new family is going to stop the world. So get your top off, get into bed with your partner and baby and join in this hour of wonder. If he seems upset but doesn't want to catch the free-falling boob of his hovering mother, offer a thumb or little finger to suck and ensure that your baby is snug on her warm lap.

If your partner is exploring and your baby wants to suckle, it's fine for you to help him muddle on. Don't try to do anything in particular or look closely to see how you should 'get him on'; just get him close enough to be touching the underside of the breast and, as long as you aren't holding his head and stopping its free movement, he will fiddle and faff and sort it out for himself. It can involve a fair bit of snuffling and chuntering at the boob but this is his gig and he will go about it in his own sweet way.

Questions and answers
Sleepy baby
I had a lot of drugs in labour and my baby is so sleepy. Isn't it better to let him sleep for now, rather than strip him off for a cuddle?

Babies who have been exposed to labour drugs can take many days to clear their systems and fully wake up. They may miss sucking times and, therefore, the opportunity to feed if tucked up in a crib. These babies need skin to skin and handling more than most and, if he is nursed closely in this way, he will behave more normally more quickly. Furthermore, skin to skin reduces the baby's workload for keeping warm (you do the work for him) and so his need to take food is lessened (though not his need to suck). Skin to skin may help reduce your baby's risk of getting low blood sugar.

Bruised baby
My baby has a nasty bruise from forceps and seems really upset when I cuddle him. What do I do?

Poor you and poor baby. You will both be pretty sore for a few days. Babies born with the help of forceps or ventouse can have a cracking headache and want to keep a low profile. The good news is that skin to skin and freedom to nurse causes the release of painkilling endorphins in both mums and babies. Instead of sitting to snuggle, lie down safely and let your little one take his time to suckle. It is easy enough to press out a drop or two of colostrum every 20 minutes or so and gently put it into his mouth from your finger. If he is very bruised, your midwife might suggest a small dose of paracetamol, which could help.

Scheduled feeding
I thought I was meant to demand feed but the midwives tell me to feed every two hours. I'm confused.

This is a complaint I hear from mums every single working day. The cause of this confusion among staff is that, after the first day or so, most babies want to suckle much more often than mums anticipate and many mums try to space these nuzzlings in the mistaken belief that baby 'can't be hungry *again*'. Midwives often use the two-hour rule to get the message of normality across. In reality, for the first few days, some babies suckle all the time, but others do so quite infrequently or erratically. The more frequent pattern comes a wee bit later, but it still won't be evenly spaced through the day and night. However, remember that babies who have had difficult births or have been exposed to labour drugs often don't behave normally and these babies need watching carefully to make sure they don't drop their blood sugar, get dry, or become deeply jaundiced. If you keep your baby really close, skin to skin – and don't hide your boobs away – your baby is more likely to wake and suckle when he needs to, which will be pretty erratic. In my experience, the more you resist the urge to dress a baby and put him quietly in a crib, the less likely you are to run into feeding difficulties, even following a difficult birth.

Special care baby

My baby is in the special care unit. Can I still enjoy this exploration?

You can, but you may have to delay it. Talk to your baby's carers about your desire to hold and explore your baby. They will explain why it isn't sensible just yet and help you find other ways to enjoy some moments (see Chapter 1 about comfort holding and kangaroo care). Both of you will really benefit from an hour of gentle looking and touching when the dust has settled and baby is on the mend, so don't despair.

Large lump at belly button

My baby has a large, soft lump at the belly button. Is this normal?

Sometimes, because the tummy muscles are a bit stretchy in the newborn baby, the belly button bulges out more than usual and, when your baby cries, it will pop right out. This is a small hernia and, although it will most likely settle by itself, do tell your midwife or doctor about it so that they can keep an eye on it with you and tell you what treatment is available if the hernia doesn't go away.

Sneezing

My baby sneezes all the time. Does he have a cold?

No! He just has a lot of labour gunk up his nose and a very good sneeze reflex. If he is otherwise well and has a good colour, just get a muslin cloth and catch anything that explodes out of his nostrils.

Hand-cleaning

Should I use hand disinfectant whenever I pick up my baby?

No. Just use normal personal hygiene with regular soap and water after going to the toilet. There is no need for you or your partner to be extra-clean. Hand rubbing gels are less effective than normal soaps and, in any case, your baby has your healthy bacteria on him to fight infection and antibodies from your placenta, and, if suckling, your own human milk is also protecting him.

Baby still cries after feeds

My baby cries even after feeding and I don't think I have any milk. Should I give him a bottle?

No need. If you don't try to put your baby into a crib after he stops suckling, he will stay soothed next to you. He may want to suck again in half an hour or sooner – this is the number one way in which a new baby calms and soothes. His tummy is tiny and your milk is hyper-concentrated, just as it has evolved to be. If you let your newborn suck as often as he wants, your body will respond naturally. Turn to Chapter 4, devoted to feeding, for more information and reassurance.

Sore nipples

I already have sore nipples and blisters! What am I doing wrong?

The biggest problem facing mums who suckle their babies is that they are taught to 'latch and attach' and this fundamentally interferes with your highly evolved baby's natural reflexes, leading to biting and soreness. I cover the whole issue of feeding in Chapter 4, so turn to that now and unpick your problem.

Epstein pearls

When my baby cries or yawns, I can see a white lump on the roof of his mouth. What is this?

It sounds as if your baby has an Epstein pearl. This is a small, white or yellow lump and one or more are sometimes found on the roof of a baby's mouth or on his gums. About 80% of babies have them and, when they are on the gums, parents may mistake them for teeth! These little lumps are filled with fluid, are completely harmless and disappear within a week or two of birth. Tell your midwife or GP if you are at all worried, so that they can check and reassure you.

3 The babymoon: recovering and adjusting

Reaching back ...

The days melt into each other and the young mother is slowly emerging from her shelter more and more each day. Recovered now from the immediate rush and jangle of birth, her energy still low, she spends her days joining her companions for short periods of time to carry out daily tasks before being drawn back to her small bundle, who is never more than a reach away.

It is time for her daughter, still warm and flushed from a night of constant suckling at her mother's filling breast, to have her first wash. Scooped in the crook of an arm and held touching close to the ever-present nipple, the new mother makes her way slowly to the river and gently washes her child with dampened hands. The bundled baby blinks and scrabbles with surprise at the chill, occasionally managing to grasp the nipple for reassurance while her mother is occupied with baby grooming.

Washed and refreshed, mother and child return to the edge of their cave shelter and sit in the sunlight to dry. The mother replenished with nuts and berries, the baby with a deep, warming guzzle of a newer milk – thinner and more flowing than yesterday, and which comes spilling out of her lips, causing her to pull away and splutter before diving back on and drinking deeply.

Resting now, the mother turns to simple tasks, enjoying brief moments of chatter and activity before lying back and resting again. Her body reminds her of the need to heal and recover.

When she moves too far from her little girl, the wail builds quickly to a howl, bringing everyone running. The baby is scooped up and rocked energetically by her father, who calls loudly for his mate, and she rushes up and grasps the child back.

She cuddles her baby, drawing her close and quickly leaning in to drop her heavy breast over her face in an effort to quieten her daughter. After a few days of golden drops, now there is a dripping flow of milk leaking out over the tiny face while the eager mouth pants and licks around the dark circle of skin, sliding on the slippery milk rink. The baby still cries, with tiny, flailing hands and a desperate mouth lapping while our mother tries to hush her child, who is raging in her arms.

Sitting on the ground, this new mother is lost for a moment, panicked by the intensity of the feeling in her chest and head, brought on by her little one's need. What should she do?

Nothing. She simply cuddles the baby warmly against her body, ssh-ing, jiggling gently, and waiting. Her baby bashing and fretting, bobbing and ducking while this new mother simply watches and waits, keeping her baby cuddled up below her dripping nipple, flesh pressed lightly against her mouth. Her child's bottom resting in her lap and the tiny shoulders held firmly on her arm, she can't see what is going on below her hanging breast, but she can feel the soft mouth licking and kissing, panting quick warm breaths. And then, in the twinkling of an eye, all by herself, the baby slips on and settles into her steady, pulling rhythm. Both sigh with relief and relax back into the moment.

Emotions

The week after your baby is born seems both a minute and an eternity. It seems only yesterday that you were still pregnant and yet, at the same time, you feel as if your baby has always been here.

While you are already becoming competent at juggling nappies and cotton wool, each day brings new questions and different emotions. Your hormones are driving you and you swing from moments of calm and delight to sudden outbursts of tears and panic. Everyone has told you about the 'baby blues' but you didn't realise that you would feel so ridiculous: crying at news stories and feeling overwhelmed for no reason. And yet you have just brought a new human into the world and your body is adjusting fast to ensure her survival, so why wouldn't you feel overwhelmed? The hormonal rush has caused your breasts to swell and fill so that it seems impossible for your little one to get on and suckle, and you feel hot and achey and rather a long way away from the safety of the hospital call bell.

Not so many years ago, newly birthed mothers, living close to their family home, had immediate support from the women in their family to cook, clean and tell them, indulgently, that they were just fine; that babies are always a bit of a pickle when the milk 'comes in'; and all babies get spotty; and, yes, baby poo does change colour every day. Today, we often live far from our families and there is not even the promise of daily midwife visits. Indeed, while you are still bruised and breathless, you may be expected to travel some miles on busy roads to see a care assistant in a hospital clinic for a somewhat rushed appointment at a time when what you really want is someone to sit with you for an hour and just calmly help you get to grips with being a new mum.

How can we regain that time to recuperate, get to know our baby and understand the changes that are taking place in us and them? In the 1980s this first week or two was often called the 'babymoon'. Just like the time after the anxious, full-on months of preparing for a wedding, this was a time to lock the doors and spend some vital days laughing, sleeping, romancing and crying with exhaustion and relief. It is also the time when we look at one another, like overenthusiastic children caught stealing the trifle, and say: 'What have we done?'

Postnatal depression

The 'baby blues' pass in a few days as hormones settle a little. Sometimes the 'baby blues' seem deeper and more prolonged than expected and it is important to know how to spot signs of impending postnatal depression so that help can be sought sooner rather than later. If you have experienced a period of mental unwellness before, you should be able to remember what, for you, signalled its arrival. If at any time you think that your recognisable symptoms are returning, see a GP quickly. If you have not experienced mental unwellness before it can be trickier to spot the signs emerging. So, if you feel emotionally unconnected to your baby (as if this might be someone else's child), find yourself unable to sleep even when your baby is settled, feel unable to leave the house, or feel unusually anxious and on high alert, see your doctor as soon as possible. The hormonal swings caused by pregnancy and birth can lead some women to tip into postnatal depression and prompt treatment is essential. Your doctor will ensure that the correct plan of treatment and support is put in place and that any drugs that you might need are fine to take when you are nursing your baby. Don't wait for the symptoms to pass – this really is a case of 'better safe than sorry'.

Your physical recovery

Resting

We can feel as if we have been hit in the solar plexus after birth, even a straightforward one, and taking a flight of stairs leaves us breathless and shaking. It is easy to wonder why we feel like this because we forget that we are not just recovering from giving birth but also from nine months of significant bodily changes. Overnight our bodies and minds have to adjust to the new arrival: there cannot be a few days of 'getting our heads around it' before we feed and groom ourselves and our baby. So we are recovering and firing up, all at the same time. We cannot expect to take day trips to the shopping centre or make stressful visits to photography studios without our bodies complaining loudly.

Plan to have a week of recuperating, allowing your body to heal and to make the changes necessary to support both you and your baby. A trip to your hospital appointment does not mean that you are then 'back to normal', but simply taking a short break in your resting-up.

The fidgety among us know very well how to be busy while resting (we are past masters at writing emails, taking calls and planning our week while putting our feet up), so there is no need to feel anxious at the thought of doing nothing all day. You will quickly learn that simply soothing and changing your baby takes most of your daily hours and all those items on your in-bed or on-sofa To Do list get relegated to next week or the week after ...

Perineum

Your after-pains should be subsiding by the second or third day, but stitches and bruises can take longer to heal, so take simple painkillers if you are happy to do this. There is no need to put any creams on stitches or bruises, and salt in the bath serves no useful purpose except to deprive the fish and chip industry of a vital resource. Just enjoy having soothing baths or showers without any products, and lie on your side to snuggle and suckle your new child. When you do sit, a bed pillow, folded in half along the long edge and put just behind the knees, will tip you off your perineum and bring instant relief.

Some women swear by a chilled sanitary towel, sprinkled with witch-hazel and then put in the freezer for a few hours before use. Be careful to warm the towel a little before use (a frost-bitten vulva is no fun) and do warn your mother-in-law before she goes to the freezer for tonight's meal that she might find more than she bargained for!

At some point during the first week, take a mirror and look at your perineum. It rarely looks as bad as you expect and it is vital that you are happy that it looks 'normal for me'. You might notice that, just inside the vaginal entrance, there are some frilly bits that weren't there before – a little like tiny bits of earlobe around the vaginal wall about half a centimetre in. Women see these and panic, thinking 'The midwife who stitched me up has missed bits.' The frilly bits are almost certainly hymen tags, which are the remains of your hymen and which tore with the birth of your baby's head. They should not be stitched and are entirely normal, but do find an opportunity to look with your midwife or doctor who can check your perineum with you and reassure you that all is well.

If you have never had a really good look at your perineum and vulva, it's time to get acquainted: if you don't know what you look like normally down there, you may not know if there is a problem in the years to come. Men check their testicles; you should check your vulva. Simple.

Legs

Until you are ready to be much more active, keep your legs moving. Circle your feet and pull them backwards and forwards regularly to prevent clots in your calves. If you have had a Caesarean section you might be given daily injections of blood thinners, and elastic stockings, but all women need to be aware of the need to fidget.

Bladder

Your bladder gets a bit of a bashing during labour and birth and, although it has evolved to cope with this pretty well, help it along by drinking plenty of fluids and peeing regularly. It is not too soon to start doing your pelvic floor exercises again, so ask your midwife or mother how to do these if you do not already know. After birth you may initially be completely unable to feel anything move when you clench, but keep trying and the feelings will return.

You should be able to feel when you need to pee, be able to get to the loo in time, start and stop the flow and feel completely finished at the end of a pee. If you don't think that everything is okay, tell your midwife or doctor.

Bowels

Most women have a jolly good clear-out in the long, early warm-up phase of labour and then find that they do not 'go' again until some days after the birth. Eat and drink well, fidget frequently and potter a little and your bowels will come back to normal. If you get uncomfortable and can't open your bowels, a simple over-the-counter remedy such as lactulose or senna can work wonders. When the force moves you and you do manage to 'go', don't panic about splitting your stitches. This just won't happen and the stitches really won't hurt.

Breasts

The biggest change you will notice in your body is in your breasts. For the first few days, the nipples feel hormonally warm but the boobs are soft. Then, as the remaining placental hormones reach a critical low in your bloodstream, your milk 'comes in'. Of course, you have had milk in your boobs since about 17 weeks of pregnancy, but it was the tiny amounts of super-rich, highly specialised milk we call colostrum.

Now the milk changes gradually to become thinner and thinner and more and more plentiful, and your breasts feel full and heavy. Women who keep their babies close by, skin to skin, and allow free suckling rarely describe the engorgement they are led to expect. Women who wrap their baby and pop them in a crib, or who cover their baby's hands with scratch mitts, are more likely to experience raised temperatures and hot, flushed, stiff breasts. Babies have evolved to stay close and suckle frequently, if somewhat erratically, and they do this best when nursed in arms. Scratch mitts can interfere with the subtle feeding messages that a baby's brain gives out, suckling becomes less frequent and the normal mother–baby 'conversation' is interrupted. Interrupted conversations are rarely satisfactory and lead to misunderstandings on both sides.

Your baby is the best person to sort out your boobs, so, if yours are over-full, rather than expressing, which can just cause a troublesome and confusing three-way chatter, let your baby get in and do her thing while you watch TV, write your emails, doze or eat more chocolate.

How your baby's doing

Baby sick

As your milk volume increases, you might notice that your little one brings some milk back after suckling. Human milk is very runny and a baby's oesophageal sphincter (the flap that keeps food down) is pretty loose, so anything she takes down that is over and above what she actually needs will be blurted back easily.

This works like a little pressure valve and prevents the tiny stomach becoming so over-distended that breathing becomes harder. The healthy breastfed baby doesn't overfeed but puts on just the right amount of weight for her, protected as she is by her clever blow-back system.

Suckling patterns

After the first day or two you might start to notice that your baby suckles more at some times of the day than others. Generally, babies are at their least sucky and most easily soothed in the morning hours, between about 7a.m. and midday, and are a little more edgy and sucky between about midday and 5p.m. Babies the world over are at their most wiggly, unsettled and sucky between about 5p.m. and midnight and then again between about 2a.m. and 4a.m. As the days and weeks go by, this pattern will become more and more obvious.

As the pattern becomes more apparent, you may notice that, through the night-time hours, every time you have finished suckling and go to pop your baby in the crib, she stirs quickly and cries. So you soothe her and try again to put her in her cot but she just won't have it. Most parents discover that, as long as she is close to her mother's skin through the night, the newborn baby is much more settled and quiet. The new mother also finds that, whenever she nurses her child at night, she dozes off into a deep sleep, only to wake when her baby murmurs. And even the gentlest murmuring causes a sudden and full wake-up.

The fact that I am telling you about this pattern and can describe it so well should tell you everything you need to know about how normal it is. If something affects all babies to some degree or another, it is normal and has a purpose in the evolutionary survival picture. Suffice to say that it really is normal for babies to behave in this way. By demand suckling your baby, you do not have to worry about 'getting it right' and can just accept that your baby cannot get the normal business of being a baby wrong! Your highly evolved baby is simply doing all the right things to stay close, safe, fed and warm.

We will dig down deeper into this behaviour in the next chapter, so if you are desperate for answers right now, turn straight to Chapter 4 and find solace. Otherwise, if you can wait, do whatever seems to work for your baby and, if you decide to co-sleep overnight, check out the safety guidelines on page 77.

Hiccups

Your baby may get hiccups after feeds. They can really make your baby rock with their strength and look as if they must be uncomfortable. Women sometimes worry so much about their baby's hiccups that they call the hospital in the early hours of the morning asking for advice. They find that the only advice they get is to ignore the hiccups and try to get back to sleep. They really are not a problem and, if you cast your mind back, you might remember your baby having hiccups when she was still inside you – a rhythmical tap on your abdomen that went on for some minutes and then just stopped. If they worry you, let your baby suck on your boob or a finger. It might help, but it might not.

Baby poo

As your baby takes more and more milk by the day, so her poo will gradually change colour, from the black meconium through a blacky-browny-green to a browny-greeny-black, to a greeny-yellow, to a yellowy-green and finally to a mustard yellow. The poo is sloppy and contains little seedy bits like tomato pips, which are actually milk curds. Sometimes the poo is mucousy, sometimes it is very runny and sometimes it explodes out noisily and flows out of the nappy legs like a tide of runny custard – what is affectionately known as a poo-nami!

Baby pee

Her pee will also change day by day. The first day you may see just one strongly coloured pee and there may be urates (the pinky brick-dust type of hyper-concentrated pee that newborn babies make). On day two you should expect two pees that are a little less strong, but you may still see urates. On day three you should see at least three pees that are bigger and then the number of pees increases day by day until, from day six onwards, you should see at least six pees a day that are big and clear. You will get used to feeling and seeing the pee in the nappy and working out what is normal, but your midwife or doctor can reassure you if you are worried and don't have family nearby. Full and wet nappies are a great way of judging that your baby is taking in enough milk.

Your daily exploration of your newborn during a nappy change might turn up a few other surprises.

Baby spots

Most common in the first week are little bumps that look like heat bumps. They come and go in crops and look red and raised with little watery heads. This common rash is seen in almost all babies in the first week or two of life and is called erythema toxicum neonatorum, which might sound scary but simply means 'your baby is red and spotty and looks as if she has something grim and we really don't know why'. It is harmless, so leave it alone, but it seems sensible to point it out to your midwife so she can check that your baby is otherwise well and that the rash really is erythema, and so reassure you. There is absolutely nothing that you eat or drink that will either cause or cure erythema, so simply ignore people who tell you otherwise.

Dry skin

Have you noticed that your baby's beautiful peachy-soft, downy skin of a few days ago has turned to dry snake scales? Every time a blanket is removed, the air is filled with a snowstorm of skin cells and your baby looks dry and flaky. Even if your baby was born a wee bit early and came covered in vernix, she will still flake off her first skin layer. This is completely normal and underneath this scaly layer is a virgin layer of fresh, soft skin that's just like the original. Friends and relatives may tell you to oil your baby or put something in the bath water to help, but the skin is dead and oiling it will not stick it back on. Besides, exposing your baby's delicate skin to lotions and potions may make her itchy and uncomfortable as well as potentially cause an allergic reaction. The human skin is more than capable of looking after itself.

Yellow baby

If your baby looks a bit yellow, she probably has jaundice. Turn back to 'Let's talk about colour' on page 30 to understand why babies have high haemoglobin levels. Once born, babies breathe for themselves and so get all their oxygen first-hand. Now the extra haemoglobin is unnecessary and can gradually be broken down and got rid of. But the clearing out can't happen quickly enough to keep up with the speed at which the haemoglobin is broken down, so there is a bit of a backlog in the system, which leads to jaundice. Jaundice is a yellowing of the skin and it is generally seen in a mild form in babies from about three days old until about a week of age. It sorts itself out perfectly well as long as your baby is free to stay close to you so that she can suckle as often as she wishes. Some people suggest putting the baby in a light window so that the ultraviolet rays in sunshine can work on the skin and reduce the bilirubin (the yellow pigment), but the evidence for this is not very good. It is nice to keep the curtains open so that you can all enjoy the day, but it is more important that your little one can feed freely and that means her being close to you rather than in a cot in a window. If your baby looks very yellow, has dry nappies or seems sleepy even when you change her, call the midwife or doctor. Normal levels of jaundice are fine, but high levels can be dangerous. Your midwife or doctor can do a simple check to see if your baby is okay.

Cord stump

The little cord stump will be black and hard after a day or two and, at some point, it will get very smelly and come off without any help from you. Once the cord stump is off, you may notice that the belly button gets a little damp and oozy at times. A little damp cotton wool will clean what you can see and the body will take care of the rest. As time goes on, the belly button becomes dry and just like yours, complete with fluff!

Bathing

Although it is safe and fine to bathe your baby in the first week of life, there is no need at all: she hasn't taken up mud-wrestling just yet (give her time), and it is better to leave her natural oils on during this scaly stage than to rinse them off. If you want to freshen your baby up after a night spent in a milky snuggle, simply use damp hands or some warm, damp cotton wool and do the minimum. We look at bathing on page 137, so turn straight there if your baby really needs a bath today.

Lip blisters

After your baby has been suckling, and often in between times too, you may see a small, white, watery blister on her top lip. This is called a sucking blister. Don't worry – sucking blisters do not go deep and do not bother babies one little bit, so don't be tempted to prick it. Sometimes you might even notice a sucking blister on a fist or wrist where your baby has sucked so hard that she has rubbed one up. Some babies are born with sucking blisters on their hands or arms and they are simply a sign that your baby is a normal human baby with a phenomenal urge to suckle.

Sticky eyes

Your baby can't make many tears yet and many babies get sticky eyes as a result. This looks like a bad case of 'sleepy dust' and is pretty gunky. The goo can stick the eyelids shut and take some coaxing to come away, but the condition does go away after a few days to a week.

- Every time you have changed a nappy, wash your hands carefully and then get a little pot of cool, boiled water and some cotton wool.
- Wrap your baby in a soft towel and then use some really damp cotton wool (don't wring it out too much) to clean the eye from the nose outwards. Use one cotton wool clump per swipe and use separate cotton wool clumps for each eye.
- Now dry the eyes carefully and gently with dry cotton wool and then lean over your baby and squeeze a few drops of your own milk into each eye. Your milk is warm, clean and contains millions of friendly bacteria, which will eat up any bad bacteria and help prevent infection. It is the ideal first-line treatment for sticky eyes in a newborn.

Partner ponderings

As the first couple of days pass, your new family arrives home to flags and trumpets (of course) and, as you emerge from your exhaustion and adrenaline fluctuations, you can look forward to a week of settling, alongside keeping the show on the road. Time to call in all those favours and offers of help so that you and your new family can have plenty of time together. If you do not have family locally or reliable friends who can cook casseroles to pop on your doorstep or take away a spot of ironing, then wing it by doing what absolutely must be done and leaving the rest until a few days before you have to return to the world of paid work.

Essential housework

It really is too soon to expect a new mum to stand and cook or push a vacuum cleaner around and she will not want to spend hours without grown-up company or watch you slaving over housework hour after hour. A babymoon is for both of you: a time to celebrate and hang loose.

The things that must be done before you join your partner in bed or on the sofa are:

- Preparing regular, simple but nutritious meals (if you have been really smart, the freezer will have been filled a month or so ago). Your partner may not think to ask for food, so keep in mind that she needs three good meals and two good snacks a day as well as regular drinks. She needs water handy all the time as feeding gives women a tremendous thirst.
- Keeping on top of your partner's medication schedule. She may lose track of time and then find herself too sore to think straight. Keep painkillers to hand and make a note of when they are given and when they are next due.
- Ensuring appointments are kept. If you believe that your partner is not up to a car journey, call the midwife or doctor and ask for a home visit and, if this is not possible, see if the appointment can be safely rescheduled for the next day, when she may feel more up to a trek.
- Making sure that any older children are taken to nursery, school or the childminder. If your child is full-time at home, she can join the babymoon too and have a few snuggly days in front of the TV.
- Basic housework. Laundry that cannot wait, simple tidying and doing the washing-up are essentials, but dusting, vacuuming and building extensions really can wait for at least two days and almost certainly longer.
- Essential shopping. Unless there is an emergency need for medicines, you should have all the food and drink you need for a few days and it is likely that your partner has already nested to the extent that there are enough baby clothes and nappies to do most of the country's babies proud. If you do need to go out to the shops, be quick – your partner may feel quite vulnerable if left on her own for too long.

Visitors

Enjoy having close friends and family over to celebrate, but decide on your house rules first. Visitors should not expect to be waited on hand and foot – if they are close family and friends, they will not expect it and, in any case, they will know where your kettle is.

Ensure that you are both dressed in a manner that says 'We are tired and need to relax, so don't stay for long' and then tell them to leave well before they outstay their welcome. Your partner may not feel emotionally strong enough to tell people to go and then may feel overwhelmed and tearful by bedtime, so do the thinking for both of you for a few days.

Rest

Don't underestimate just how emotional you both may be. Ensure that you both grab a daytime nap and have relatively early nights as well as eating properly. If you get tired and hungry, you will be of little use to your partner and baby, so look after yourself too.

Support

Your partner will need lots of reassurance that she is doing well. Your baby makes little sense to either of you right now, but mum is the one who has to fulfil her basic needs, so cross your fingers behind your back if necessary and tell her that the house is still standing, food is in the oven and she is doing a great job of nourishing your baby.

Be reassured that, if your baby is being wet and dirty, is a good colour and stirs when you touch her, she is fine. Babies cry even when they have been suckled if they are put down in a crib during the day. They cry even when they have been suckled and are in your arms during the evening unless being rocked or patted or suckled yet again. Babies under about four months old want to stay close and in arms all the time. This is normal and protective and you can reassure your partner that your little one is not poorly or hungry but simply a brand-new human being who cannot yet be alone or far from the breast. In time your little child will want space of her own to explore the world that is beyond a milky boob – but not just yet.

Questions and answers
Stitches

I've looked at my perineum and the stitches seem to have come undone. Do I need to be re-stitched?

No, you don't. The stitching material used today is designed to dissolve and how long this takes varies from person to person. Do get someone to have a good look at you to check that there is no infection, but if all is otherwise okay, don't worry, keep an occasional eye on the stitches, stay normally clean and your perineum will heal up.

Aching legs

My legs ache. Is this normal?

It is common to feel achey and heavy in your legs after giving birth and you might find that your ankles swell (especially if you had an epidural in labour). Keep them fidgeting to keep the blood flowing and the puffiness shifting, but do remind your midwife or doctor to check your legs for you to make sure all is well. If you notice a hot, red, hard lump anywhere on your legs, tell someone quickly – leg clots, though quite rare, do pop up and can pose a real danger.

Mastitis

My breasts are heavy and tender. Do I have mastitis?

If, during the first week, your breasts become mottled, tight, over-full, painful and heavy, the likelihood is that you have engorgement. The tightness is caused by tissue fluid (oedema) and you have to get rid of this as it causes a sort of gridlock in the breast. Rather than expressing, which can simply make matters worse, try something called reverse pressure softening (RPS) to reduce the oedema, help milk to flow and allow your baby to get herself on more easily to suckle. This can also help stop mastitis from occurring. To do RPS, use a flat hand with fingers together. Place your hand above or below the nipple with the finger closest to the nipple just at the base of it. Now use a rolling wave of very strong, slow pressure away from the nipple, backwards, to force the tissue fluid back into the lymphatic system. Do not move your hand over the skin surface as the friction can hurt (simply press firmly with each finger in turn so the wave moves) and do not move the wave of pressure towards the nipple or the oedema will move that way and further harden the areola. If you don't mind a cold breast, you could then chill it to constrict the blood vessels and minimise further engorgement. Simple pain relief remedies (paracetamol every four to six hours or ibuprofen every eight hours) taken regularly and according to the packet instructions can reduce pain and inflammation. Remember that engorgement is caused by a gridlock and not an infection. There is a temptation to get a prescription for antibiotics, but this is rarely necessary. This is a self-limiting problem if you continue to demand suckle, and antibiotics can lead to thrush and resistant 'super-bugs'.

Baby won't settle in her crib

My baby won't go in her crib at night and I'm worried about falling asleep and rolling on top of her. What should I do?

Don't panic! This happens to almost everyone because it is normal, protective baby behaviour kicking in. Turn to page 77 and read about safe co-sleeping, why babies behave like this at night and what you can do.

Urates in pee

My baby is three days old and is still peeing urates. Should I worry?

A newborn baby is able to concentrate urine right down until it is almost a red powder. This strong solution is called urates and passing urates is normal for the first day or two when the volume of a mother's milk is low. During the first 24 hours a first-time mother may produce as little as a teaspoon of colostrum over the entire day. This is normal and completely adequate for the newborn, who has evolved to 'expect' this. A second-time mum tends to produce greater quantities, but the amounts will still be very small. The milk is very concentrated and so your baby really is getting everything she needs. In the second 24 hours mum produces more – maybe a few teaspoons in the day – and then the day after that the amount moves into tablespoons. Once the milk 'comes in', the volume increases greatly. You should expect your baby's pee to increase in line with this pattern of growing milk supply as described earlier in the chapter. If this doesn't happen, there is a very good chance that, although you will undoubtedly be making milk, your baby is not managing to suckle it off. More often than not, this is because mum has been taught to 'latch and attach', but sometimes there is something else going on, such as a tongue-tie or unusual palate. Rarely (but it does happen), a mum fails to make milk. This can be due to a bit of placenta being still inside her, interfering with her hormones. Sometimes it is medication she is taking that causes a lack of milk. Whatever, once your milk is in, if a baby's nappy seems 'dry' it is essential to get thoroughly checked over. See a midwife or doctor to make sure you are both essentially well and then see an infant feeding specialist for help with baby-led suckling. It can be harder than it should be to find someone who doesn't teach 'latching and attaching', but persevere and, if you are reassured that you are both well, you could simply try following the advice in the next chapter, which is free from this over-complicated and thoroughly unhelpful approach.

No poo

My baby hasn't pooed for two days. Is this okay?

Babies generally poo every day and at least once a day for the first couple of months before settling into a daily poo routine that is normal for them. If your baby is doing plenty of pees, the hold-up might be caused by drugs that you have taken (opiates such as codeine only get into mum's milk in small quantities, but that may be enough to slow a baby's gut), a bottle of formula (even one bottle can slow the gut) or simply that she had such an enthusiastic pooing session the day she was born that her gut is not yet filled up enough to poo again. Give her time and get ready for the poo-nami! If your baby is not peeing either, read the question and answer above.

Blood in the nappy

My baby girl is passing blood in the nappy. What's wrong?

This is almost certainly pseudo-menstruation. While she was inside you, your daughter had all your hormones from across the placenta. Now she is born, the hormones from you have stopped and, once they reach a critical low in her bloodstream, she may bleed from her vagina. This is just like the withdrawal bleed that women get when on the contraceptive pill and is absolutely nothing to worry about. It can be as little as a smear on one nappy to being enough to bloody her vulva and every nappy for a few days. It can look very scary. Ask your midwife or GP to check for you so that you can be reassured. You should be asked about any family history of blood-clotting disorders and whether or not your daughter had an injection of vitamin K at birth. If there is a family history of issues and your midwife or GP is worried, your baby may need more specialised checks. If she didn't have vitamin K at birth and your midwife or doctor feels that this is more than the usual blood loss of pseudo-menstruation, it might be suggested that it is given now. If you are told that this is normal, then it really is normal, so try not to worry. Some baby girls never have pseudo-menstruation and this is fine too.

Angry heat bumps

My baby's heat bumps (erythema) look really angry. Is this normal?

Take a careful look at the bumps. If the head on them is clear or pale yellow but watery and your baby is otherwise well in herself (in other words, she rouses when you handle her, feels comfortably warm to touch between her shoulder blades and is being wet and dirty), her erythema is just a bit angry. Keep a careful eye on her and don't be afraid to call your midwife or doctor. If the heads on the bumps are yellow, crusty or look as if they have pus in them, they might have got infected. Don't put anything on them but do make an appointment to see your midwife or doctor today. She needs checking over. Keep allowing her to be close to you and free to suckle so that, if she does have a bit of an infection, your healthy bacteria and your milk can help towards making her better.

Baby boobs

My baby has little boobs that are pink and hard. Why?

The answer to this is hormones. Your placenta hormones are causing your baby to grow little breasts. Sometimes there is even a little milk that comes out. Leave these tiny breasts alone and, as the hormones seep away, they will disappear too. Never poke or squeeze these mini-boobs or you might cause pain and inflammation. If they get really red and hot, let your midwife or doctor know and they can check your baby over and reassure you.

Stinky cord stump

My baby's cord stump stinks and the skin above it is really red. Is this normal?

Infection in the cord stump is unusual but it does happen. If you notice a red 'flare' coming up from the belly button area, if your baby seems hot and unwell or if the skin around the belly button looks angry and crusty, your baby may have an umbilical infection. This needs sorting out straight away, so call your doctor now. A simple antibiotic treatment will clear up any infection quickly – this is not a time for herbal remedies, homoeopathy or a liberal squeezing of breast milk.

Red eyes

My baby has red eyes. What should I do?

If your baby has gunky, sticky eyes but the whites of her eyes are normal, simply follow the advice above and keep an eye on her day by day. If the whites of the eyes are red, she has conjunctivitis and this needs treatment. Call your doctor, who can ensure that your baby has the right eye drops to kill the bacteria that are causing the problem. There is no evidence that breast milk, herbal drops or homoeopathy can safely treat conjunctivitis, but the right drops will bring about a pretty rapid cure.

4 Suckling made really easy

Reaching back ...

The nights and days merge into a milky tangle of woman and child, this new mother barely able to tell where she ends and her baby begins. Her body is hormone-hot, her breasts heavy and full at times and soft and yielding at others, but always there is the sweet breath of her daughter hanging close by and fingers reaching out to connect with her flesh – once her own but now seemingly forever mingled with the plump skin of this new creature.

Just a few days ago, this young woman drew her child to her breast for the first time, rocked by the raw urges following birth. There, in the dim corner of her stone shelter, while her body continued to squeeze itself free of the afterbirth and she scrambled to understand what was happening, her new baby simply searched for and found her place. And stayed.

Now this couple melt and muddle together, unthinkingly. The fresh-faced woman, driven simply to soothe her baby moment by moment, knows only that, once she is cradled in her arm, pressed warmly against her aching breast, the world falls silent.

In the warmth and bright of the day, her child sleeps sporadically in her lap or on her back as her mother sets about her work. She stops whenever her baby wakes and searches; hauls the tiny wriggler closely under her falling breast; and then gives her attention back to her task, trusting her daughter to find what she craves. Sometimes she howls and fights away before diving back again for another try; at other times she instantly draws on.

The pitch dark of the long night only allows the mother to feel her child, never to see – the moon is too new to offer any light through the cave entrance and even the nights that she and her companions spend tucked together under the sky hold only the very darkest of shadows.

As long as she can feel her child pushing and wriggling her small, urgent face into the soft underside of her breast, she knows that in a moment the pushing and wriggling will ease and the strong, steady pulling will begin.

Where we are

Almost all mothers I speak to are unable to tell me clearly how the first sucking took place. Awash with adrenaline and endorphins, staggered by the enormity of their experience, they clutch their much-awaited child to their breast and, the next thing they know, their child is drawing deeply. The mother often can't recall the long searchings and muddlings that have preceded this moment, let alone the actual second that her child hits his target.

Then, some hours later, she tells me, she 'went to latch him' ... and so the trouble starts.

Astonishing as it may seem to you, the fashion of 'latching and attaching' has been with us for only a generation or so. Your own mother may not have heard the term until you introduced it into her vocabulary and my mother looked at me as if I was crazy when I asked her whether she was taught to 'latch and attach' her babies.

Women trying to nurse their babies today look neither like women in parts of the world where suckling babies is the only way to feed and soothe, nor like your grandmother when she nursed her babies.

For over 20 years now, women have been taught how to 'get their babies on to feed' and the only thing we have to show for our efforts is a generation of despondent, confused and bitten mums.

Without exception, every woman I see with their first baby tells me that she is trying really hard to latch and attach 'properly' and she

believes that it should look like the image to the left.

Without exception, when I see them, they are holding the baby with the opposite arm to the breast to which they are putting baby, bringing baby's bottom up off their lap, rolling him in so that he is looking under her armpit and then making a gap between her breast and the baby's mouth so that she can see what is going on and 'wait for the big mouth'. Just like she has been told to, repeatedly and ever more forcibly. Except that, for these mums, and no doubt for you, their little one is not lying contentedly like the lady here, but is snoozing, yelling or biting them. The baby puts his arms and hands in the way, apparently pushes away from the breast, closes his mouth a bit and simply gets frantic or drops off to sleep.

Poor mum is doing just as she was told and yet feels as though she is fighting an octopus.

So let's try to unpick what is going on and what you can do to reclaim the happy intimate picture that you imagined you were signing up for when you bought your first nursing bra.

A few years ago I had a client who had come to the UK to work shortly after becoming pregnant. Her background was like mine as far as feeding babies was concerned: she had never seen a baby bottle-fed. I never asked her how she intended to feed as it always seems to me to be a faintly ridiculous question (like 'How do you plan to change a nappy?').

She planned to attend some hospital birth preparation classes and also a feeding workshop. The feeding workshop was being run by well-trained specialists and, the week after she had attended it, she came back to see me for a regular pregnancy check.

'How did you get on at the feeding workshop?' I asked.

'Well, it's a jolly good thing that I went along.'

'Really?' I asked incredulously, knowing that, with this woman's background, she probably could have run the session herself.

'Well, before I went, I thought that feeding a baby was the easiest thing in the world. But now I know that it is actually pretty tricky and I really have to work at it and learn!'

She wasn't joking, but I roared with laughter. Then I picked up my baby doll and sat down with her. I put a pillow on my lap, laid my doll on it and pretended to 'latch' my baby 'nose to nipple, tummy to mummy and wait for the big mouth'.

'Like this?'

'Yes, yes. That's exactly it. It's new to me but they say it's the right way.'

So I threw out the pillow, swapped arms so I was just cuddling, dropped the baby onto my lap, rolled the baby out to 'look up' at me. 'Is this how your friends and family do it?'

'Er, yes!'

'And everyone nurses their babies, right?'

'Yes, of course. Everyone.'

I asked this mum-to-be whether she was used to seeing women have such terrible problems with soreness and loss of milk that they stopped feeding their own milk in favour of formula. Of course she wasn't. 'So maybe you should simply forget every single thing you learned at that feeding workshop and just bung your baby on your boob like every other woman you've ever known.'

I saw this woman again after she had given birth and, needless to say, she had ditched the simple but devastating mantra 'nose to nipple, tummy to mummy and wait for the big mouth' in favour of bunging her baby on the boob with one hand while eating a

sandwich with the other and we laughed about 'English women and their crazy baby-feeding style'.

She looked like the image to the left (with both hands free!).

Back in her bedroom after food, I watched as she did exactly what I had done a hundred times with my own babies: she fed one end while she changed the other. This was her first baby and she was only a week into motherhood.

Where we came from

Your great-gran didn't 'latch and attach' your gran, and your gran didn't 'latch and attach' your mum. Your ancestors had never heard of foremilk and hindmilk and, as my own mum once said to me, 'Sweetheart, if I'd had to worry about "latching and attaching" and "foremilk and hindmilk", you'd have starved!' If I asked her how she had gone about feeding me, she'd get exasperated. 'For goodness' sake! I don't know. I just dropped a boob in your face and let you get on with it.'

Whenever I see a client wanting support with nursing and we are lucky enough to have her gran there, as soon as I have shown the new mum how to simply cuddle her baby on her lap and let this instinctive human just find his own way on to nurse, without exception the gran will point and smile and say: 'That's it! Your way. That's how I did it. I didn't want to say anything because I thought maybe it was different now.' Indeed. After millions of years of evolution that have resulted in babies with perfect reflexes and mums with perfect cuddling arms and responsive breasts, we have decided that we know better and have wrecked things, causing untold misery.

How the first humans did it

Ponder this: it seems that the very first human-like creatures (*Homo habilis*) walked the earth just under two million years ago. Evidence for the earliest control of fire comes from about 1.4 million years ago. And these very early humans lived at and around the Equator, where the sun comes up at about 6a.m. and goes down, fast, at about 6p.m. Then it is dark. Very dark. This is where you and I evolved.

So now imagine yourself at the Equator, in the middle of the night, safe in the shelter of a roughly made stick hut or the opening of a cave shelter, without any source of light at all. You cannot see your hand in front of your face. How are you going to 'latch and attach'? Can you see the mouth opening? Can your baby get a good look at your breast?

Our earliest ancestors simply snuggled their babies in to their breast in a very close cuddle so that they could feel their babies bumping frantically against the fleshy underside, and the babies, touching the flesh, lifted their heads, bobbed about with opened mouths in the dark and the nipple simply dropped in.

Now, in the daytime, our ancestors were busy, nomadic people. They walked long distances across the plains looking for food and water, making good use of the morning and early afternoon daylight hours to hunt and gather and avoid dangers. In the late afternoon they might have been looking to stop and settle down to eat and prepare for the night, when they huddled safely together wherever they could best protect themselves from dangerous animals and the cold night-time air.

So the evolved baby might have slept either in his mother's arms or wrapped on her back through the morning, rocked continuously while his mother walked and gathered, warmed by the sun. In the afternoon, sitting in his mother's lap as she rested and ate, he would have had an opportunity to nurse more, which would have kept him warm as the sun fell in the sky and the air began to cool. In the cold and dark of the night, he would have stayed permanently on his mother, being nursed and snuggled and never put down. If he was put down, how would his mother find him again when she couldn't even find her own hand in front of her face?

All the time that women have nursed their babies, right up to the invention of the electric light bulb, the majority of the sucklings have taken place in darkness.

How your highly evolved baby finds the nipple

Look at your baby now. Snuggle him in very close under your dropping breast, using a cuddling arm on the same side as the feeding boob, and roll him out so that you can see his eyes looking at you over the top of your nipple. See how he immediately draws back his head and then bobs frantically around, reaching and wobbling about. But if he is in close enough for you to feel his mouth on the underside of your breast, you can't see his mouth. Now draw away just enough so that you can see his mouth. It doesn't look very big, does it? Bring him in and relax again as his mouth touches the area under your nipple. You can't see his mouth! Well, you really don't need to. In fact, if you try to see his mouth, you will make a space between your breast and him, and his mouth will close a little. Self-defeating.

You have been told repeatedly, no doubt, that your baby has a 'rooting reflex'. Now, a reflex is something that is inherent – not learned, not improved with practice, not able to be done wrong – and it triggers every time it is stimulated. Think about sneezing. Your new baby has probably already sneezed many times in his short life and yet you have not stopped to consider whether you should help him. Nobody has suggested that it is your job to learn the art of baby-sneezing and to assist him. In fact, if we interfere when someone is about to have a good sneeze, we are likely to get pretty messy! Your baby won't sneeze better as he gets older, he won't forget how to sneeze, he won't ever decide that he needs to sneeze differently. This is a reflex. And so is suckling.

The trigger for the reflex is not a look but a feel. This is why your baby will root onto pretty much anything. Hold him against your cheek or neck and see him go – bouncing about, little mouth open and grasping. A reflex that guides him even in the pitch dark. Every time your little one touches the underside of your breast, that reflex triggers and his mouth opens wide enough for the breast to get in. Why wouldn't it? It's a reflex and reflexes always fire if triggered. It's just that you can't see it happening.

The problem with 'nose to nipple'

Have you tried it? If you have, you will have noticed how your baby overshoots the nipple and then flails around before bringing his head forward a bit to find the lost nipple (which is now down by his chin somewhere) and gives you a good bite. Helping him by doing the 'nose to nipple' move will still trigger his reflex because he has had a touch trigger from you, and the reflex is to look up and throw his head back. Always, every time, forever. And so his mouth zips straight past your nipple and then flaps up at you, looking like a hungry bird.

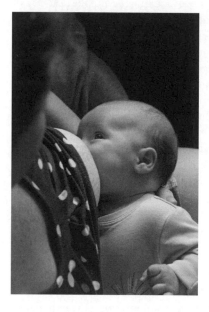

Bring your baby in right under your breast, pulling him into your waist rather than up so his mouth is well below your nipple. Your nipple will probably hit him between his eyes and now, when his reflex makes him reach back and up with a wide mouth, he will get his reward. You feel this. You don't see it. All the breastfeeding books and videos show you how it looks from the watcher's perspective, but you get to see this:

You never evolved to see what was going on under your breast, so you can stop trying. Left alone, the reflex will work perfectly fine. Your baby doesn't need to see, either, just to feel.

The problem with 'tummy to mummy'

The distance from the breast to your face is the perfect viewing distance for a baby. Roll that baby tummy to mummy and he ends up looking under your armpit. You can't roll him tummy to mummy *and* see his face.

Mothers have always looked at their babies while they nurse them. It is here that babies learn how to read emotions and words. We gaze at each other, tease, smooch, tickle and kiss. As soon as you allow your baby to roll out a bit, you get that eye-to-eye contact. Mums who roll their babies tummy to mummy get sore nipples from their babies desperately trying to twist to get a view of mum. The nipple angle is actually just right to remain unbent if a baby is rolled out, under the dropping boob, looking up at his mother. No twisted baby's neck and no twisted nipple.

The problem with 'wait for the big mouth'

If our highly evolved baby is the survivor, the fittest, then surely he must have evolved to nurse easily and so must we. Breasts hang down and babies look up. When a baby gets a face full of soft breast, a reflex is triggered to make his mouth open wide and his head drop back to free the little snub nose and bring his chin in even more closely to the underside of the breast. Baby opens up and the elastic breast drops right in. For the baby sitting on the mother's soft thigh and facing up towards his mother, the breast falls naturally towards his mouth, which is already open, thanks to the touch reflex. Now there is no need to support the breast with your other hand and it is free for dealing with emails or eating more chocolate.

Step by step

- Rather than getting into a special feeding position, just sit where you normally feel comfy – maybe on the sofa, enjoying some TV time.
- Now simply cuddle your baby in close to you with the same arm as the breast on which you have chosen to nurse him. You will find that, when his mouth is right down low under the dropping breast (look at where your breast drops to and bring your baby into that 'drop zone'), his bottom will probably be sat down on your opposite thigh. Don't try to lift his bottom up as this will bring him too high and roll him in and, in any case, he will get too heavy in weeks to come.
- Roll him so that he is looking up at you and then bring him *in*, not *up*. Really well in. Don't be frightened about handling him confidently:

he was handled very confidently by your womb not long ago. His mouth will then get pressed deeply on the soft, round underside of your breast, well below the nipple. Maybe close your eyes and just feel this. If you have small boobs you will have a view of your nipple; if you have large boobs you may not. In any event, both you and baby need to feel rather than see.

- He will bob and muddle about like crazy for a while, trying to get his line of action just right. This is his reflexes working just fine. It looks a bit erratic but, after a while, your baby will make a dive for it and either get it right first time or get on a bit wonky, come off and try again. *Remember:* try not to look for the mouth or you will pull your breast away just enough to mess with his reflex.
- Once you can feel that your little one is really on and drawing, shift about until you are comfy and then let him do what he wants while you turn your attention back to the TV, emails or that chocolate bar with your name on it!

Remember that your baby has evolved over millions of years to get onto your breast by feel and reflex. He doesn't think about this and so cannot get it wrong (any more than you can sneeze wrong). You have evolved to have arms that are the right length (and don't need a pillow under them to hold them in place), breasts that fall down, and to nurse by feel even in the pitch black of the darkest forest or cave shelter.

So you can see that our very modern shopping list – 'nose to nipple, tummy to mummy, wait for the big mouth' – fundamentally takes the power away from your highly evolved baby by switching off his primitive reflex. You were never evolved to latch and attach under an electric light.

If you can reach back in time and reconnect with your primitive ancestors and simply let your highly evolved baby lead, that easy, natural suckling that you so looked forward to will be within your grasp.

How does a baby nurse?

So your baby has muddled onto your breast. What next? Once your baby has got himself on and has settled (and babies can faff about for some long minutes), he will pull hard to bring your elastic breast tissue deep into his mouth. You will feel a strong draw which can be very surprising. The first few days, before hormones make everything more elastic, you might feel a hot stretching that is a little like a friction burn. It should not feel like teeth biting you, but if it does, pull back at the corner of your baby's mouth with a fingertip until the vacuum has broken and then slip him off. Now, get your little one right under your breast again (really right under so your boob drops right down onto his face) and pull him into you so that he can try again. If his head is really free to tip back and his chin is pressed deep against the underside of your breast, his reflex will kick in again and he will have another go.

Once he is on, don't fret about how much of your nipple, areola and breast tissue is in his mouth. If you have not tried to see his 'big mouth' but have kept him pressed touching-close to the underside of your breast, his reflex will have ensured that his mouth is open just the right amount for him and your breast. Is it comfy? If yes, all is well. If you feel a pinch or a bite, take him off and let him have another go, again without trying to take charge.

Once you are both comfy, expect to feel some strong pulling draws followed by some fluttery ones and then some complete stops. Expect your baby to appear to doze off (that is the endorphins in your milk causing a state of blissful dreaminess). After a minute or so, the endorphins will wear off and the cycle will start up again. This will go on for as long as it goes on. Then, eventually, after anything from a few minutes to about 40 minutes (longer if your baby is more than a few weeks old or it is between 5p.m. and 5a.m.), your baby will turn his face to one side and let your boob come out of his mouth.

If you do not immediately lift him away and try to put him down in a crib, your baby will happily snooze on you for a while.

Nipple issues

Are sore nipples normal?

No. Suckling a baby should not be sore. In the vast majority of cases, when a woman is experiencing soreness she is simply trying to 'latch and attach'. One nipped nipple and even the most laid-back mum will begin to look at and manoeuvre her baby, hovering and pulling away slightly to avoid another nibble but, paradoxically, causing just the thing she dreads. Try lying down to feed for a few days and close your eyes so that you can feel what you are doing. Ensure that your baby is very low down – your nipple needs to be at eye level, not nose level, so that when the lifting head reflex kicks in, your baby automatically hits his target! If this doesn't help in a day or two, ask an infant feeding specialist to check for issues such as tongue-tie or infections.

Painful and throbbing nipples after feeding

Your nipples could be painful due to: trying to 'latch and attach'; letting the baby 'hang' from the breast, causing the internal breast tissue to be pulled down; tongue-tie; Raynaud's syndrome – caused by an unusual sensitivity to cold; or thrush, which is a yeast infection that some mums and babies can get.

Try to let baby get himself on to nurse, pull him in very close to prevent dragging and stretching of the internal breast tissues, dry and warm your nipple with your hand or a heat pad after feeds to prevent Raynaud's syndrome if you are a sufferer and also get yourself checked out by an infant feeding specialist as soon as you can to exclude thrush. Your health visitor or GP may not be experienced enough with feeding issues to spot the differences that signal exactly what is wrong.

How much?

Because there is so much emphasis on the word 'feeding' in the baby world, mums understandably worry about how much their baby has taken in a given time. They say 'He hasn't been on for very long, he can't have had enough' or 'He has been on for ages! He must be full now.' Neither of these things need be true. Think of it like this ...

It is cold outside. The wind is howling, the rain is clattering and you have £2.50 and a jolly good book in your bag. You want to go to a café, enjoy a good read over a cup of coffee and stay out of the rain. How will you drink your coffee? You will nurse your drink for an hour or two, taking occasional sips between chapters. If the barista comes over to take your cup away (after all, she gave it to you half an hour ago so you must have finished by now) you are likely to grab it back and reassure her that 'I'm still enjoying it, thank you.'

Over the course of an hour or two, on a different wet day and with £10
in your pocket, you might get through two coffees and a sandwich while
enjoying your book.

The point is this: you are in the café for more than just refreshment. You
are keeping safe and enjoying a lovely, restful lunchtime. You don't want
to bolt your food without breathing so that you can rush on to the next
thing. And you can take as much or as little in the way of refreshments
in the same amount of time as your needs, and purse, dictate.

Equating time spent at the breast with amount of milk taken misses
the point. Your highly evolved baby is safe and warm, protected in
your arms from the forest bears, and the suckling steadies his erratic,
immature nervous system, as we will see in Chapter 6. If he takes more
milk than he needs to grow just right for his genetic make-up, he will
easily bring it back up. There is a natural overflow fail-safe that makes it
impossible for the breastfed baby to take too much and get overweight.

You will never know how much milk your baby has taken. If you try to
guess, you might be like the barista and try to take away the cup before
your customer is physically *and* emotionally completely finished. Grab
a book or the TV remote and join your baby in a nice long snuggle. This
phase will not last forever and you will miss it when it is gone.

How often?

An average adult's daily intake of fluid and food might look like this: a
morning cuppa on waking and another with breakfast; a quick drink of
water while brushing teeth; a mid-morning coffee and snack and then
sips of water until lunch with a glass of juice; 3p.m. obligatory cup of
tea; back to sips of water until 6p.m., when they may have a glass of
something refreshing before dinner; after dinner, perhaps a cup of tea
or nightcap.

This is a pretty average intake for an adult human. We put something
in our mouth (fluid or food or both) very frequently and often take a
long time to finish our drinks rather than glugging them down.

Your baby is a human being. Stop fretting about how often he wants
to nurse and turn your attention to something else while he gets his

emotional and physical needs met. His reflexes and needs for that moment will determine whether he nuzzles in a way that delivers a little or a lot of milk during his time there and how that milk is made up (he needs to meet his food as well as his fluid needs).

If you have to be somewhere, simply 'wet your baby's whistle' with a quick look at your boob before you go to wherever you have to be, and then nurse him for as long as he wants once you have arrived. If you are due to see your friend for the morning, a snuggling baby keeps you there and catching up happily for longer, and your friend can be on tea and cake duty.

One boob or two?

Always offer both boobs at each feeding session. Your baby will decide how long to spend at each, and if you try to second-guess him, you run the risk of guessing wrong. Pop your baby on whichever side feels heavier: you can try different ways to remember which he went on last but you will forget so just do what all mums do and weigh your boobs quickly in your hands! Let your baby muddle on and then do something else with your time. When he comes off (after 5, 15, 30 minutes or whatever), don't fret about whether he has had long enough. Hold

him over a shoulder or on your lap for a while and pat his back. This patting helps to relax his gut while his food goes down a bit. Then, after 10 minutes or so, change his nappy before sitting down and offering the second boob. He may or may not take it – that is up to him.

If you find that when you change a nappy, your baby always yells, start the change on your lap and, if the noise starts, simply feed while you carry on changing.

If you realise that you need to be somewhere, then go now and offer the second boob when you have arrived. If your baby doesn't take the second boob now, he may do in an hour or so or it may be a while before he wants to nurse again (unlikely, but he may have a long nap).

The next time your little one wants to go on the boob, you will find that the refused breast is now the heavier one and so start on this side. You will quickly get used to the changing weight in your breasts and find it quick to work out which one to offer first. As long as you always offer both each time, don't over-worry about this. There is no need for apps and charts that just give you the impression of having a control that you are just not 'meant' to have.

The foremilk and hindmilk conundrum

Remember I said that our parents had never heard of foremilk and hindmilk? In spite of everything you have been told, you too never need worry about this again. The foremilk is just the name we use to describe the thinner, more squirty milk; the hindmilk is thicker and more droppy. But the two are in your breast together at the same time. Your baby, if you have let him get himself onto your boob and then allowed him to manage his time there in the way he chooses, will get exactly the blend of milk he needs at this moment. He doesn't think about this; he just gets it right because he doesn't know how to get it wrong. Sometimes, maybe in hot weather, he will want a little more foremilk in the blend and, at other times, a little more hindmilk. Sometimes I like more salad than potatoes; at other times it has to be carbs all the way; and, on occasion, I have very little appetite at all but still enjoy the company at the dinner table ...

Weight gain

There is no need for weekly weight checks after the first couple of weeks. If your baby is being nicely wet and dirty, is well in himself and is following a centile on his growth chart, he is getting enough.

What is a centile? If you look in your Personal Child Health Record (PCHR or 'Red Book') you will see your baby's weight chart. There are curved lines on the graph called 'centiles' showing the average weight of a baby at different ages and above and below average. The numbers on the centile lines (2nd, 25th, 75th) can be a little confusing but basically ask you to imagine a line of 100 babies in order of weight. If your baby is on the 25th centile then he is 25th in the line, with another 75 babies out of the 100 heavier than him. The baby on the 75th centile is 75th in line, with 25 babies heavier than him.

The centile on which your baby is born seems to be more affected by mum's genetics than dad's (after all, it is mum who has to push the baby out through her pelvis) and some hospitals adjust the chart for this.

Mark which line your baby was on when he was born and expect him to wobble around that line or the one below or the one above. Don't expect him to climb upwards across more than two centile lines or fall down across more than two either. Sometimes, however, mum is genetically geared towards growing and birthing a big baby but baby is destined to be small like his dad! I birth *big* babies and have a 'bijou' husband, and so, despite being extremely healthy babies, after the first few months my sons sank down the centiles to reach their own genetically determined size. If this happens to you, it can be useful to measure your baby's length from tip to toe (this is common practice in many countries at birth but is not routinely done in the UK) and chart that on the height page. Expect your baby to be on the same centile line for height and weight or for the weight one to be one line lower than the height one. Then take the information to your health visitor and get advice about whether you need to act. My sons were the right weight for their height, just very short for their age!

In any case, when you do have your baby weighed, it is essential that this is done with the scales on a hard surface (never a carpet) and *immediately after* a full feed. Any weigh-in that does not follow these criteria simply does not give you an accurate reflection of what is going on. Seek out a healthcare professional who understands this and is happy to comply. This will save you the unnecessary anxiety of having your baby weighed incorrectly, him not following his curve and needless bottles of formula being suggested.

Pee and poo

The healthy baby pees a lot! After the first week, expect at least six pees a day. Some nappies are sodden and these may contain two or three pees. You will get used to what is normal for your baby, so if he becomes less wet, check that you are not trying to space his sucklings or curtail them more than is really needed.

Your baby will poo daily to begin with and then, after a month or two, he will settle down to his own pattern, which could be after every visit to your boob or just once a fortnight. If he is not having formula (which can cause constipation) and he is being wet as usual, don't worry.

Breast milk never causes constipation.

Nights

You will quickly discover, after the first week of your baby's life, that he prefers to be on your boob far more between 5p.m. and 5a.m. than between 5a.m. and 5p.m. This is an evolutionary safety measure (of course) and, try as you might, you cannot beat millions of years of evolution. If you succeeded in getting your baby to sleep well in the darkness hours before he is developmentally ready, you would increase his risk of coming to harm.

Safe co-sleeping

Babies have evolved to stay close and nurse all night and women have evolved to sleep in a very restorative fashion while nursing, even when their sleep is very broken. This is why the vast majority of women who nurse their babies describe falling asleep while they snuggle their babies at night. If you sit up in an attempt to stay awake, evolution will win and you will drop off to sleep anyway and you could drop your baby. In order to be as safe as possible at night, always lie down to feed and, even if you plan to put your baby back in his own crib, prepare for safe co-sleeping: it is better to intentionally prepare to safely co-sleep and then find that you can actually move your baby into his crib than to assume you will stay awake and end up unintentionally co-sleeping unsafely.

- Keep your baby skin to skin with you.
- Use light covers that keep you both comfy but are not too heavy or too hot.

- Ensure that you are on a firm mattress and that baby is free to move (do not put pillows behind him to stop him rolling).
- Don't cover your baby's head.
- No smoking, drugs or drunkenness.
- You should be present in the bed. Do not leave your partner to co-sleep without you in the bed.
- No safety measures will ever reduce the risk of SIDS to zero, no matter where your baby sleeps, but remember that breastfeeding him reduces the risk by around 50%.

It is worth noting that babies who are slept 'back to back' appear to sleep less deeply than those slept on their tummies. This more wakeful type of sleep is normal and protective. Anything that you do to try to make your baby sleep more deeply (swaddling warmly, using a sleep nest, sleeping your baby on his tummy) may indeed cause deeper sleep, but this is not safe sleep. Babies who co-sleep wake their parents less but continue to sleep in the safer type of sleep. They appear to be protected from harm through a combination of their mother's instinctive behaviour; her ability to regulate baby's temperature, breathing and heart rate; by increasing protection against infection; and by frequent suckling.

Forget feeding routines

Trying to wrestle your baby and his 'feeding' into some sort of arbitrary shape dictated by parents, friends, healthcare workers or books is pretty much guaranteed to lead to a sense of failure and frustration for both of you. Try to let your baby just be a baby. After all, you can't cure him of being a baby. Stop fighting him and let your highly evolved baby do what he is so instinctively brilliant at – being the very best survivor that he can be.

Expressing

Many women want to try expressing, to give themselves a little flexibility. This is of course possible, but do proceed with caution. Your highly evolved body is set up for a two-way conversation with your baby and may get quite confused if you express as well. Ideally, unless there is a clinical reason to do so, do not express until your baby is six weeks old as this will give your body time to understand your baby's unique needs.

Express using your hands or a pump (electric or manual – your preference) for 20 minutes on each side. This will be a good enough equivalent to a feed. Just as when your baby is at your boob, sometimes you will get a big 'feed' and sometimes very little. This is normal.

Your milk can be stored at room temperature for up to six hours, in the back of a good fridge for up to six days and frozen for up to six months. Defrost your frozen milk in your fridge, and then, because the freezing process kills off your friendly bacteria, treat it like formula milk and dispose of any undrunk milk straight away.

Sour milk

For reasons that we don't fully understand, some women produce more lipase in their milk and, though it does not affect your baby at all, it can quickly cause your expressed milk to go smelly and your baby to refuse it. If you use your milk soon after it has been expressed, all will be well. If you want to freeze it, scald it first by bringing it close to the boil – until little bubbles form around the edges of the pan – then cool it and freeze it. Once defrosted, you must treat it like formula milk (see page 97).

When you give your baby expressed milk in a bottle, you'll find it is very difficult to guess how much your baby needs at each feed. As you have read, and probably experienced, babies nurse for food *and* nurse 'just because' each time they go on the boob and mum never knows whether there has been more or less of each type. You can't replicate this properly when you bottle-feed, but you can bottle-feed with boob-suckling in mind. See Chapter 5, where we'll look at how you and your baby can achieve a boob-suckling approach to bottle-feeding.

If you plan to exclusively bottle-feed your baby your breast milk from the very outset, express for 20 minutes from each breast every three hours, including at night. Don't worry about being tired as when you express your body produces hormones that cause you to sleep more deeply, with better quality, no matter how often you wake up. Once you have got a good supply going, you can very gently experiment with reducing the amount of times you express in a day (but be careful before cutting out those night-time expressings; night-time pumping is good for protecting your supply, and cutting down can cause a loss of milk).

Anything that is used only for breast milk (bottles and teats and pumps) need not be sterilised each time: sterilise it once a day and then simply wash it out in hot soapy water in between.

Partner ponderings

Breastfeeding a baby is pretty intimate and time-consuming. Most women really want to nurse their babies and yet most women stop pretty soon after birth. Of course you want to help and support, but you might well feel a whole confusing mess of emotions. Your emotionally charged partner may well also feel overwhelmed, trying to understand the needs of this seemingly ever-sucky baby, and be asking you what is wrong that he never seems satisfied.

If you can't feed the baby ...

If you are offered a bottle of expressed breast milk to give to your baby so that you can 'feel more involved', it may have come after a miserable hour of fighting with a pump, and then the actual feeding isn't anywhere near as intimate as the breast-suckling seems to be. Sure, he wolfs the milk down greedily in 10 minutes flat but then he still squeals to suck again and you can't soothe him. He goes back to your partner, she pops him on her boob and he nuzzles on and off for the best part of an hour and still won't sleep in his crib and none of this makes any sense at all.

Moreover, when I talk to partners, what they actually want is to be part of that on-the-sofa mother–baby snuggle that looks, when the feed is a settled one, rather romantic. Your place in her arms has been taken by this interloper who you both adore and resent at the same time.

These feelings are pretty much universal but little talked about. You are a grown-up. Surely you do not feel jealous of a little baby? Well, a bit of you does, actually. And a bit of you is genuinely perplexed that this baby who you both wanted so much is making your partner cry with his never-ending demands and does not seem to be in the slightest bit interested in you.

The harsh truth is that evolution doesn't need you to be brilliant with the baby stuff just yet. Evolution does not need your baby to 'bond' quickly and deeply with you. Evolution certainly does not need you to feed your baby! But evolution really does need you around for a very important role that secures your baby's well-being as well as that of your partner.

What can you do?

What your partner needs from you right now is the reassurance that, over and above everything else, she is doing a really great job of mothering. You telling her that breastfeeding is not the be-all and end-all and that you can run down to the supermarket for some formula will just confirm her worst fears: she can't do this and was a fool to think she could.

Take tips from dads who were themselves breastfed and come from families where it is the accepted norm rather than something quite remarkable requiring canonisation. They use the sort of reassuring language of a gran who has been there, done that: 'You're fine; you're doing just great; these things take a bit of getting used to; I'll put the kettle on and push the Hoover around while you get the hang of it – shout if you need an extra pair of hands.' Midwives with women in labour don't break into a sweat every time a woman panics during a contraction, or rescue her from her experience by offering drugs, or join in the panic with her. The midwife calmly gets on with her note-writing or simply and usefully rubs the woman's back while saying gently, 'You're doing just fine!'

Women do not want rescuing; they want reassurance that they can and will overcome this challenge and that you believe in their ability. It costs nothing to say the reassuring words, even if you do not, in truth, quite believe them yourself.

Look back at 'Partner ponderings' on page 54. All those tips remain important: regular food and drink, household tasks, etc. But also consider these:

1. Share a glass of wine in the evening. If part of your grown-up relationship has always been to enjoy a drink together, a tipple with supper will not upset your baby but may reconnect you both to that grown-up world and help your partner relax after a stressful day with your baby.

2. Avoid asking her what she has done all day! This can feel very challenging when she is asking herself why she hasn't managed to get out of her PJs until midday all week. Instead, tell her that you can't imagine how she has managed to look after a baby *and* still look so gorgeous!

3. Run her a deep bath and then walk the baby around the garden (an umbrella will keep the rain off). Fresh air soaks up the sound of a fractious baby who can't bear to be apart from his mother for the 20 minutes or so that she needs to freshen up and have some free time. Remember that, in the evening hours, what your baby needs is not more food, just constant, in-arms soothing. You can provide this beautifully.

4. Walk the baby around and pat his bottom firmly but gently while your partner goes up to bed a little early. Keep walking and patting and doing anything else that soothes him (don't stop doing whatever works or the crying will return). When nothing soothes, tiptoe upstairs, bung the baby on the boob while your partner sleeps (ensure that you follow the safe co-sleeping guidelines above) and then hop in too so that you can get some sleep before morning. NEVER sit on the sofa with your baby if you think that you are too tired to stay awake. Sleeping with babies on sofas is dangerous.

5. Accept that suckling a baby is just suckling a baby and does not have to be wonderfully snuggly every time. Much of the time, nursing our babies is quite functional: it stops the noise and it just needs doing. Hand your crying baby over when he won't settle, get up and make a sandwich and a cup of tea for you both, put the linen in the washing machine and then rejoin your partner to keep her company while she pops the baby to her boob, yet again. Parenting is relentless at times.

6. Reclaim your spot on the sofa while baby snuggles at the boob and hold him in place while your partner eats her supper! Partners generally make the mistake of waiting until *after* the baby has stopped suckling before moving in for a cuddle with their woman, but women feel all touched-out after nursing their baby. Move in during that oxytocin-soaked feed and you might get a much warmer reception!

Questions and answers

There are enough feeding questions to fill a book all by themselves, so here are a few of the most common and the simplest ones. If there is something more problematic for you, such as a cleft palate or a loss of milk, see an infant feeding specialist as soon as you can.

Breast care

How should I look after my breasts?

It is helpful to prevent problems rather than try to sort them out after they have occurred. Look after your breasts by adding a regular check to your daily wash routine. Either in the shower or after a wash, feel gently but firmly all around your boobs. Use flat fingers and not knuckles and feel for tender areas and lumps. If you find a tender lumpiness in the breast tissue or something that feels like fishing wire just under the edge of the areola then you have a bit of engorgement and this needs sorting out in order to reduce the likelihood of mastitis. Using the pad of a finger, massage deeply in circular movements and then do some reverse pressure softening (see page 57). If you want to, next time you put your baby to your boob, you can massage the lump again (make sure that you don't pull the breast out of his mouth when you do this). Simple pain remedies such as paracetamol and ibuprofen will reduce inflammation and pain until the problem subsides. Daily breast care will help to keep your breasts functioning well and flag up any potential problems before they get too troublesome. If you notice a lump that doesn't go away within about four or five days of massage, see your GP for a check-up.

What can I eat?

I love spicy food but I'm told it will affect my milk. Is this true?

No! Your milk is made from your blood, not your food. When you eat, your food goes into your digestive system, where it is broken right down into its component parts. These go into your blood and the fibre and bits that can't be used come out of your body and down the loo! That curry may be spicy, but your blood can't be spicy; onions may make gas in your bowel, but you can't have gas bubbles in your blood to make your milk windy; all those grapes might give you heartburn, but your blood cannot become too acidic. Air or acid in your blood would kill you, so just forget what people tell you about the foods you eat and get back to enjoying your mealtimes! Interestingly, flavours *can* get into your milk in tiny amounts (you know how you sweat garlic sometimes?)

and this may be why the breastfed baby tends to be easier to wean onto family foods. If your baby wants to wean onto curry or Marmite, we know who to blame …

Mastitis

I have a hot, red breast and feel awful. I think it is mastitis. What should I do?

Mastitis is an inflammation of the breast tissue. It is almost always a result of engorgement and, as such, does not need antibiotics. If you continue to let baby nurse freely, avoid expressing unless you can't get your baby on your breast, and take regular pain relief in the form of paracetamol and ibuprofen, mastitis sorts itself out pretty quickly. There is more detail on page 57. Don't express at all unless baby can't nurse, as expressing may make matters worse. If baby really can't get on the boob, express for 20 minutes each side and no more.

Lump in the breast

I have a hard, tender lump in my breast. Should I worry?

No need to worry yet! Most lumps turn out to be blocked ducts and the treatment is quite simple and as mentioned in the answer to the first question above. If the lumpiness doesn't improve within about four or five days, or if the area becomes very hot and hard, see your GP so that you can be checked for other problems.

White spot on nipple

I have a painful white spot on my nipple. What is this?

This sounds like a 'bleb'. A bleb is a blocked milk sinus and looks like a large whitehead. Blebs hurt! Some people use a really hot flannel on the bleb and then squeeze it out but I find that, although this can help in the short term, the bleb tends to come back quickly. Better to practise the daily breast care detailed on page 83. Feel deeply under the edge of the areola and you will find a tender area that feels like a bit of fishing wire just under your finger. Feel back from this area and you will almost certainly find a blocked duct, which feels like a tender lump under the flesh. Massage this entire line from the areola backwards to the lump and further in order to clear the tissue fluid back into the lymphatic system and this will lead to better milk flow. Do speak to an infant feeding specialist if you are unsure.

Baby can't latch and nurse

My baby just can't get on and nurse at all. He tries but seems to be clueless! What is wrong?

The majority of babies simply need less 'latching and attaching' and, in my own experience over more than 30 years, I have yet to meet a mum who found it easier to 'latch and attach' than to simply feel her baby cuddled very close in and let her baby's reflexes do the rest. So always start from that point. Even if there is another issue, all babies benefit from having their reflexes freed up to behave normally. However, some babies need extra time nursed lying down to recover from birth trauma and about 10% of babies have skin (called a frenulum) under their tongue that shouldn't be there. Some people call this a tongue-tie, but this is not helpful because about 75% of these babies do perfectly well with sensible support and time. The other 25% may need further support or a snip of the skin to release the tongue to do its thing unhampered. Until you can get really good help from a specialist, use a nipple shield. Many people worry about the use of shields but it is the underlying problem that has driven you to use a nipple shield that causes issues, *not* the shield itself. A nipple shield can help you nurse for the short time it takes to get really good help and support. Not all infant feeding specialists are trained to assess whether a baby has a frenulum under the tongue and, if he does, just how it affects the tongue movement, so do ask carefully. If your baby does have a problematic frenulum, a specialist should help you to decide what to do next as well as support you in the weeks to come as things settle down.

Large breasts

I have really big boobs and am terrified of smothering my baby. What should I do?

Your baby has flared nostrils and a pretty gristly nose tip. This provides a little safety air channel when he is at the breast. Also, if, as described above, you are careful to hold your baby across his shoulders so that his head can drop naturally back with his chin digging into your breast, his nose will be quite free. Listen and you will hear the gentle sniffing. If your baby is trying to pull away and is fighting, check that you are not holding his neck or head in such a way that he is not free to tip his head back and sniff the air.

Breast surgery

I have had surgery to my breasts. Will this mean I can't breastfeed my baby?

Not at all, but, depending on what the surgery entailed, your supply might be affected. If you have had a breast reduction, or any removal of breast tissue for whatever reason, you might have to work harder to produce a full supply. If you have had a lot of breast tissue removed and find that your supply is on the low side, a supplementary nursing system (SNS) can work wonders in the short or long term. If you have had a breast enlargement, as long as this was not done because your puberty did not take place normally, you will be quite able to nurse normally. If you have had a mastectomy on one side, you will be able to feed on the remaining breast (twin babies only ever get one breast each, after all!). If you are in any doubt, talk to an infant feeding specialist.

Suckling in public

I am keen to get out and about but nervous of suckling in public. Any tips?

We all worry about this at least a little. We worry that people might stare or be offended or that we might feel uncomfortable or embarrassed. There are breastfeeding drop-ins in most towns and villages now, so search one out and try that first. If you have followed the advice in this chapter and are simply cuddle-suckling one-handed, most people will be completely unaware of what you are doing – it is the faffing around with pillows and strange holds that attracts attention. Wear a light camisole or T-shirt under your main top, pull this down under your boob and pull your main top up to create a sort of letterbox through which to pop your boob into your baby's mouth. This keeps your back and chest warm as well as providing some privacy if you need it. Finally, don't assume that the person who has caught your eye is about to get cross about your feeding in public. Most people simply love babies. I discovered that, if I smiled back, a conversation usually started and I would often end up having some delightful company over a cuppa.

Dummies

Is it okay to use a dummy if I am a suckling mum?

Yes, but! Your body really needs to work out how much milk your baby needs day by day and the best way to achieve this is by letting your baby do all his suckling on you (or his thumb if he does this naturally at times). If you use a dummy too much your supply can suffer. Avoid using a dummy until your little one is at least six weeks old and, preferably, until he is three months old, as all the boob-suckling he does during those colicky evenings provides much better soothing, nourishment and protection for him.

Contraception

Can I get pregnant as a suckling mum?

Yes, you can. However, suckling is actually a very good contraceptive if: (1) your baby is under six months old; (2) you are *exclusively* nursing your baby day and night (no top-ups and no dummies); and (3) your periods have not returned. If you are not exclusively suckling your baby or if another pregnancy is absolutely *not* what you want right now, use another contraceptive method alongside nursing. The mini pill, injections, implants, coils and barrier methods are okay options. The combined pill is okay after six months but not recommended before that as it may interfere with your supply too much.

C-section

I have had a C-section and the staff told me to use a pillow or feed 'rugby ball' style. I'm struggling to feed. What should I do?

Putting a pillow on top of your tummy will squeeze your abdomen onto your scar and, with a baby on top of this, you will be sore. Feeding under the arm, 'rugby ball' style, is not as easy as healthcare professionals seem to think. Ditch the pillow, feed lying down for a week (you have had a major operation and need time to recover) and then, when you want to sit up to nurse your baby, simply sit baby on your opposite thigh and cuddle him like in the pictures earlier in this chapter. Your milk might take an extra day or two to increase in volume, so do hand-express from the outset if he seems uninterested and get help early on if your baby seems sleepy or is struggling at all.

Twins

I have twins. Can I still feed them myself without topping up with formula?

Of course you can! Your breasts simply respond to suckling, and if two babies nurse freely, you make enough milk for two. People who tell you that you won't make enough milk simply do not understand how it works. After all, every breastfeeding mum gets to the point when she is making enough milk for a 14-pound baby because a 14-pound baby is suckling. Two seven-pound babies seem the same to your breasts as one 14-pound baby and they respond in the same way. Over time you will discover that you can feed one at a time, two together, and even walk about with two feeding. Women are masters at adaptation. Just get going without fretting and follow the basic advice above.

Diabetes

I am diabetic. Is there anything extra that I should know?

Yes. Exclusive suckling of a baby reduces his risk of diabetes in later life by up to 50%. If at all possible, express your milk (see page 78) in the week leading up to the expected birth and use the drops of colostrum after the birth to keep your baby's blood sugar stable without him needing formula milk. Exclusively nurse your baby for as long as possible before starting weaning (see Chapter 9) and then wean alongside continuing to give your own milk. Eat healthily yourself and keep a careful eye, as you always do, on your own blood sugar. If you do need or choose to give formula milk to your baby, there is some evidence that a goat's milk formula might offer slightly less risk of diabetes in your baby.

Poorly baby

My baby is small and poorly. How can I nurse him without needing to top up with formula?

Every situation is different, but some things are common. The female human lactating breast makes more milk when stimulated more and less when stimulated less. If, for whatever reason, your baby is unable to get everything he needs through suckling, you can do a couple of things.

- Express using your hand or a pump every three hours day and night. Do 20 minutes each side. Give this from a feeding cup, finger feeder or bottle until your baby is able to nurse on you.

- Use an SNS, as discussed on page 94, using your own expressed milk.

- While your baby nurses, compress your breast with a constant, steady squeeze using a hand. When the suckling stops, you pause. When it starts again, squeeze again. This is like a top-up directly from your boob and is great for small, weak or poorly babies. It can also be good for a baby with a pesky frenulum while you wait for good help and support.

Adopted baby

I have adopted a baby and want to nurse him. Is this possible?

Yes! How amazing is that? It helps to get started with stimulation before the baby arrives and you can use a hand pump every three hours (20 minutes each side) every day for a couple of weeks while you prepare for your baby. Even more helpful is to ask your GP for some Domperidone. This commonly used drug is given for acid reflux but has the weird side effect of causing people (even men) to lactate. If you can't start before baby arrives, buy an SNS online and use this to nurse your new baby at your breast using formula or donated breastmilk. The stimulation alone can make many women lactate, but Domperidone at the same time will really help. Even if you don't fully lactate, you can enjoy the practicalities and closeness of suckling your little one.

Lesbian parenting

I am in a lesbian relationship. Can my partner share the suckling?

Of course! Some lesbian couples have the birth mother boob-feed the baby until all he wants is soothing and then the non-birth partner takes over the soothe-suckling. This is no different from settling a baby with a dummy after he has had a good milk feed. Some couples use an SNS with or without Domperidone to allow suckling in the non-birth partner. See the answer above about adoptive nursing. It seems to me a shame that more women do not know about using an SNS when feeding in difficult or unusual circumstances.

Topping up

I need to 'top-up' my baby because he needs more than I am making right now but I don't want to use formula. Is there a solution?

Yes, there is. Except in a few circumstances, women make enough milk as long as their baby is free to suckle and doesn't have a problem such as tongue-tie or prematurity (both of these can cause a suckle that under-simulates the boob). While you wait for your supply to pick up, look into getting hold of some donated human milk (see useful resources section, page 233). You can use this with an SNS or a bottle and keep your little one exclusively human-milk feed.

5 Suckling the bottle-feeding way

Women arrive at the destination of bottle-feeding from a variety of starting points. For a few, the decision is taken happily and heartily before their baby is born.

The vast majority of women, however, start out wanting to nurse their baby but, due to illness (mum or baby), separation from their baby, long-standing medical conditions or, most often, through lack of good support and help in the early days, they hit the rocks and can't row back. If you are part of this group, my heart goes out to you. Many people underestimate the grief women feel when they are not able to nourish their child in the way they would choose, but I see it every day and I understand the frustration, anger and sense of betrayal you might be feeling.

Because of the way our society views *feeding* as somehow separate from suckling and soothing, women have become split into two camps – breastfeeders and bottle-feeders – and this causes, as sectarianism always does, antagonism, suspicion and fighting. The assumption is that women who bottle-feed do not want to mother in the same way as those who breastfeed, that they want to measure and schedule and separate from their baby and certainly do not belong in the 'attachment-parenting', 'baby-wearing' cliques!

Some women really do believe that, by bottle-feeding, they will get a baby who is routine-led and 'easy' from the word go. Most get a nasty shock when they discover that, however you get food into a baby, she still has her highly evolved DNA set to 'cave baby'; but most women have imagined themselves, throughout pregnancy, parenting in a more baby-led way, enjoying long, languid snuggles, the intimacy of skin on skin, and the delight of looking down on a downy head as it peeps out of a cosy sling. They find themselves bottle-feeding and quickly discover that they are not seen by others as being part of that picture anymore. Now, not only are they not nourishing their baby in the way they had anticipated, they are not even mothering in the way they had wanted. A double grief.

So in this chapter, I want to reintroduce you back into the world of suckling ... as a bottle-feeding mum.

We will look at a variety of ways of feeding and suckling, from expressing and giving your own milk through to exclusive formula milk feeding. We'll also look at how to breast-suckle your baby in the rare circumstance that you are unable to produce milk.

Now, obviously, no matter how you parent, it is not possible to negate the risks associated with giving a baby formula milk and, if this is how you are feeding your baby, it makes no difference whether you got here by choice or not – the risks are there. We will look at the safest way to make up formula feeds, and this will solve some of the common problems – but it will not negate the risks. That is simply how it is and no amount of hand-wringing will stop that being so. Being a mum involves having to accept tough truths. There will be many more really very tough moments through the years to come as a parent, so don't bellyache over this too much – it's just life.

Everyone feels guilty!

Don't assume that, because she is suckling her child, your breastfeeding friend is having an easier time of it with the professionals and family than you are. You imagine that she is not being put through the same guilt-mangle as you and that she is having her halo polished every day by midwives, health visitors and every other Tom, Dick and Harriet. Nothing could be further from the truth.

After the birth is when breastfeeding mums have a really tough time. The umbilical cord has barely been cut and she is being asked, 'How long do you plan to breastfeed for?' Then, and many times a day, 'How do you know how much you are giving?'; 'Why are you feeding him again?'; 'Are you sure you have enough milk?'; 'Are you winding him enough?'; 'Why is she crying?'; 'What have you eaten?' Your friend is probably feeling pressured towards bottles after the birth just as you felt pressured towards breastfeeding before it.

If you are reading this as a suckling mum, open your arms, hug your bottle-feeding mate, read this book together and haul her back into your world. Sure, it is a muddled, chaotic and confusing world, but it is the way the baby world has evolved, so share it openly, honestly and generously. Your bottle-feeding friend may think you are judging her parenting for being too structured even as you think she is judging yours for being over-indulgent. Every time she says that her baby is settled, you may reckon she is suggesting that yours would be too, if only you would sneak a good glug of formula into her; she may think that, whenever you relate how delightful it feels to know that your bundle of joy is growing just from your milk alone, you are giving a coded message that says, 'Your body has failed!'

Talk to each other without needing to compete about which way is 'better'. Between you, ditch the guilt trips that you are both susceptible to: you are both struggling enough with the realities of motherhood right now without having this battle and misunderstanding.

Now then, bottle-feeders, enough of all that guilt: read on to learn how to suckle as a bottle-feeding mum with a breastfeeding mum's sensibility, hold your head up and get back in there to rejoin that clan from which you thought you'd been banned!

Take the lead from suckling mums

Wherever you can, find a way to give your baby at least some of your own human milk. Virtually all women are able to produce some milk, even if you had a supply and then 'lost it'. Even if you need to supplement the amount you can produce with formula milk, the smallest amount of your milk can reduce some of the problems associated with giving formula. Every bit of human milk helps, so if you run into problems, don't throw your baby out with her bath water; find someone who can help you get the very most out of your boobs. Then learn to bottle-feed as safely and smartly as possible and behave as if you were a breastfeeding mum in every other way.

You and your little one still need those early days of total skin to skin, the endless in-mum's-arms time, the long snuggly feeds. You really can combine bottle-feeding your baby with all the other aspects of baby-led parenting that we have looked at so far and you and your baby will benefit enormously from doing so. Babies who are kept close to mum in their arms have less risk of infection; babies who are soothed in arms as often as they need to be cry far less than those who are put down after feeding; and babies who have all their emotional and physical needs met immediately in the early months of life appear to go into primary school more confidently and show more sociability and independence.

Bottle-feed like a breastfeeder

First, many women who want to suckle but find that their milk has gone move to bottle-feeding when they could use a supplementary nursing system (SNS) and give the formula while still enjoying boob-suckling. An SNS is a tidy little gadget with a bottle device which sits between your own boobs and delivers formula or expressed human milk from tiny silicone tubes. These tubes sit along the nipple and your baby simply suckles the breast in the time-honoured fashion and gets whatever you are able to produce alongside whatever is in the SNS. Even if you produce no milk at all, you can exclusively boob-suckle your baby, and many of my clients do just that. When I suggest this to mothers, they are astonished. 'Is it okay for me to do that?' they ask. Of course it is. You can put your breast wherever you jolly well like! Giving infant formula milk from a supplementer means that the baby gets ample non-milk suckling time alongside the milk-getting suckling; she only takes what she needs rather than how much she is fed from a bottle; and she gets the great palate-rounding benefits of boob-suckling that can reduce the likelihood of ear infections and wonky teeth.

A shop-bought or even home-made SNS can also be used perfectly for 'finger-feeding' a tiny, sick or pre-snip tongue-tied baby who just cannot suckle a boob but can manage a finger. I'm sure you will work out how, but if you get stuck, speak to an infant feeding specialist.

Even if a mum decides to give milk from a feeding cup or bottle, there is no reason why she can't then offer her breast as a soother instead of a dummy when a no-milk suckling is needed.

This is wonderful news for those heartbroken mums who desperately wanted to suckle but, through lack of good support or because of other factors beyond their control, have lost their milk.

Don't be robbed of the experience you craved all those months. Just be creative and do things the quirky way. Will baby become confused? Of course not. She doesn't get confused between a bottle, a dummy and her fingers. She simply loves to suckle and is adapted to suckle whatever reaches her mouth. If the reason you stopped in the first place was due to soreness, get good help to discover the cause (there is *always* a cause) and then confidently move forward in the direction you wish to go.

If you are cup- or bottle-feeding and have no desire or intention to ever suckle your baby at your breast, there is still no need to miss out on all the great stuff that keeps mums and babies most settled and soothed. You just need some pointers to help you bottle-feed your baby as if she were a boob-suckled baby and to help you experience some of the benefits enjoyed by your breastfeeding friends.

So whether you are feeding your baby your own milk from a cup or bottle, using an SNS, giving just an occasional bottle of your own with formula milk, or exclusively bottle-feeding formula milk, read on.

Kit

First of all, get shopping! You are going to be spending a lot of time and money, so choose carefully and don't be caught up in this week's bottle and gadget hype.

Even very small babies can take very happily from little feeding cups and they are less fiddly to clean than bottles and teats. These can be ideal in the early days for ready-made formula or your own expressed milk. But if you are using powdered formula or giving larger amounts of your own milk, SNS devices and bottles are generally the most straightforward option as you can measure and mix and feed all from the same receptacle.

You will need preferably two SNS devices or six to eight bottles and teats, something to sterilise the kit, a bottle brush, a small airtight tub, a small thermos flask that can hold boiling water, sharp scissors for ready-made formula boxes, a kettle that does not have a filter, and a few dummies.

Bottles

You will be astounded by the sheer number and variety of bottles, teats, sterilisers and dummies. Most bottles now have gadgets in the teat or bottle that are claimed to 'prevent wind, colic and reflux'. These make absolutely no difference to a baby's natural daily gut churnings. As you will see in Chapter 6, evolution dictates that your baby is very uncomfortable a lot of the time, which causes her to complain and you to pick her up. You cannot and should not try to cure this. These valves and buttons also make putting together and cleaning the bottles and teats unnecessarily complicated and fiddly. Always choose bottles that are made without BPA (bisphenol A) plastic as BPAs are affected by heat and can leak chemicals into the milk that may harm your baby. Some parents choose glass bottles.

There are numerous teats on the market that are, apparently, 'just like your breast'! Most of these are very badly designed from a baby's point of view as they do not allow a good amount of teat as well as the 'nipple' bit into the mouth to work with the tongue and jaw. The baby ends up just sucking on the 'nipple' and this is not so good for the development of the palate, jaw or teeth. Save your money and buy standard bottles and teats. Look for teats that have a high profile: they should have the 'nipple' part and then a soft, fatter bulb below that which is at least as long as the 'nipple'. Teats have different flow rates and you need the ones for a newborn baby. If there is a good silicone bulb for the tongue to work on and a steady, not over-fast flow, your baby will have better control over the feed.

Sterilising

You can either get a steam steriliser or use the cold chemical sterilising method. You can even sterilise your kit in a pan of boiling water. Anything that will come into contact with non-human milk needs to be thoroughly sterilised, so make sure your sterilising kit is easy enough to use so that you won't be tempted to cut corners.

Even new bottles and teats must be sterilised. Clean everything first with hot, soapy water. Then rinse thoroughly to remove the soap. Now sterilise everything (teats, bottles, retaining rings, caps) using your chosen method.

If steam sterilising, follow the instructions on your steriliser very carefully and ensure that the bottles are open-side down. Leave the steriliser closed until you are ready to take a bottle out: this ensures that no bacteria get in.

If using a cold chemical steriliser, make up the solution according to the instructions on your product and then get the bottles and teats right under the water, making sure that there are no air bubbles. They must stay put for at least 30 minutes and the solution must be changed every 24 hours. Shake off the excess fluid before making up a feed, but don't run the bottle under a tap to get rid of the chemicals.

If you are boiling your kit in a pan, ensure that everything is below the water line and there are no trapped air bubbles, then boil for 10 minutes. If you do not plan to use the bottles straight away, store them with the caps on to prevent bacteria getting inside. Boiling causes teats to crack sooner than using other methods, so check the teats weekly and replace them if you see even the tiniest cracks – this is where bacteria can lurk.

If you are using any amount of formula, all your bottles, teats, retaining rings and caps need to be washed and then sterilised after every feed and it is good practice to get in the habit of putting your brush and dummies through at the same time. Gastroenteritis (vomiting and diarrhoea) is potentially dangerous to small babies. Don't take the risk.

If you are using human milk, see below for expressing and cleaning instructions.

Human milk

Whenever possible, express your own milk and give that to your baby. It will help cure a bout of constipation; it will give vital antibodies when there is a bug going around your neighbourhood; it will soothe your baby's gut spasms with its high level of endorphins; and it will taste different every day according to what you have eaten. Even one feed a day or a week or a month of your own human milk is better than nothing. If you can express some milk but not enough for a full feed, it is completely fine to mix your milk into a bottle of infant formula. Despite what your grandma says, this will not curdle in your baby's tummy.

Express each breast for 20 minutes in total (either 20 on the right then 20 on the left; or 10 on the right, then 10 on the left, 10 on the right and then 10 on the left, or five left, five right, five left, five right, five left, five right, five left, five right; whatever works best for you). The amounts will differ each time and this is completely normal. Give whatever you get and, if you know your supply is too low and this is why you are needing to use formula, give your milk first and then top up with non-human milk afterwards, taking it very slowly to avoid overfeeding. Remember that your own human milk can stay on the counter top for up to six hours, in the back of a good fridge for up to six days, and in the freezer for up to six months.

Anything that has only been in contact with your human milk can be washed in hot, soapy water and rinsed rather than sterilised. Simply sterilise once a day.

If you are using your own milk in a bottle, it is smart to get one bottle ahead. Express and store your milk until the next feed and then feed the bottle of your milk while expressing at the same time: to begin with you will need someone to help, but, before long, you will be able to do this on your own. It just takes a bit of practice. If this is too tricky, feed the stored milk first and then express afterwards. Don't make your baby cry while she is waiting for you to express. Always have a bottle ready and waiting.

Ready-made infant formula milk

When your baby is very young and if you are not ready to start making up feeds from powder, consider buying ready-to-feed cartons of milk. Choose the smallest cartons – whatever the manufacturers say about storing opened cartons in the fridge for 24 hours, bacteria will get in and will feed on the milk and multiply. You will be creating a perfect bug incubator!

Powdered cow's milk infant formula

Cartons of ready-made formula are expensive and quite wasteful (the carton may contain five ounces and your baby needs only two). So, before long, you may want to move over to powdered infant formula milk.

Read the ingredients list on your chosen tub of powdered milk every time you buy. The formulas change recipe fairly regularly and you may not know, unless you check, that the formula you chose because it was suitable for vegetarians now has added fish oil. Equally, if you eat a halal or kosher diet or avoid beef, read the ingredients and, if you are still not sure, contact your local faith community support team. Some formulas will be suitable for your baby, but some will not, and it is better to be safe than sorry.

If you have a family history of allergies or atopy (eczema, asthma, hay fever and migraines), it may help to avoid milks that contain extra allergens. Dairy is a common allergy in any case, but fish and eggs are also common, and many of the better-known brands add these ingredients to the powder so that they can claim that the essential omega oils are needed for your baby's health. This was the same reason given for adding peanut oil to formula many years ago and, due to the rise in peanut allergy, it had to be removed. Exposing your delicate baby to one allergen is unavoidable when you use formula; exposing her to numerous ones is unnecessary and avoidable.

Goat's milk and soya milk infant formula

There is recent evidence supporting the use of goat's milk formulas. Goat's milk appears to be easier to digest and may be less likely to cause constipation. It is every bit as carefully manufactured as cow's milk-based formulas.

Likewise, soya-based formulas must also abide by exactly the same strict guidelines for nutrition and safety as the more common dairy-based formulas. Just read the back of the tub and buy carefully. If your baby is likely to be prone to allergies, she is just as likely to be allergic to goat's milk and soya milk as to cow's milk. You may discover that she is allergic to one but not the other, to none of them, or to all of them.

Switching between brands

Brands like your loyalty, so myths have been allowed to circulate that, once you have chosen your brand, you must stick to it or your baby will have an upset tummy. This is simply untrue.

There is an argument that exposing your baby to different flavours is a good thing. It has been well known for many years that the breastfed baby weans onto family foods more easily because she is exposed to a wide variety of flavours through her mother's milk. Formula-fed babies have the same flavour meal after meal after meal, day after day for up to six months. Give your baby a little variety. As long as you never swap scoops between different brands and don't mix two brands in one bottle, it is fine and dandy to give one brand in the morning, a different one at night and another one altogether through the middle of the day.

If you are away from home and can't get your usual brand, don't panic; simply use a different one and be glad that you baby is being given a new flavour experience.

Always choose a basic first milk rather than a follow-on milk or milk for 'the hungrier baby'. These are not recommended by healthcare professionals and do not offer any benefits to your baby. Furthermore, they are invariably more expensive.

Once a tub of powder is empty, throw it away *with* the scoop: don't keep the scoop to use with a new tub as the ingredients change often and the scoop size changes accordingly.

Making up the feeds

It is essential that you do not cut corners when you are making up feeds. Your mother may have made up all her bottles in the morning and kept them in the fridge, but this is really not safe. She may have boiled the water and then left it to cool right down before making up a bottle. This is not at all safe either. She will tell you that she was sterilising the water. But it is not the water that is the issue here: it is the powder.

Infant feeding formula milks are not sterile when they leave the factory. They are as clean as they can be, but they are a tub of sweet food, which bugs love! It is the milk, therefore, that you need to sterilise, and that means adding boiling or very hot water.

How to safely make up formula

1. Wash your hands and wash down the preparation surfaces thoroughly.
2. Ensure all your kit is freshly sterilised (if using steam or boiling in a pan, you can do this immediately before making up the feed).
3. Fill a kettle (without a filter attachment) with at least one litre of fresh tap water. Do not use previously boiled water or bottled water.
4. Boil the water while you get out your sterilised bottle and extras. Put the bottle on the cleaned work surface and keep the teat, retaining ring and cap on the upturned lid of your sterilising unit or in the pan of boiling water until needed. Do not put them on the work surface.
5. Either use this water immediately or allow it to cool, in the kettle, *for no more than 30 minutes*: you need very hot water (70°C or above) to kill any bacteria in the powdered milk.
6. Standing the bottle on a cleaned surface, follow the instructions on the back of your milk tin and carefully pour the right amount of boiling or very hot water into your bottle. Crouch down to look at the markings on the bottles from straight on because looking from above can give you an incorrect guide.
7. Using the correct, dry scoop that came with the tin of powder, carefully measure in the correct number of scoops of powder according to the instructions on your milk tin. Be very careful not to press the scoop with powder against the side of the tin as this can compress the powder into the scoop and cause over-concentration of the feed. Use a sterile knife to carefully slice off the excess powder from the top of the scoop.
8. Holding the teat by its edge, put it on the bottle and hold it in place with the plastic ring. Now put the cap on firmly so that it closes off the teat hole.
9. Shake the bottle very well to mix the feed properly. *Take care!* The liquid will be very hot and may spray back when you take the cap off the teat hole.
10. Once you are happy that the feed is completely mixed, run the bottom part of the bottle under a fast, cold tap until it is cool enough for your baby to drink. Do not let the tap water touch the bottle cap. Do not let it stand on the work surface to cool down and do not put it in a jug of

cold water: neither of these approaches brings the formula temperature down quickly enough and this can lead to bacterial growth.

11. Test the temperature on the inside of your wrist. It should feel comfortably warm and not at all hot. Some babies are happy with their milk much cooler than others.
12. Use it immediately.
13. Throw any leftover milk away after two hours.

Formula-making machines are not recommended as they cannot guarantee a sterile feed. As tempting as they sound, the evidence suggest you should 'steer clear'. Bottled water is not recommended for making up feeds, as it's not sterile and may contain too much salt (sodium) or sulphate. If you have to use bottled water to make up a feed, check the label to make sure the sodium (also written as Na) level is less than 200 milligrams (mg) per litre, and the sulphate (also written as SO or SO_4) content is not higher than 250mg per litre. It's not usually sterile, so, like tap water, it will still need to be boiled before you prepare the feed.

Going out

If you are going out for the day, you will need to prepare the components of a feed like this:

1. Carefully measure the right amount of formula powder into a sterile pot and put the lid on it.
2. Boil some fresh water and then measure out the correct amount of boiling water, using a sterile bottle, into a clean vacuum flask that is only used for this purpose. Secure the top on the flask.
3. Pack the flask, tub of powder and a sterile bottle in your bag and make the feed up fresh where you have access to a cold running tap for cooling the feed down quickly.

If you have to make a feed in advance (maybe for nursery), carefully make up the feed as usual, and put it straight into the back of the fridge for at least an hour. Take it out of the fridge just before you leave the house and pack it in a cool bag with an ice pack. This feed must be used within four hours of leaving your fridge.

I realise that this seems like an almighty faff. It is, but you really do need to be this careful. Taking short cuts puts your baby at unnecessary risk.

Giving the feed

Giving a baby a bottle can be every bit as snuggly and intimate as suckling her at your breast. Remember that suckling a baby is about far, far more than ensuring that she gets human milk. Just being held in her mother's arms helps to protect against infection; skin to skin can help your baby's autonomic nervous system (ANS; for more on this see Chapter 6) to soothe, and snuggling helps with the early and essential attachment that babies and mothers need in the first few months.

Wherever possible, ensure that just mum gives the bottle. Of course, it is nice to share the baby around for feeds and this is one of the reasons some women opt for bottle-feeding in the first instance, but it is not so good for babies.

My experienced bottle-feeding clients try to avoid letting anyone else give a feed as others often give it too quickly, which can lead to discomfort and vomiting. Besides which, your baby is less protected from infection if she is having infant formula milk, so passing her around the family is not sensible.

Although the milk tin will give you an indication of how much milk to make up per feed, be guided by your baby. The breast-suckled baby will take very little sometimes and a good deal another time, and she is in control of switching the flow on and off. With a bottle, it is easy to give too much. If this happens, some milk will come back up and some won't. Formula-fed babies can quickly become overfed and overweight if repeatedly given more than they need.

To avoid overfeeding, copy as far as possible the way a baby naturally needs to suckle. Like this:

1. Snuggle up really close with baby right in against you with her turned to look up into your face. Try to get some skin to skin by having a bare arm against her neck or unbutton your blouse a little bit. Have your freshly made bottle and a clean dummy close by. If you'd prefer not to introduce a dummy, your clean little finger or, if you want to, your boob will do nicely.
2. Hold the bottle teat just above her nose, touching her skin, and let her reach up onto the teat rather than pushing it in. Remember that feeding

is baby-led for a good reason. It is her suckling time and she needs to be in charge – only she knows how this needs to pan out.

3. Make sure that the teat is full of milk to prevent your baby gulping down air.

4. Now, let your little one suckle and take milk for around 10–15 seconds. Take the bottle out and pop in the dummy, your finger or your boob.

5. Let your baby suckle on the dummy/finger/boob for another 10–15 seconds, then swap back to the bottle.

6. Keep swapping in this way. Sometimes let the dummy/finger/boob-suckling last a bit longer (a minute or so).

7. After your baby has had about half the made-up feed, stop completely and let her have a good break of about 10–15 minutes. Wind her over your shoulder by rubbing her back or patting her gently, and ensure that your shoulder is protected by a cloth. Bottle-fed babies can take down air in a way that breastfed babies can't, so she will need winding. Change her nappy.

8. After a good break and a nappy change, start again as above.

9. As soon as your baby has finished, she will turn away. She really is done. Don't try to encourage her to take more. If you were suckling her at the breast, you'd have no idea how much she had taken and this is exactly how it should be!

How much?

The only way to be sure that your baby is taking the right amount for her is to allow her to lead. The breastfed baby takes really different amounts throughout the day, just like you and me. It is unrealistic to expect the bottle-fed baby to want exactly the same amount of milk at every feed.

The approach outlined above allows your baby to do what she would instinctively do at the breast: move between suckling-for-milk and suckling-not-for-milk. She will therefore get all the milk she wants as well as all the suckling time she needs and will be far less likely to vomit or be over-full.

You will discover that babies take very different amounts at different times and not 'three ounces every three hours'. This is normal and should not be interfered with. Your baby is not trying to guess how much she needs – she is driven by instinct, so she cannot get it wrong. In contrast, you *can* think about it – and you may think wrong!

The chart on the tin can only give you a guide to get started with. Make up a bottle with the suggested amount and then feed as described above. Try really hard *not* to keep checking to see how much your baby has taken. Checking can lead to a parent-led feed, with you encouraging her to take 'just a little bit more' because you're worried that she hasn't taken as much as yesterday. It is also a commonly held myth that if you can encourage your little one to take 'just a little bit more' she will sleep better. But none of us sleeps well when we are stuffed full.

The well baby will take what she wants. If she takes a bit too much, she will bring back much of the extra. She may not bring back *all* the extra if she has taken too much, as formula milk tends to sit a little heavier in the stomach. This is one of the reasons why a formula-fed baby is more likely to become overweight. So let your baby lead and, if she has a little feed at one time, she may take more next time, or tomorrow ...

If your baby settles easily with a dummy/finger/boob, or with rocking, white noise, patting, etc., after she has turned away from her bottle, she's had enough. If she cannot be soothed, offer a little more milk.

Remember that your bottle-fed baby is still a highly evolved human and so will go through all the same unsettled periods of the day as her boob-suckled friends. Particularly between 5p.m. and 5a.m., be careful to try other soothing strategies before giving yet more milk as it may be that her gut spasm needs settling with something other than food.

Nights

There is no doubt that dealing with bottles and making up feeds at 2a.m. can be arduous. It is tempting to cut corners by making up feeds in advance, but just don't do this. If you cannot face making up a bottle properly overnight, it is better to take a sterilised bottle (firmly capped) and an unopened carton of ready-made formula to bed and use that when you are woken. However, any formula that you do not pour out at the first waking needs to go straight in the fridge and be thrown away after 24 hours.

It is risky to co-sleep if you are giving infant formula milk because the milk-making hormones that help women respond instinctively to their babies at night and keep them safe while co-sleeping disappear when you formula-feed. So, if your baby does not settle, you will need to offer something to soothe her. The best option is a dummy, as the sporadic suckling on a dummy appears to offer some protection against SIDS. The dummy may fall out and you will need to pop it back in again, but, if the crib is very close to your bed, this need not be too difficult.

> ## A word of caution about dummies
>
> When a baby is given a dummy to suckle at night, she is at a decreased risk of SIDS. However, for reasons that are not fully understood, if the baby who is used to having a night-time dummy has it removed, her risk of SIDS goes back up and is *higher than* the original risk level; so it seems that she may be *more* at risk than she was before the dummy was introduced. If you use a dummy for night-time soothing, make sure it is available every night.
>
> If a dummy doesn't hit the spot and you don't think your baby is needing milk, it might help to do any of the things mentioned on page 126: rocking, massage, white noise and shushing, a bounce in the pushchair or pram or even a car ride. You might be surprised by how many parents are out driving their babies around at 2a.m. just to help soothe them!

Room sharing

It is just as important for the bottle-fed baby to share her parent's bedroom until she is at least six months old. She is also no more developmentally ready to sleep through the night or get into a routine. Trying to get your highly evolved baby to act against her survival strategies is a fool's errand, so give yourself a break and try to mould to her for now. Routines and sleeping through the night will come along in good time when they are sensible and appropriate. That time is not yet.

Remember that baby monitors are not protective against SIDS, so do not replace round-the-clock close attention and soothing with a listening device.

Partner ponderings

You may have very mixed feelings about your baby being bottle-fed, and even more so if your baby is having infant formula milk rather than his mum's human milk. If your partner really wants to express and feed her own milk, you simply need to help her in whatever way you can.

It looks like hard work to keep expressing, and it is, but she does not need rescuing or being advised to give formula 'to make things easier for yourself'. She needs extra emotional support and ongoing physical help around the house so that she can continue the work of collecting her own milk to feed your child.

If your partner decides to give infant formula milk, she may need plenty of reassurance that you are happy to support her decision as well as to help her with the more complicated task of bottle-feeding.

Giving a bottle

Many women who choose or end up bottle-feeding (either their own human milk, donated human milk or infant formula milk) say that one advantage is that other people can do the feeding. As you will have read above, as nice as this sounds, this is not ideal for mother or baby. In the first few months of life a baby ideally needs to have one main carer to deeply attach to, and this should preferably be mum. This may be disappointing, but it is just the way it is. However, giving the occasional feed will not cause problems, so consider, if asked, offering to give one regular bottle a day.

If your partner is a late riser, set your alarm clock to get up for work that bit earlier and give your baby her first early morning bottle (this is often at about 5 or 6 a.m.). Then wind and settle your baby before taking her back to mum, who has benefited from a bit of a lie-in, before heading off for the day.

If your partner needs earlier nights than you, your daily bottle could be the last one before midnight. Be very careful to follow the advice on page 103 on how to give a bottle appropriately. It is tempting to rush, or to get more formula down the baby to help her sleep, but you may just be creating a night of tummy ache and vomiting. Whenever you give a bottle, slow your pace right down and indulge yourself in some nice long snuggles with your baby.

How else can you help?

Cleaning and sterilising bottles is a task you could well make your own. Many mums find it a real daily grind and, even with your help, your partner will still spend a lot of time sterilising kit and making up bottles safely, so anything you can do to relieve her of this task will be welcome.

When a mother is bottle-feeding (whatever type of milk she is using), remember that giving a baby a bottle-feed should take as long as giving a breastfeed, so extra help will be needed with cooking and housework in just the same way. One of the many reasons why suckling helps mums and babies bond so thoroughly is because of the time spent suckling and not having the option of handing baby over. This is a good thing, inbuilt over millions of years of evolution, and it serves everyone very well in the long run. The bottle-feeding mum and baby need space and encouragement to build that same intense, all-encompassing relationship in the first 12 weeks.

Our breastfeeding mums are constantly berated for holding and suckling their babies too much and for 'never putting that baby down!' It's more sensible to help our bottle-feeding mums to emulate close suckling behaviour. The more settled the mother–baby attachment is, the more easily your baby will turn outwards towards you for a good relationship a bit later on, so be patient.

Questions and answers

Mothers who are bottle-feeding their babies have just as many worries as those who are breastfeeding and deserve thoughtful, in-depth help and support. Don't be afraid to ask for it and, where possible, get help from someone who specialises in feeding: an infant feeding consultant or lactation consultant should be as skilled with helping those who bottle-feed as those who suckle their babies.

Winding

How long should I wind my baby for?

That is a tricky question to answer. In general, bottle-fed babies take down a fair bit of wind during a feed. Feeding as described above can help a bit, but she will probably still need winding. More often than not, babies bring up any gas easily within a minute or so of being brought upright. There is often a very full-throttled burp. Gentle back rubbing or patting can help bring wind up and keeping your little one over your shoulder with her back straight helps too. Some mothers sit their small babies on their lap but they tend to slump and this can make winding more tricky. If your baby doesn't burp after about five minutes she probably doesn't need to. Remember that, just like all breastfed babies, your baby will have the normal hormonal gut spasm at various times of the day and this is easy to mistake for wind. Using the same winding technique will certainly soothe a gut spasm a lot of the time but, if that doesn't work, try soothing your baby with one of the other strategies mentioned on page 126.

Bringing back milk

My baby brings a lot of milk back up. Am I overfeeding her or does she have reflux?

Reflux actually just means 'bringing back'. However, it tends to be used to describe a situation where a baby brings back so much food that they lose weight and become ill. If your baby is being wet and dirty, is gaining weight and is otherwise well, she is simply bringing back excess milk. Bottle-fed babies still need lots of suckling time that does not give them milk, which is why giving a bottle interspersed with a dummy/finger/boob as described above is so helpful. Do not be tempted to get a little more down your baby to aid sleep: an over-full tummy does not lead to settled sleep. Babies have evolved to have little and often, and this is just as true of the bottle-fed baby as it is of the breastfed one. If you carefully follow the advice above about how to give a feed, and your baby still vomits a lot, she may – or may not – be better on a different formula recipe. It is just very difficult to stop a bottle-feeding baby getting too much and the excess needs to come up. Always keep a muslin cloth to hand and feed your baby slooooooooowly! If your baby or her nappies seem dry, or she has diarrhoea or is at all unwell with vomiting, see a doctor urgently: she may have a tummy bug. Tummy bugs are a real risk to the young baby, so they need quick treatment.

Weighing

How much weight should my baby gain?

As much as she needs to stay well. See page 75 for information on how much weight your baby should gain – the advice for bottle-feeders is exactly the same as if your baby is being suckled. Ideally, the formula-fed baby should follow the centiles in the same wobbly way as the breastfed baby does. Feeding as described above will help her to follow her own, true centile.

Constipation

My baby has not pooed for two days. Is this okay?

It may be okay, but it may spell a bit of bother. Formula milks do not contain any human milk at all. Human milk stops babies from getting constipated and, even when a breastfed baby has not pooed for many days, it would not worry a healthcare specialist if the baby were otherwise well. The exclusively formula-fed baby can quickly get constipated and uncomfortable. If your baby has not pooed for three or more days, if you can express some of your own milk, this may be enough to clear the blockage. If this is not possible, give half an ounce of cool, boiled water and, if this does not bring relief within 24 hours, offer another half-ounce of water and also see your doctor. Sometimes a little medication is needed. *Never* put anything other than properly made-up formula, expressed breast milk or cool boiled water in a baby's bottle. Do not add fruit juice or 'baby tea'. This is simply not sensible, whatever your friends and family say.

Allergies

There is a family history of allergies. Should I give a special milk?

This is a tricky one! A genetic likelihood of being prone to allergies is easy to inherit from our mums and dads, and being fed something other than our mum's own human milk makes it more likely that the wonky gene will appear. Even if we only ever have our mum's milk, the gene can act out but it tends to be less severe. Just one bottle of infant formula milk can trigger the gene to start working and allergies to be set off. Many people will tell you to use a goat's milk or soya formula, but your baby is just as likely to be allergic to these proteins as to a cow's milk formula. It is worth considering choosing a formula that has fewer allergens for your baby's system to cope with, so read the labels and avoid those that contain fish and egg lipids. If your baby develops a rash, eczema, wheeze or other symptoms, see your doctor quickly for advice. There are formula milks available for sensitive babies, but these should only be used on medical advice. If you want to give your own milk but are struggling, get good help from someone who is very experienced.

Moving from formula to breast milk

I have changed my mind about bottle-feeding infant formula milk and want to start giving my own milk. Is it possible to get my own milk coming through again?

It is, but it may take a bit of work. The easiest way to get a supply going is to suckle your baby. If you don't want to suckle your baby but do want to bottle-feed your own milk, you will need to start expressing regularly. It is worth hiring or buying a hospital-grade pump, but if this is not possible, use a good domestic-grade one. In order to trick your body into thinking you have given birth again, pump every three hours, including at night, for 20 minutes each side. In addition, speak to your doctor and ask for a prescription of Domperidone. Some people will tell you to take fenugreek or fennel, but these are slightly more risky than Domperidone and less effective. Your doctor will check your medical history to make sure that you do not have any illnesses or conditions that would make taking Domperidone a problem. It may take a week or so before you start seeing any signs of progress, but as soon as you start to make milk, give it. It might be that, with patience, you get a full supply and can stop giving formula milk. If you do not get a full supply, don't worry. Just give whatever you can express. Remember that your human milk does not need to be kept in the fridge or thrown away after two hours. It is fine at room temperature for up to six hours or in the fridge for up to five days. Give it fresh whenever possible. If you mix your own milk with formula, it is best to throw away any leftovers straight after the feed has finished.

6 Making sense of your highly evolved baby: the autonomic nervous system

Reaching back ...

The sun comes up and a cool breeze freshens the air, waking the young mother from her deep slumber. She gazes down at her snuggled, bare child, warm against her own skin. So quiet now, after a night of suckling and nuzzling.

She steals away, leaving her dreaming child curled up like a tree frog, comfortable in the glow of the day as it reaches into the modest stick shelter that she and her companions have shared for the last few days. A few older children are playing happily on the ground nearby, looking up every now and then from their game, and the woman, still slow from her sleep, takes this time to stretch and yawn before settling on a tree stump with some of her companions to reflect on the night and enjoy some food.

The sound of her baby's waking grizzle brings the woman back for a brief cuddle, soothe and suckle on the soft fur bed. The baby settles back into her dream and can be safely left for a few more moments. But before long, she senses her mother's absence and howls to be safely back in her arms. Pulled away from her tasks by the wails of her daughter, the young mother grabs a loose cloth and deftly ties it around her body before picking up her wailing child and popping her into the wrap where, after a short suckle, pat and jiggle, she drifts back into a doze.

Today there are tasks to attend to and the women of the tribe quickly settle together to mend the damage to their shelters caused by last night's sudden downpour and prepare some meat and roots for tonight's meal. The young mother knows her child well now and, with her baby safely knotted to her body in the wrap, she can get on with the task at hand, stopping whenever needed to briefly suckle and soothe her baby. She must make the most of these hours of light to prepare for the long night that is just another sun-swing away.

As the day wears on past noon and the sun shifts steadily downwards, the young mother is pulled away from her tasks more and more. The cooler the air gets, and the darker the sky, the more her child searches for the steady warmth of a human body. Any attempt to free herself from this tiny girl causes immediate fretting and searching and so the women take turns to break from work and soothe the baby with hushing and patting, enjoying the respite this gives them. As long as she is close in someone's arms, the mewing bundle quietens a little and the mother can enjoy a moment's pleasure of seeing her child at a distance.

With sudden speed the sun falls from the sky, the stars appear and the hunting animals begin to prowl. As the returning hunters reunite with their companions and settle down beside the warmth of a crackling fire to share some food, the baby lurches onto her mother's breast. From now until dawn, she will need to be kept safe, warm and breast-close. Even the shortest of moments away from her mother's arms will cause the child to wriggle and cry until she is gathered safely back to the breast to suckle.

Through the cold fear of these long nights, filled with danger, the ever-watchful mother and her precious baby will cling together, sharing warmth and comfort, never out of touch for a second.

Days are for working and travelling, nights are for huddling close, resting, watching and protecting.

Our newborn baby can seem like a mystery to us. He cries when he has just been fed, he sleeps for ages in our arms and then wakes up within a minute or two of being 'put down' in his crib, and he sleeps in the day and keeps us awake all night! What on earth is going on?

We have spent some time watching a young primitive family and now it is time to unpick some of what we have seen and think about how it relates to the new baby in our arms. Once we understand why our baby behaves as he does, it is easier to ride with the apparent chaos that is our new life, letting it just be, safe in the knowledge that it will pass and a new phase will emerge.

For now, let's look at why your baby behaves in this confusing way, how his behaviour may actually be beneficial for you and him, and how you can mother him in a way that calms him down, keeps him well fed and ensures that he doesn't grow into a clingy, anxious child.

Survival of the fittest

Look at your baby and remember that what you see is a highly evolved little creature. Given that evolution works by survival of the fittest, everything that your baby does has to be a part of a survival strategy that is deeply set within him. Fighting evolution never works. Better to understand it and work with it.

In Chapter 4, we reflected on how dark it might have been between dusk and dawn for our ancestors right up until relatively recent times and how, in the very early years of human evolution, there was not even the light of a fire to guide night-time parenting.

The autonomic nervous system

All humans have an inbuilt system, called the autonomic nervous system (ANS), that governs the bodily functions without us thinking. If we had had to worry about, for example, keeping our heart beating as we were out searching for food, it would have meant certain death. Likewise with our breathing and temperature. So the essential workings of our bodies take place without our needing to think about them. An adult's ANS is steady and measured; a newborn baby's is all over the place. Let's think about why this might be.

If the primitive baby could have managed his own systems easily, keeping warm and settled and quiet, he could have been safely popped down while his mum got on with the day or took a quick nap. Safe, that is, until a wolf came by and found him ...

If the baby was very unsettled, breathing erratically, getting cold easily, and crying because of his internal distress, he would have been picked up by his mother – a crying baby could alert hunting animals to his whereabouts as well as rattling his mother's nerves! – and kept close. Easy to see why the unsettled baby survived.

Put your baby down for a minute and watch him. Very quickly you will begin to see how his ANS is unregulated: his breathing is erratic; his reflexes are very wacky; he quivers and waves his arms around; and his simple, primitive reflexes kick in at odd times, making him bob his head about and stamp his legs. Listen to his chest and you will hear that his heart rate is irregular compared with yours; he can get warm and cold but he can't regulate his temperature properly like you; and, although you can't see it, his ability to fight infection is very poor. Now, if a baby with his wonky ANS is put skin to skin with someone with a functioning ANS, the baby's wonky ANS settles. The combination of heat sharing and endorphin release helps to calm the baby and keep him safe. So pick your baby up now, cuddle him in and notice how his breathing calms a little and his reflexes settle down. He will still need more than just a simple cuddle, but a cuddle is better than being on the ground.

So you can see how a primitive baby with a wonky ANS will have been cared for more intensely than one with a fully functioning ANS and, therefore, would have been more likely to survive.

A primitive baby cannot have worked this out by himself and *decided* to be unsettled so that he could stay in arms more; a system will have evolved. Think about what your baby does that makes you pick him up. When he is in his crib for any length of time, he will start to wriggle. Then he will start to move his head about and suck his fist. Then he will start to cry, louder and louder!

Skin to skin

When he sucks his fist, what is the first thing that goes through your mind? He's hungry! So you pick him up and he will settle a little. Then, if you do nothing other than sit him quietly on your lap, after a few minutes he will start to root around frantically. So you get a boob out and put him to it. Bingo! Skin to skin! Food on tap, if he needs something more than just ANS soothing. You've responded to his needs, thanks to an excellent evolutionary driver.

But this cannot answer the question of what actually happens inside your baby to make him yell and search for a bit of skin to skin. Something must be causing the yell.

We all have various hormones and systems in our body helping us to function without even thinking about it: digesting, growing, sleeping and so on. Along with the ANS, these other regulating systems are immature in our newborn baby. The hormone melatonin that helps us relax and sleep is lower in newborn babies, the system that regulates adrenaline is less settled, the system that causes our gut to contract is immature, and the wonky ANS means that your baby is hypersensitive to all these seemingly chaotic internal shenanigans. Poor baby! His gut is churning, his night-time/daytime clock is not yet settled, his adrenaline sparks at every hint of bother and his erratic ANS is firing like crazy. From an evolutionary point of view, this is perfect. The highly evolved baby human, unable to crawl, let alone run, from danger or to feed himself is driven to distraction every time he is out of arms by his immature, cramping gut and erratic ANS, and the crying isn't going to stop until his mother picks him up and gets him skin to skin.

Why does picking him up, patting him, shushing him, suckling him and putting him next to your skin (even if it is only the warm skin of your neck) stop the yelling? Because all these things cause the release of endorphins.

Searching for endorphins

Endorphins are our very own opiates. Better still for your poor, sore baby, they relax smooth muscle (the involuntary muscles). So every time you pick up your baby, the gut spasm eases. That's the good news.

The bad news is that endorphins last for only a few minutes before they wear off. Every time you soothe your baby and then move to put him back in the crib, the endorphins wear off, the spasm kicks in and the yelling starts again. Your baby is an endorphin junkie!

ANS in brief

- Your highly evolved baby keeps his ANS stable by being in arms.
- Skin to skin settles the ANS best of all.
- Baby is oversensitive to the normal gut spasm due to his immature system.
- Endorphins stop his gut spasm and promote rest.
- Being skin to skin releases endorphins.

Now you can see how it all fits together and starts to make sense.

Suckling to calm baby

Where does suckling fit into all of this? Well, your human milk is rich in endorphins, and suckling also produces endorphins (in a baby and his mum), so whenever a baby suckles and gets milk, not only does he get fed and grow but his tummy ache stops for a short while. Of course, when a baby sucks his fist and you think he is saying 'I'm hungry', he's actually saying, 'Get me skin to skin and let me suckle.' The reason why your baby spends so long suckling is so that he can stay longer skin to skin, settling his ANS and therefore being much safer. Remember the 'café baby' on page 72? Well, here he is, keeping a steady flow of endorphins trickling through his poor, erratic system, calming both him and you while he remains safely away from those bears and wolves hunting just outside your cave shelter!

We have already seen that when he suckles, your baby sometimes sucks deeply, pulling quite strongly; at other times, the suckle feels like a tickly shiver. During the deep pulls, your baby is taking down a lot of endorphin- and nutrient-rich milk and during the tickles he is keeping his endorphin levels up without taking much milk. So the time it takes him to satisfy his hunger and thirst is spread through the total suckling time. Even if your baby only needs five minutes' worth of suckling-for-milk time, it is essential that he spends a long time at the breast to keep him skin to skin and full of endorphins. Evolution has ensured that this happens whether you like it or not – it's survival of the fittest. If you are bottle-feeding, keep in mind the slow feeding approach on page 103, with plenty of time for snuggles as you give the bottle, and keep your baby in your arms for as long as he needs.

The difference between days and nights

If we think back to our primitive baby, we can see how he was more vulnerable at night than in the daytime.

In the daytime, he might have been kept warmed by the sun on the ground or the lap as his mother worked, or on her back if she needed to travel. He could be seen when he wriggled or needed cleaning and many of the hunting animals would have been in their dens waiting for nightfall or, at least, easily spotted in the bright daylight.

If you think of your own highly evolved baby, you might have noticed that his 'best' times are during the day (particularly in the morning). This allows you to pop him safely in a pram and go to the shops to do a little hunting and gathering! As you go back to your centrally heated cave shelter to eat and rest, the gathering gloom will mean that your baby has to up his game a little to stay in arms. He will be a little more unsettled but still fairly easy to soothe. But watch out as darkness falls, from 5p.m. onwards. Out come the foxes, the warming sun goes down and it gets colder, plunging your cave shelter into the dangers of the night. Now your little baby had really better work hard.

No wonder, then, that babies the world over, girls and boys alike, are at their best between about 7a.m. and midday, a little more restless from midday to about 5p.m. and then at their 'worst' between 5p.m. and midnight and 2a.m. to 5a.m.

'This is all well and good,' you say, 'but how am I supposed to cope when my highly evolved baby keeps me up all night soothing his poor, sore tummy?' How do you, as the mum, fit into this evolutionary survival of the fittest picture? Don't worry – you haven't been left out!

Your altered sleep state

Have you noticed that during the day when you suckle your baby you feel quite relaxed? When you suckle at night, you feel positively incapable of keeping your eyes open.

Women often say that breastfeeding makes them tired, but it doesn't. It makes you sleepy, and that is different. As our primitive baby evolved, his mum evolved alongside him in such a way to ensure that she could keep baby safe without dying of exhaustion herself. Brain/sleep studies show that, when a mum suckles at night, she can't help but fall into a very deep sleep. While she is asleep, she only experiences the deepest, most restorative type of sleep.

Now, so that baby didn't get forgotten while mum slept deeply, primitive mum evolved so that she was aware of baby even in her very deep sleep state, touching him and keeping him warm instinctively and waking immediately and completely at the slightest baby noise.

So now you know why your partner doesn't wake quite as quickly and fully when your baby cries at night as you do and complains of being so very tired in the morning when it's you who has had the fewest hours with your eyes shut! Every second you spent asleep, you were in the very deepest sleep, while your partner beside you was wasting time going through light sleep, REM sleep, deep sleep, light sleep and so on. Just one waking will wreck your partner's working day, while you will quite surprise yourself by managing well enough after a night of frequent disturbances.

Staying safe at night

Most breastfeeding women report falling asleep with their babies in bed, despite their best efforts. No matter how hard women try to stay awake and feed at night, they fall asleep. Even when they manage to settle baby into a crib, he refuses to stay put and, in no time, mum is awakened again.

By safely co-sleeping, keeping baby close to mum, skin to skin under light covers, and by being certain that no one sharing the bed has been smoking or is drunk or drugged, you can be reassured that your highly evolved baby alongside highly evolved you is as safe as possible. So, even if you plan to put your baby back in his crib after a night-time suckling, anticipate that you might fall asleep and prepare for safe co-sleeping. Better to do this than to assume you will stay awake and then end up co-sleeping in a non-safe way by accident.

In any event, it is never safe to try to stay awake by going downstairs to the sofa as, when you naturally fall asleep (as you have evolved to do), your baby is at increased risk of getting caught between you and the back of the sofa. This is dangerous.

Likewise, because it is you who has evolved to be alert and responsive to your baby, he should always stay close to you rather than anyone else at night. By being the one to soothe your baby at night, you ensure that the whole household is more rested next day.

Remember: Safe co-sleeping assumes that you are suckling or exclusively expressing for your baby. See the safe co-sleeping information on page 26; and for coping strategies if you are formula-feeding your baby, see page 155.

Sensitive babies

Babies whose parents (either or both) have a family history of eczema, asthma, migraines, hay fever or food allergies may be more unsettled than normal. A family with this group of issues is called atopic and the gene for it is highly heritable. Atopic babies tend to be more sensitive than most and require far more soothing. The atopic baby boy can be extremely challenging as he may need constant, intense soothing (suckling *and* rocking *and* shushing *and* patting all at the same time!). If this is you, as the mother of four atopic sons myself I completely understand and share your pain. The excellent news is that these babies grow up to be more sociable, confident and independent. Let's be honest, they have had three or four months of grown-ups trying endlessly to cheer them up, so their social skills should be legendary.

The three-month howl

Just a few days of dealing with an unsettled baby is hard enough, but this seems to be going on forever. Surely something is wrong!

As ever, you can relax, knowing that you are in the safe hands of evolution, which, as we have seen, has survival at the centre of everything. Your baby needs to be in arms and suckling a lot until his ANS is more regulated and he is more able to survive on his own for short periods of time.

By about four months, your baby's ANS will have become regulated and so the risk of hypothermia, infection and SIDS will have dropped right down. Also, by the time you have spent three solid months soothing your little one and trying to make him feel better, you will be very well 'attached' to each other and this also ensures ongoing survival. But the three months before the ANS settles down can be very difficult.

Your grandparents had a name for this unsettled stage – 'three-month colic'. Colic is a painful spasm: it isn't 'wind', it isn't 'cluster feeding' and it isn't caused by acid 'reflux'. The picture you are seeing is simply the entirely normal evolutionary mechanism for keeping your baby safe. Medicines cannot, luckily, change your baby's ANS or hormones and so will make no difference. In any case, you do not want to cure your baby of something that protects him!

By now, it should not come as any surprise to you that, if your baby became more vulnerable during this three-month period, his crying and pain would increase. Well, that is just what happens. Your baby hits peak vulnerability during weeks six to eight, having gradually become more and more susceptible week by week. So expect to hit peak 'colic' during these weeks. Batten down the hatches, call in support, hunker down in your safe cave shelter and weather the storm.

As week eight moves to week nine, and week nine moves to week ten, things will gradually settle. By the end of the three-month mark, your baby will be far less sore, his ANS will be more regulated and so his need to be skin to skin will reduce. Your baby will still need a lot of time in arms – he can't run away from the wolves and bears just yet – but the need to be at your breast will just not be the same.

> ## The gender divide
>
> When you talk to other parents about your unsettled baby, you may discover that parents with baby girls are generally having an easier time than those with baby boys. When you look at gender ratios at birth, marginally more boys are born than girls. There are various hypotheses for why this might be, which all amount to the same thing – boys are a little more vulnerable than girls. This might account for why, generally, baby boys need more soothing in the early days than baby girls. Within the boundaries of 'normal', there will be settled boys and unsettled girls, but the trend is the opposite.

Too soon for routines

How we long to get some routine back into our lives. Some rhythm into our days and some predictability into our nights. That will come, but not just yet! If evolution determines that survival must come first, who are we to argue with that? As humans, we love to see patterns. Being able to see tiger stripes in the undergrowth signals the need to run, so we have evolved to see patterns wherever we look.

There are so many books claiming to help you get your newborn baby into some specific routine and it seems so tempting. But let's remember that we cannot beat evolution, no matter what we do. It would spell disaster if we could teach our babies how to stay in their cribs all night – what about the wolves and bears and the cold, cold corners of the forests? Not to mention the risk of SIDS and infection in the early months.

Your baby is no more able to learn a routine than to read a book or ride a bike. He will in time, when he reaches the right developmental stage, but not until then.

Try to get your baby into a routine from a month old and you will discover that after three or four months of really working at it, he will do it! Of course, you could have waited until your baby was five months old and saved yourself months of misery trying to teach your baby something he was incapable of learning. Babies in the early months have evolved specifically *not* to be able to learn routines as this would not protect them. So beware of anyone trying to tell you how to get your baby into a routine before his fourth or fifth month (at the earliest). They do not understand how babies have evolved and may inadvertently put your baby at risk.

Some parents will insist that they *did* manage to get their baby into a routine by a few weeks old, but numerous studies around the world of thousands of babies tell us that this just isn't true. It is just that some babies need less soothing than others and others just spend a lot of time crying or sucking dummies.

There is no need to worry that all this in-arms time will lead to clinginess. Think of it like this.

When you met the love of your life, you did not sit down on day one and say to each other: 'I can see that ours is going to be a deep and powerful relationship that I hope will last. To this end, we should limit ourselves to only one night a week in the other's bed, only one 10-minute hug every four hours and only one phone call a day. After all, we don't want to become too needy.' Imagine the wedding vows in that universe.

The truth is that, in a new relationship, we build up trust by spending every waking moment thinking about each other, calling each other, clinging to each other at night, and our lips rarely part long enough to declare our love. Once we know the relationship is secure, then we can have more space without feeling worried. Imagine if our new-found love kept leaving us, ignoring our calls, pulling away from hugs. Then we would become more clingy and needy.

So it is with our babies: the more we meet their needs in the early months, the more able they are to develop confidence in the relationship and spend time away from us in due course. Be patient and trust the process of evolution that brought us here safely and successfully kitted out for survival. Once you relax and accept that your baby doesn't think about how to be a baby and so really can't be 'wrong', life just seems far less fraught. Take away those modern expectations and constraints and babies seem much easier to live with all of a sudden.

Go with, not against, your baby

By the time humans discovered the light from fire, the human baby was already beautifully evolved to survive. Through a process that favoured survival of the fittest, the most successful human baby was one with a wonky ANS, driven by his oversensitive gut to search for the endorphin-stimulating environment of his mother's arms and, even better, the warmth of his mother's skin and nourishment of her milk. This highly evolved baby needed to be picked up and put next to his mother's breast but, after that, he was in control. He could suckle for hours without getting too fat and then take little catnaps in his mother's arms before going back to suckling. If his mother put him down, loud cries would soon ensure that someone else would gather him up and soothe him with rocking, patting, shushing and warm skin to skin, keeping those precious endorphins ticking over and his ANS settled.

At night, this amazing baby became so sore and erratic that his mother kept him next to her skin, quiet, warm and soothed, ensuring that he neither died of hypothermia nor was taken by wolves. The primitive baby's mother could care for him in the very darkest corner of the forest or cave shelter, simply cuddling baby close to her bare chest and letting him suckle whenever he needed to without ever asking why her baby needed to suckle – again!

Your highly evolved baby is just as able to be safe and secure as long as you can trust your own instincts to pick him up and soothe him without asking why. This is a developmental stage, evolved to ensure that your baby survives these first few vulnerable months in the outside world and forges a strong tie with the person who can protect and nourish him the best. Like all developmental stages, it has to take place and it will pass, as sure as day follows night and light follows dark.

Partner ponderings

If you have read all of the above, you will have a much better idea of why your baby doesn't seem to want to be in your arms quite as much as he wants to be in his mother's.

You can, though, use what you have learned to help you understand what to do when your partner needs a break from constant suckling and your baby needs to be soothed. Remember that your baby simply needs endorphins. Do those things that ensure your little one stays chock-a-block full of those and you will be the hero of the hour.

Soothing strategies

- Try rocking your baby in your arms. Hold him upright against your chest with his head nestled in your neck to create that much-needed skin to skin (cuddling him in your arms lying near your nipple area is a sure-fire way to create havoc as he roots frantically around for what he thinks you are offering) and rock your body strongly up and down or side to side.
- Pop him in his pushchair and push it firmly and rhythmically back and forward over a slight bump (a thick magazine or the edge of a rug will do nicely).
- Take him for a car ride.
- Give him a warm bath. You need a nice deep bath, and let your baby lie with his body fully submerged and his head back so that his ears are under water.
- Give him a massage.
- Turn up some white noise or pop him in a sling on your chest and get hoovering.
- Hold him firmly in your arms, sway, and go sh-sh-sh in his ear.
- Hang him tummy down over your forearm and pat his bottom firmly and rhythmically.

All these things push up your baby's endorphins and provide temporary relief. If you stop doing the soothing strategy, after about five minutes your baby will become sore and resume crying.

Keep it up

During the worst hours of the day, expect to have to combine a few of the above strategies to work up enough endorphins to soothe your little one.

The mistake that all new parents make is to think that when they have soothed the baby, they have cured the baby. It then comes as a shock when the noise starts again within minutes of stopping the soothing. All you are doing is easing the distress of your poor, sore, unregulated baby from moment to moment. You can't cure him of being a baby.

The 'rooting' reflex that carries on most of the time when your baby is unsettled just means 'soothe me'. It is never wrong to suckle a baby whenever he roots, but, if his mum can't suckle him right now, you can soothe him in different ways. You will quickly discover non-boob soothing strategies that your partner is not so good at. You may envy her the ability to always quieten your baby with a boob; she will envy you your ability to soothe the little one *without* needing a boob! Such is life as a parent. Don't take it personally.

Guilt in the nursing mum

Try hard not to ask why your baby is still crying. Is it something you have eaten/not eaten/drunk/not drunk/done/not done? Babies behave erratically, no matter how we choose to feed or parent and no matter what we eat, drink, think or do. There is remarkable pressure on women who choose to suckle their babies to examine every element of their lives to see if something they are doing is 'affecting' their milk and causing this baby-ness. Remember that formula is made from cow's milk and cows eat grass all day, but nobody ever says to a formula-feeding mum, 'It must be all the grass the cow ate that is making the baby so colicky.' Simply acknowledge that babies are puzzling and hard work at times and take your crying baby out into the garden for yet another bout of fresh air ...

Being a couple

As much as you want to have some in-arms time with your partner, she wants it just as badly, but not at the expense of putting the baby down and listening to him cry. Nor does she need to feel that she has to stop nursing her baby in order to soothe your need for closeness. Women can quickly feel overwhelmed by all these needs they are meant to both interpret and meet. Just join in the mum–baby cuddle by sitting next to them both and holding the baby to the breast with one hand while you cuddle your partner with the other. This allows you both to share these baby-soothing moments while reassuring each other that you are still a couple. I know this sounds so obvious, but I rarely see it, and, when I suggest it to couples, they often express genuine surprise. 'Of course! We hadn't thought of that!'

Remember that this phase passes. These erratic days are numbered but essential, so try not to fight them. Instead, watch evolution unfold before your eyes.

There are no Q&As for this chapter. All parents ever want to know as they struggle, hot on the heels of all other parents down the generations, through this difficult and confusing first three months is 'What am I doing wrong? How do I cure it? When will it ever end?' Now you understand that this very particular behaviour is written into your baby's DNA and it simply reads 'Survive!'

7 Instinctive baby care

Reaching back ...

The young, primitive family is ready to move on.

This young woman is more physically and emotionally recovered by the day, and her appetite is growing along with her confidence. Gradually she is venturing out more and more to gather food and water and prepare for evening meals with the group. She is never short of willing arms to share baby-soothing but she knows that, within minutes of passing her baby away from her, no matter how warm the companion's cuddle, her little one will quickly come back to her.

Today she and her companions must find a new place to call home for a while. There are many days of walking ahead and so, by first light and after a nourishing meal for the young mother and a warm milky suckle for the little one, the baby is wrapped securely inside her mother's clothing, head bobbing between her mother's breasts, and the gentle padding rhythm of walking feet as the tribe moves off rocks her immediately into sleep. The warmth of skin and sun and the light burr of wind through the trees draws her back to dreams every time she wakes.

Under the strong midday sun the group sits in the shade of some large shrubs and enjoys the food they have gathered along the way. The padding has stopped, the sudden stillness wakes the baby and, searching quickly, she finds the full breast. As baby nuzzles and drinks, her mother laughs with the adults and shares the food.

This mother has already learned to free her daughter's bottom from her clothes when she suckles, but she is a little late this time and her companions laugh as a torrent of warm pee flows from her baby and down her legs!

The baby gasps and cries as a slop of tepid water poured from a hollowed-out gourd is poured over her rump and legs before her mother's swift hands rub her dry. Then up over a shoulder for some rocking before being dropped briskly back into her mother's clothes. The group has to get on and can't sit around all day patting fractious babies ...

Getting 'back to normal'

The babymoon is over, the relatives have disappeared, leaving a swathe of wrapping paper behind, and your partner has re-entered the world of work.

You have been used to having a contract of employment, a shape to your day, deadlines to meet and a brain ever-ready to solve the latest problem to hit your desk. And here you are, panicking at the thought of a few hours alone with a tiny human being!

We all feel like this. We all fear being unable to make it through the day with a baby whose neediness seems endless, without another adult with us to share the emotional as well as the physical trials. We were never meant to be alone with the newest member of our tribe, ours the only arms to rock and soothe, and yet in our modern world we often find ourselves with no support except from a book and no adult company except from the TV.

As we saw in Chapter 4, we are not at all helped by the 'latching and attaching' fashion which leaves us stranded on a chair with a pillow on our lap and both arms employed in the feeding wrestling match. We can make life with our baby so much easier and regain some of what has been lost over the millennia. As always, it helps to reflect on our ancient roots, look back to those women who gave no thought to how they would cope with a baby *and* still gather the food for the day. If, like them, we allow our babies to be like an extra appendage for a while, life can get back to some semblance of what we like to call normality.

Going with the flow

Until the fourth month, the immature and unregulated baby needs no structured routine or bedtime and allowing her to go with our flow and us to go with hers will not create bad habits. She is unable, thanks to evolution, to learn how to be either bad or good. If she were able to learn habits, she might learn how to sleep alone and, as we now know, this would be potentially unsafe. Every time you pop your baby down, you can almost hear evolution scream: '*No!* Not safe. Get back in arms, *now!*' Stop fighting and adapt. You can, she can't.

Structuring your day

Look back at Chapter 4 and you will see that the least sucky times of day are likely to be between 7a.m. and midday; the hours between midday and 5p.m. will see rather more fractious and sucky behaviour; and the evening and overnight will need maximum soothing efforts.

Morning

If you are feeling very tired from last night, you may feel a few hours catching up on sleep while your baby dozes either in her crib or next to you are in order. She will doze for longer if suckled while you sleep but she may well be happy for an hour in her crib. If your baby is in those middle 'colicky' weeks, it is highly unlikely that your baby will settle alone at any time of the day out of arms and so safe co-sleeping often becomes the only option for the tired nursing mum (see page 26). If you do not want to safely co-sleep, remember to nurse lying down for safety (falling asleep sitting up can lead to a dropped baby) and then set an alarm clock to go off after about half an hour. If your baby has nodded off, you can try gently moving her across to her crib so you can carry on catching up on some well-earned rest. Your baby may well waken pretty quickly in her crib but you will, at least, have caught a few moments of deep sleep.

If you're formula-feeding, you may need to use a dummy, rocking crib, white noise generator or a willing mother-in-law to soothe your baby during the really tricky weeks while you grab some catch-up snoozing. If you've got a very 'colicky' baby boy, you might have to get through the day and then grab an early evening nap when your partner gets home and can walk the poor, sore baby for an hour.

As tough as this is, it just isn't possible to cure your baby of being a baby and she is simply incapable of adapting to you at this stage, no matter how hard you try. It's much better to accept what you cannot do and turn your attention to what you can.

If you feel rested enough – and remember that any seconds spent with eyes shut as a nursing mum give you deep sleep so you will feel better than you expect, even if your night has been very broken – you may decide to use the morning hours to 'get on'. Of course, if you try to put your baby in her crib while you do whatever you need to do (laundry, meal preparation, cleaning), you can fully expect to get less than an hour's peace.

How to carry your baby

Take a note out of primitive mum's book and strap your baby onto you. Many people now talk about 'baby-wearing' and there are even people trained as 'baby-wearing consultants' or 'sling consultants', but you are really just carrying your baby in the way women have always done. It does not need a gimmicky name or great expenditure.

Grab a cotton cloth, shawl or pashmina you don't mind getting baby sick on and that measures about 2.5 metres long and about 1 metre wide and make a quick knot sling:

- Pop your baby down while you fling your cloth around your waist and up over a shoulder. Once knotted, it will sling around you in the same way as if you were to wear your handbag across your body.

- Knot it with a reef knot (see right) at the shoulder. It needs to be pretty tight so baby is held firmly against you.

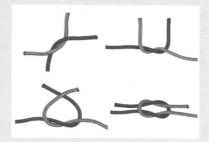

- Holding your baby over your shoulder, gently lower her into the wrap with one arm and, with the other, bring the lower edge of the shawl up under her frogged legs and bottom to make a pouch. The top edge needs to come right up to hold her firmly around the back of her head.

- When she is in properly, her legs and bottom will be sat, froggy-style, in the pouch and she will be held upright with her head in your cleavage, chin right off her chest. You will be able to see the top of her head. She should not be slumped down at all.

- As she gets older and bigger you will find that her legs can come out of the pouch and the weight of her bottom will keep the pouch firmly under her so she doesn't slip out. Even bigger and she will be able to sit with her arms out, on your hip, looking at the world around her. This is where our children learn about human life and also where they might get their first tastes of non-milk food from about six months while you prepare supper with your companion on your hip.

A baby held snugly in the very simplest of wraps will allow her mother to do whatever she needs to do (except showering!) with her hands completely free. If your sling allows your baby to be too loose when you bend over, re-knot it a bit more tightly. Go shopping (done that), paint the car (done that), teach a class (done that), even go to the loo (definitely done that!) knowing that the normal rhythm of life on the move will keep your baby soothed and nice to know. When she needs to suckle, grab a drink and a snack, sit down and ease the sling down low enough for your little one to find your boob, or, if you can't or don't want to sit down, feed on the go ...

You will have bleak moments of wondering if this stage goes on forever, or if you are creating a bad habit. The answers are simply 'No' and 'No'. This is an important phase for your highly evolved baby and it will pass as surely as night follows day. You can get on with your life, but baby must come along too for the ride. Her next phase may not allow you quite the same amount of freedom, so try to treasure these weeks as best you can.

Afternoon

In the afternoon, when your baby is a little more wakeful and needing more soothing time but still pretty manageable, you might want to take a trip out. A refreshing walk to a friend's house, a trip to the shops, a drive around the countryside just for the heck of it. All these will create enough movement and distraction to keep you and your little one settled. Ensure that you have factored in somewhere to stop to feed you both over the course of the afternoon.

If your morning did not pan out as planned, an afternoon on the sofa with baby held snugly near your breast, interspersed with a little pottering around the house if she becomes too wiggly, may be in order. Many women use the afternoon to catch up with friends – the company of other adults can really soak up the stress and noise of a mid-afternoon colic burst and we were always 'meant' to parent in groups. If you have a particularly good friend, she may well soothe your baby while you nip off upstairs for a nap!

Many babies prefer being carried in a close sling, but some are more than happy to be in a moving pram or pushchair. It is, however, very common for a baby to be pushed into town in the pram at 2p.m., only to be carried home in arms with the shopping in the pram at 5p.m., so shove your knotted sling into your handbag for that walk home if you take your pram or pushchair.

Evening

Oh dear, evenings! These are simply going to be full-on. There's no getting away from that, but rest easy in the knowledge that not only is it entirely normal, you are also witnessing a protective evolutionary behaviour. Seeing behaviour as normal and healthy frees you and your partner from the exhausting stress of looking for reasons and cures. Worrying that our healthy baby is unwell and that it is in some way our fault drains away the pleasure we would otherwise get from delighting in seeing our baby ease into her life with us. You have not caused this endless evening and night-time discomfort through your diet, behaviour, indulgence, overfeeding or anxiety. But you can help her manage her discomfort through close, soothing parenting and the suckling that brings everyone's ears at least a little peace. Of course, within minutes of dropping off the boob, your little one starts wriggling and complaining and hunting around to nurse again, but this doesn't mean the suckling has created the upset; it is the *not* suckling that causes it.

When your partner rocks your baby and soothes her, then tiptoes across the room to pop her in her crib, she rouses almost instantly, but no one ever says, 'You see? All that rocking and soothing makes her worse!' Your partner probably sighs heavily, picks baby up and rocks again – after all, it worked before. With nursing, however, when the inevitable evening colic picks up steam and the baby cries harder and harder every time she is put down after suckling, the poor mum gets blamed for overfeeding, for not having enough milk, for having 'obviously eaten something', for just creating more wind.

Remember that your boobs will feel softer and less milky in the evenings. If your baby is going to be soothe-suckling for hour after hour, it really wouldn't do for her to get over-filled with milk. On top of dealing with her painful tummy spasms, you do not want to have to deal with lots of vomit too. So do not be drawn into the idea of cluster feeding. This is cluster suckling (which is different) – it is normal, protective and universal.

All you can reasonably do through the evening hours is soothe and suckle, suckle and soothe.

Don't shun visitors if you'd like to continue to do some socialising in the evening. I remember many happy evenings with family and friends enjoying a 'bring and share' supper while we all took turns rocking and soothing. Eventually, my baby would find his way back to my arms and my boob and have a deep suckle until his spasm eased before going off around the circle of willing adults again. You simply need friends and family who 'get' little babies, and hopefully you have these.

If you are bottle-feeding (either your own human milk or formula milk) you can really help your baby by organising your feeds around soothing and dummy-sucking. Formula can increase painful gut spasms, so you may need to pace the floor and jiggle quite enthusiastically, but don't be tempted to think, because of the frequent rooting reflex, that your baby needs yet more food! She needs more in-arms time and sucky-soothing.

As we discussed in Chapter 5, space a feed well by interspersing the bottle with a dummy and this will ensure that your little one has both enough food *and* enough non-milk suckling.

If your baby has siblings, engage their help too. Older children make great baby-soothers and often find creative ways to entertain a colicky baby and they learn all about family life into the bargain. Children enjoy watching TV or reading a book with a warm, wiggly baby tucked skin to skin. The age of the older child will determine just how close an eye you need to keep on the siblings, but, in any case, make sure you are quickly available. Never ask your older child to give the baby a bottle-feed. Feeding needs to be done properly and this makes it an adult-only task.

Night

Once you start to get tired, go to bed. This sounds so obvious but I regularly hear parents say that they wait until baby has made it into the post-colic hours to turn in for the night. In fact, I did much the same myself with my first. Not, needless to say, with the other three!

Take your still-crotchety baby upstairs and lie down to soothe-suckle so that you can rest and relax ready for the night. Once the colic has passed for now (generally somewhere between 10p.m. and midnight) you can pop your baby in her crib (or keep her close to you for safe co-sleeping) and grab some good, deep sleep before the second colic bout hits sometime in the early hours.

If you are creative, these early months of constant soothing and suckling needn't be a chore or spell the end of anything resembling a life outside the home. Integrate your wiggly, sucky baby into whatever it is you want to do and stop chasing rainbows.

Cleaning and bathing

Some babies love being bathed. Some hate it. No babies *need* to be bathed. Even children who have spent the day digging for dinosaurs in the garden don't need a bath: washes with flannels, a tickly shower or a hosing down on the patio will work just as well and can be fun for the bath-decliner. Your baby simply needs to have her bottom properly cleaned at nappy changes and any milk or sick gently washed away when necessary.

Cleaning

Whenever possible, wash with water rather than using wet wipes at nappy changes. If you have access to a sink, strip off the bottom clothes or roll up the bottom of a sleep suit, run a sink of warm water and thoroughly douse your baby's bottom and genitals. This ensures that all urine and poo is cleaned off and will reduce the likelihood of nappy rash. Use a soft towel (carry one in your changing bag instead of a mat – towels are easy to wash) on your lap for drying off and, if you feel it is needed, a tiny smear of something basic such as petroleum jelly or pure jojoba or coconut oil before the clean nappy. Lotions, potions and wet wipes can cause soreness and thrush and offer no benefits to the normal, healthy skin of a human baby.

In the absence of a sink, take a pot of water with you and some cotton wool, lay a towel on your lap and change the nappy on that. There are changing facilities in most public toilet rooms, but without a towel underneath, you are likely to end up with a baby in a puddle of water, wee and poo. Keep wet wipes for emergencies only.

A milky, sticky face and neck can also be gently washed with a soft, warm flannel rather than cotton wool. Or use your own wetted hands in just the same way as our primitive mum might have done. Little hands can be held under a warm running tap and should never be soaped or have creams applied to them. Be sure to reach every nook and cranny as milk build-up under, for example, multiple layers of skin in the neck can get very stinky. Lie your baby on her back and gently expose the skin, giving it a good clean with warm water. If your baby has redness in her neck folds, use a dab of barrier cream such as Vaseline or a light smear of coconut oil.

Bathing

If you decide to bath your baby, take the advice of hundreds of my clients and don't bother with a baby bath. If you have bought one and can't take it back to the shops, use it for storage – you will be joining the rest of the parent population in keeping it for bath toys.

Instead of breaking your back over the bath, bath your baby in your kitchen sink – doing this doesn't waste too much water either.

Gather a clean nappy, a soft towel and clean clothes. Thoroughly wash out the sink and fill it to a good depth with really warm water (use a baby bath thermometer if you like, but you may find you need the water a wee bit warmer than it says). Lay the towel out on a clean, dry draining board and then gently undress your baby. If she cries, stop and suckle or cuddle her for a while. It often works best to do boob–bath–boob (or bottle–bath–bottle). Use a warm flannel or cotton wool to clean away any poo. When you are ready to bath, put your forearm/wrist under her shoulders. Now make a ring with your thumb and index finger round her farthest arm close to her armpit and let her head rest gently back over your forearm/wrist. Grasp her ankles with the other hand and lift her into the sink.

Let her body sink low into the water and her head loll gently back over your supporting wrist so that her ears are under the water. Often, the moment the ears are under water, a baby thinks she is 'home' and goes very quiet. It is not unusual for them to fall asleep. Just let her lie and be calm. Enjoy watching her stretch out in delight at the watery warmness. There is no need for soap or formal cleaning – this is for pleasure, not cleanliness.

As soon as your baby starts to seem even a little unsettled, however briefly she has been in the water, lift her straight onto the towel, wrap her up warmly, sit down and nurse her. She will dry while she suckles. Indeed, while she suckles, you can hold her in place with your drawn-up leg and use your freed-up hands to carefully dry every nook and cranny before popping a nappy on and re-dressing. If you really need to re-dress. Maybe, instead, simply gather your warm, freshly bathed baby into a soft fleece and take her for some long skin-to-skin snuggles or a soothing massage. The fuss of poppers and buttons can surely wait. If your baby seems to hate the bath, don't sweat – she needs to be clean, not bathed.

Many parents find that it is far easier to take their baby into the bath with them. Don't add products to your water, have the water comfortable but not too hot (check it with your elbow first) and have your partner or a friend hand you your baby once you are already in and sitting safely. Many mums nurse their babies in the bath – it is a wonderful experience and can soothe away your own stress and tension as well as your baby's. You will need your partner or friend to take the baby back from you before you get out, so do not do this if you are home alone.

You could try taking your baby in the shower with you, but I have not had much success with this myself and mums I speak to who have tried it find, like me, that their baby doesn't like it at all. Yours, however, may be different.

Partner ponderings

There is no doubt that, like many partners, you might do very little day-to-day changing, bathing and carrying unless you are at home full time. There is no need to feel bad about this, in spite of your desire to be equal partners. Equal does not always mean 'same'.

However, being the primary carer for a new baby is pretty thankless work and can be very exhausting emotionally and physically. You may wish that your partner greets you happily and that baby gives you a milky smile and a nuzzle. Instead, your woman smells of baby sick and is still in her nightie and your baby is red in the face and inconsolable. You are asked to 'Just take her!' as soon as you walk in the door, and you know the most fractious time of day is upon you.

Sharing the workload

Some couples find that, if the homecoming parent can have half an hour of downtime, their energy is restored enough for baby to be taken and soothed while mum has half an hour to herself with a glass of wine in the bath or a walk to the newsagent and back. Then someone cooks and someone rocks. You need to work together on this one.

Days at home

During your days off, remember that your baby will be at her most manageable in the morning hours, so this is the best time for you to enjoy her. She will still need to be in arms, rocked, patted or soothed in your own favourite way, so don't bother wasting time trying to 'get her down'. It is completely fine to snuggle her up skin to skin (any bit of your skin will do, but the neck is usually easiest) and catch up on some TV. Or use the sling to carry her around while you shop, clean or put up shelves.

In the afternoon, family walks or visits are a great way of keeping a gradually wigglier baby settled, as long as you schedule in suckling stops along the way. During the worst colicky weeks (about weeks six to eight), you may just have to accept that only mum can soothe her and your efforts will go into keeping drinks and snacks on the go and morale boosted. Don't waste time wondering why your baby is impossible to soothe out of arms and away from a breast; just accept that this is completely normal (it really is) and that your partner needs reassurance and good food.

Bath time

Many partners make bath time their special time with baby. If you are nervous about holding your baby in the sink, take her into the bath with you. Your partner will need to be around to help, but, while you enjoy the warm skin to skin of a deep bath with your little one, you and your partner can catch up.

After the bath, you might find that massaging your soft baby's barely dry skin with lightly warmed oil is soothing for you both. Take her into a warm room, still wrapped up in towels, lie her safely on your lap and then use your warm hands to firmly but gently stroke a little oil onto her skin. Jojoba oil is expensive but very light and unlikely to irritate even the most delicate skin. Grape seed and coconut oils are cheaper and also nice. Heavier oils can cause itching and rashes, so choose carefully. Go gently and slowly, ensuring that your little one stays warm.

Nights

Through the night, try to sleep. It is tempting to offer to give a bottle of expressed milk to 'help out' but, even if your baby is normally bottle-fed, your partner will wake before you and find it impossible to settle until baby has fed and soothed. Better to be really well rested tomorrow so that you can fulfil your normal commitments and still have energy left over to provide practical and emotional support when you come home. Remember that an early morning cup of tea and slice of toast in bed before you leave for work will be much appreciated, as will a prepared lunch left in the fridge.

These first four months require real patience and understanding. You are both tired and overwhelmed by the enormity of your child's needs. This may be the biggest test of your relationship to date. Try not to worry too much but work creatively with your partner to come up with strategies that give you both enough rest, space and time both with and without a babe in arms.

Questions and answers

Nappy rash

How can I avoid my baby getting nappy rash?

Babies have delicate skin, so it needs to be treated gently. Urine and poo will not generally cause nappy rash if cleaned off properly. At each suckling time, nurse on one side and then take a break before offering the other. During this break, check the nappy. Avoid all cleaning products except water and don't add any creams except, if you really feel you need to, a tiny smear of petroleum jelly or a few drops of jojoba or coconut oil. If your baby gets nappy rash, ensure that you thoroughly wash your baby's bottom and genitalia at each change, put on a smear of oil or petroleum jelly under the nappy and, whenever possible, leave the nappy off for a while.

Spotty bottom

My baby has a number of red pimples on her bottom and nappy rash. What is causing this?

This sounds like thrush and needs checking by your midwife or health visitor. If it is thrush, you should be given a cream or ointment to treat it. Make sure that you complete the treatment course and then, once it has cleared up, follow the nappy-changing advice above.

Cleaning genitals

How should I clean my baby's genitals?

Carefully at each nappy change. With both boys *and* girls, only clean what you can see and do not pull back the foreskin on a boy's penis as this can cause swelling and make circumcision necessary. With a baby girl, wring out plenty of water from a flannel or cotton wool over her vulva and this will wash out any poo. Do not poke or rub as her vulva is sensitive and you might hurt her.

Circumcision

I am considering having my son circumcised to help him stay clean. How do I go about this?

Currently in the UK it is rarely possible to get a circumcision done on the NHS except for medical reasons, and cleanliness is not one of these reasons. The foreskin cannot and should not be retracted until it can naturally be done so by the child himself. As it cannot be retracted, it does not get mucky underneath and so is not a hygiene risk. Once your son can retract his own foreskin, he needs to be taught the simply daily hygiene routine of washing under the foreskin with plain water. Girls are taught to keep their vulva fresh and clean with a daily wash and boys should do the same. Should you wish to have your son circumcised for religious reasons, this will need to be done privately and it is best to consult with your own religious leader for reputable practitioners. Be sure to consult carefully as there are potential risks to circumcision even in the hands of a skilled surgeon.

Nails

How should I keep my baby's nails properly manicured?

Looking back to Chapter 2 (page 33), you will see that it is okay to simply and gently pick or peel the paper-thin nails. Baby nail clippers look sweet, but your baby may jump at just the wrong moment and cause you to cut her. As she gets older and her nails toughen up, nail clippers or scissors can be used. Some parents use a fine emery board and gently file nails down. Remember that, in the newborn, scratch mitts can interfere with normal suckling patterns, so, if you can't bring yourself to pick or peel the soft nails, you will need to turn a blind eye to the quick-to-heal scratches.

Baby acne

My baby's face is covered with horrid red spots. What are these?

If your baby is otherwise well, with no overall rash or temperature, you are almost certainly looking at baby acne. These red pimples tend to appear within the first few weeks of life and disappear without trace within a few weeks, coming up and going down in crops. They are common and harmless and require no treatment at all other than a daily wash with plain warm water. Do not use creams and medicines designed for older children and do seek medical advice if your baby seems at all unwell or has a rash developing over her whole body. If you are at all unsure, speak to a doctor.

Eczema

My baby has red pimply skin on her face which is dry and not like baby acne. What is this?

Most likely this is infantile eczema, but a doctor will be able to tell you with more certainty. If you or your partner come from a family with eczema, asthma, migraines or hay fever, your baby may have inherited the atopic gene. Try to exclusively suckle your baby, avoid all soaps and creams and wash all clothes in a non-perfumed, non-bio laundry liquid. Never use fabric softener on your baby's, your or your partner's clothes as this can quickly lead to eczema and dermatitis.

Hair washing

What should I use to wash my baby's hair and how often should I clean it?

Plain water and no more than once a week. If you find that your baby's hair gets somewhat sweaty and milky over the course of a day in arms, a freshen-up with a hand dampened with warm water will suffice. Make sure that you dry her thoroughly after washing.

Cradle cap

My baby's scalp has thick scaly scurf and I have been told it is cradle cap. How should I treat it?

Cradle cap is caused by overactive oil glands and may be a result of your placenta hormones in your baby. It will pass but, in the meantime, *don't* pick the scales, do wash the scalp with plain water or, at the very most, a very gentle baby shampoo, rinse and dry the scalp carefully and then massage in a little olive, coconut or jojoba oil. If you are worried, see your doctor.

Tummy time

I keep hearing about 'tummy time'. What is this?

Now that babies sleep on their backs, many of them spend little awake time on their fronts so that they can experience pushing up and reaching. There has been some concern over the years that lack of tummy time leads to an odd head shape and slower development of the muscles required for crawling. While an odd head shape and later crawling are not a problem as time goes on, tummy time is recommended every day, for short periods (your baby will soon yell when she has had enough) and while you are around to keep a close eye on her. If your baby is carried by you a lot and spends a lot of time suckling, you will almost certainly find that her head shape is entirely normal and her tummy muscles firm up quickly through the normal pushing away to look around that slung babies do.

8 The fourth month: farewell to the wonky ANS

Reaching back ...

As the season changes, so does the behaviour of our primitive baby. She has spent a little over three months jiggling in arms, never a moment away from her young mother's breast. Always safe from sun and storms, carried for the day's walk and tucked safely away from nocturnal animals, she has joined the survivors.

Our young family has simply let their newest tribe member in. Wherever they have trudged and whatever they have done, the baby has been there. They have changed very little about their life and yet nothing will ever be quite the same again. They have adapted.

After the long months of endless suckling, which has kept the baby and mother tightly attached physically and emotionally, things are now subtly changing.

In the daytime, as the baby becomes more and more part of the colourful world around her and is able to lie for longer out of arms without getting too cold, she suckles briefly now. Diving in with a wide smile for minutes of deep drinking before pulling sharply away to take in her surroundings and engage with the other members of her tribe. She can sense that her mother is separate and that she can draw her in with a grin and a head bobble or dismiss her with a pushed hand.

The primitive mother, keen for some time without her arms aching from long months of baby-holding, passes the eager child to her friend. The little one beams for a few moments before sensing the loss of her mother and, crying with a panicked yelp, causes the friend to laugh and hot-potato the squeaky bundle straight back again. A brisk suckle reassures the tribe's newest member that all is well and she has not been abandoned. The mother can, at least, sit and work now with her baby at her feet, just a touch away, without needing to constantly suckle. So long as she is within a moment away, her tiny child will cope.

The evenings are cold and dark and the companions sleep tightly together, waking regularly through the night to tend the fire and share stories. The baby, after months of long dreamy night suckling, drifting in and out of dozing, is becoming more like the adults: sleeping soundly for a couple of hours before waking up with the adults and being part of the group. She is growing up.

The ANS calms down

As the third month passes into the fourth and beyond, some dramatic changes take place. More often than not, parents are so close to the scene that they cannot see what's happening. Then, suddenly, realising that the baby is behaving quite differently, they panic. What has gone wrong? My baby doesn't like my breast any more and keeps getting angry at it!

So what does this change look like? Well, you have got so used to your 'café' baby – his long suckling times, his 'only the boob will do' behaviour – that, after the initial worry days, you learned that this was entirely normal and you adapted. Now your baby roots around and, adapted as you are, you grab a drink and the TV remote and settle down to nurse him. In he dives, suckles deeply for a few minutes and then pulls away hard. Your nipple leaves his mouth with a distinct 'pop!' and you are momentarily puzzled. 'That wasn't very long. Maybe the let-down was too fast for him. I'll give him a moment and then try again.' So you pat him for a few moments and, as soon as the rooting starts again, you go to suckle him. But he pushes away and cries at you! 'Okay! So you're not hungry? I'll put you in your bouncy chair and enjoy a few moments with my arms all to myself.' You go to put him in his chair and he kicks off. You pick him up, he roots, you offer the boob and he pushes away and yells. No wonder you're confused. He is obviously hungry, otherwise why would he root? You know him well enough now to know that he usually suckles for at least 45 minutes. A few cursory draws and a couple of gulps will not be enough, but he shouts when you offer more.

Don't panic! Let's step back for a moment and think this through together from an evolutionary point of view.

Do you remember that in the first three months of life the ANS is unregulated? That the sleep mechanisms and hormones are not yet settled? This wonky stage meets a couple of evolutionary needs. Firstly it ensures that your vulnerable baby is kept in arms and skin to skin where his ANS will soothe and the bears can't get him. Every time he is away from this safe skin to skin place, his ANS and sensitive gut yell at him to get back. Survival.

Secondly, this intense time locks you and him together in a deep attachment. The relationship is now secure enough that you take care for him even when you are too tired to think. He drives you nuts but you would pull off your right arm before letting him come to harm and, even if you want to, you just cannot let him cry alone for more than a very short while before feeling utterly driven to act.

Stop and look at your baby. Think about what he can do now. Have you noticed his gaze turning ever more outwards from the safety of your arms? He will smile at others, make the occasional surprising laugh that makes you both jump. He even tries, occasionally, to vocalise. Little coos and hums. You are now so smitten with him, thanks to this three-month knotting together, that you are drawn into his every movement and noise. Try as you might, you can't take your eyes off him for more than a moment.

At the same time, there are visible signs that his ANS is calming down. His jazz hands are a thing of the past, his foot stamping is disappearing (although the evenings will remain wiggly for a few weeks yet) and his chin wobble's gone. He can now better manage his own temperature;

that crazy erratic baby breathing that had you hovering over his crib for weeks wondering if he was okay has been replaced by ... just breathing; and were you to listen in to his chest, you'd notice a slower, more settled heart rate. What you can't see is that his immune system is now functioning pretty well and the hormones that help to organise sleep are starting to kick in (more about this later).

Great! So now your baby can safely start the long process of separation. But as his gaze lengthens, and he gains the ability to engage more with the wider world, his improving immune system and more settled ANS ensuring that he is safe away from skin to skin for longer periods of time, new dangers emerge that must be taken care of.

Your new 'sandwich shop' baby

Now that your little one has a more settled, functioning ANS, he no longer needs it soothed through endless skin to skin and suckling. Remember that in the first three months your baby was a 'café' baby? He could always get his milk in five minutes flat but he needed to stay skin to skin and so spread those five minutes over a long, dozy time at the breast. Stopping and starting, drawing hard one minute and then fluttering the next.

Now he is like a busy worker on a short lunch break. He has a fiver in his pocket and just 15 minutes to run to the shop, grab a sandwich and a drink, wolf it down and be back at his workplace before the boss misses him. He can't waste time counting the daisies or sitting in the park reading his book. Busy, busy busy! Your baby can now simply grab his food and then get back to the job of learning about his world.

So you can see how there really isn't anything wrong with your baby, or your milk. As always, your baby is doing the 'being a baby' thing exactly as he has evolved to do. Of course. Why would he suddenly get this stuff wrong? When you panic that he is not getting enough to eat, ask yourself, 'Is he being nicely wet? Is he otherwise well? Is he growing gradually out of his clothes?' If the answer to all these questions is 'Yes', your older baby is simply being an older baby. Your breasts will adjust accordingly, and you can relax and watch this new stage emerge.

If you are bottle-feeding your baby your own expressed milk or formula milk, you might find that the bottle–dummy–bottle–dummy method that better ensures your baby doesn't overfeed or under-suckle (see page 103) is taking less and less time and yet doesn't lead to an uncomfortable, cranky baby. Keep that dummy there at feed times: suckling and soothing are still needed.

Don't be cajoled by marketeers into thinking that your baby needs 'follow-on' milk or 'milk for the hungrier baby'. Neither of these is necessary or advisable. Just keep using stage one formula. Some women are told that their baby needs more iron than their own milk provides and so they should use follow-on milk. However, although the iron level is a little higher in a tub of follow-on milk, the iron is not in a very digestible form. The iron in human milk is in the perfect form for digestion by the human baby. Your own milk is exactly what your baby needs and he doesn't need anything else.

So you can see that, while your baby's needs are changing, this strange fussy feed-time behaviour is not about needing more, or no longer liking, milk.

The rooting reflex remains

Now that you feel calmer about your baby's faster feeding, you are probably wondering why he pulls away but then still roots around, only to cry and push away again if you offer to suckle him. All these changes from one stage to the next take a little time. Bodily functions cannot change overnight. There is a transitional phase and this phase emerges over a couple of months, starting at around the three-month mark.

Although some of the primitive reflexes (most notably the Moro or startle reflex) disappear before the third month, others take a little longer to fade away. The rooting reflex hangs around until the fourth to fifth month and the grasp reflex is going to keep your baby hanging onto your clothes for a few months more. So, although the need to suckle endlessly is disappearing as the ANS settles, the rooting reflex sticks around, confusing things. This ensures that the breast is still offered an awful lot (for very brief but frequent sucklings), until the immune system is really more functional.

Next time your baby comes to suckle, suckles briefly and then 'pops' off, if he doesn't grin and then immediately dive back on but pushes off and cries if you try to suckle him again, simply accept that he doesn't need to be skin to skin, button your shirt, turn him away from you in your arms or sling and do something else. Before long, he will be your newest hip-resident!

> ## Won't short feeds mean he doesn't get the hindmilk?
> There is no need to worry that by only having frequent, brief feeds your baby will not get enough hindmilk – remember that your baby is in charge and can take the blend he needs at that moment by the way he suckles, not for how long. And if he has a 'light snack' now, maybe he'll have a three-course meal a little later. He has evolved to sort this stuff out and he will.

Still unable to crawl

What if you put him down? He will yell to come back into your arms. He simply can't move yet. He won't roll regularly and reliably in both directions until he is six to seven months old, and crawling may take a couple more months, although some babies are crawling a lot earlier and some a fair bit later. If you put him down, he could be okay, or a bear might get him! Evolution ensures that he doesn't leave the safety of your arms just yet.

For a few months yet, your arms will still be pretty full of baby, but at least you won't get such a frost bitten boob any more!

Stranger aware

From an evolutionary standpoint, it is essential that the human baby learns to socialise. We are social creatures, after all, and our ability to communicate through both the spoken and, more importantly, the unspoken word has been fundamental to our success as a species. So you will notice during this fascinating transition period that your little one studies faces and tries to communicate with you and others more and more. He makes efforts to engage others and try out his best smiles and head tilts, charming everyone in the vicinity to smile and coo back, reinforcing the learning of these valuable social skills.

As long as he is safe in your arms, these interactions can take place. Pass him across to another person and watch the face change suddenly from sweetness and enticement to shock and fear. As he becomes more interested in the world, it is imperative that he becomes very wary of strangers. He will be fine with those he sees daily, like his parents. Those he sees less frequently, like grandparents, will only be able to keep him happy for a short while before he needs to return to you for reassurance. Complete strangers will have to smile and engage from a safe distance.

There's no need to force him to get used to being with other people. This stranger anxiety is an evolutionary stage and is protective. It is a sure sign that your baby is actually starting to separate himself from you a tiny bit. It doesn't seem like that, but it is. As he starts to realise that he is a separate entity from you and also doesn't need to spend so much time skin to skin at the boob, it is important that he shouldn't happily go off with strangers! Don't force it and don't worry that this means your child is going to be socially awkward all his life. The more you let him develop confidence at his own natural evolutionarily determined pace, the more secure and confident he will be. Whether he turns out to be a party animal or not, who knows, but he will not be clingy for long. You can help not feed any anxiety by showing that you are not frightened of either your friends or his fear. That way, his own fear will not overwhelm him. If, every time he shows fear, you mirror his panic in your own face, you will reinforce his idea that he is in danger. Simply let him hang onto you and carry on chatting away happily.

Now you can see that your baby is not clingy, you have not 'made a rod for your own back', he is not 'trying it on'. He is simply a human baby, perfectly equipped to stay safe while he learns.

Still too soon for routines

Remember that, until the fourth month, the immature and unregulated baby needs no structured routine or bedtime and that, because he is unable to learn how to be either bad or good, we could simply take our lead from him.

From the fourth to sixth month, during this transition, it is tempting to let the pull towards scheduling take hold. So many books tell you that babies start 'sleeping through' at about three months and, because the worst of the 'colic' is behind us, we start to fantasise about a full night's sleep and reclaiming some hours in the daytime for ourselves.

Hang fire! Your baby is *in* a transition, not through it. He is still unable to learn to self-soothe and his sleep is not fully organised yet, so time spent trying to teach him something he is not ready to learn could be better spent in other ways. If routines are something you hanker after (and many of us do), your time will come in a couple of months. For now, you can start to watch the natural routine emerge and make some mental notes.

Sleep organisation (not sleep regression)

As the ANS settles, so the systems and hormones involved with sleep start to kick in. Apart from the change in behaviour at the breast, parents also start to notice that sleep gets worse! Just when you thought you were through the clouds of 'colic' and could breathe a sigh of relief, your baby starts to wake every hour or so through the night and just 'fights sleep' during the day.

Maybe you had a week of a settled baby at about 12 weeks and patted yourself on the back, only to be brought back down to earth with a bump. Your friends smile indulgently and say, 'Oh, it's that sleep regression!' This has become such a commonplace phrase that parents really think that their baby has gone backwards and they can therefore get the baby back to where he was.

This is a leap forwards, not backwards. It just needs some explaining to help you understand what is happening so that you know how to manage your life.

Think about how your baby slept for the first three months: power naps scattered through the day and night with the best part of the day being the morning and the worst part of the day being the evening and night. Your baby seemed perfectly fine on regular 15-minute naps, even though your mum told you that he needed long sleeps. This is normal new baby sleep. A bit like his nursing mum, he wasted no time in the various different types of sleep but just grabbed deeply restorative moments to keep him going while being very quickly rousable to re-trigger his suckling urge. Power naps were what was needed.

Now think about how you sleep when you do not have a baby to suckle. You may think that you sleep deeply right through the night, but you don't really, do you? You know that you drift off to sleep from an awake state, into a dozy time, then a weird half-asleep time and then right off to proper sleep. This proper sleep consists of different types of sleep, including dream sleep (REM sleep) and deep sleep, in blocks which are broken by coming up out of sleep for a very short while. You look briefly at the clock, think 'Excellent! Only two o'clock – lots of time left for a good sleep.' And then you repeat the sleep cycle. It is possible that this type of sleep enabled early peoples to be on alert and ready for action if predators came by. We all know how difficult it is to get going if we wake during the wrong phase of sleep. In a tribal group there would always be one person in lighter sleep at any one time.

Far from regressing, your baby is heading towards a more grown-up type of sleep. So now he gets tired, settles (with help) for sleep, drifts, dozes, wavers in half-sleep and then sleeps properly for a while before coming to the end of a cycle. Until he is able to develop self-soothing, he needs your help again to get him back into his next sleep cycle. And so on through the night.

His daytime sleeps are much the same and, unless he hits the restorative type of sleep before he is disturbed, he will get tired and cranky.

So much for the theory. Now, what can you do?

Sleep cues

You may not be able to get your baby sleeping in the sort of way you'd like just yet, but you can do something useful. After three months of simply going with the flow and paying little attention to your young child's patterns, now is a good time to starting making notes. Write stuff down if that is how you like to work, or simply become consciously aware. You will have noticed that your little one wakes at some point in the morning, has a brief feed and then goes back to sleep. The waking is often at around five or six o'clock and then you get a short extra sleep until about seven or eight o'clock.

Once you are up for the day, make a note of the time your baby woke (let's say 7.30a.m.) and then see at what time he starts to show sleep cues.

Sleep cues emerge as the third month merges into the fourth and all parents are aware of them when I point them out. They even say, 'Oh yes, that's what he does when he's tired,' but they don't really register it as a 'thing'. Typical cues are ear-tugging, nose-rubbing, eye-rubbing, nuzzling into a parent's neck, making odd crying-but-not-really-crying noises. All babies have something and your job is to spot it.

You will also notice that different cries are now part of his vocabulary. Rather than the newborn '*Now!* Pick me up *now!*' yell, some cries are half-cries, some are about pain, some are moany tired cries and some are frightened cries: 'Where are you? I don't feel safe!'

The first sleep cues generally show themselves about one and a half to two hours after the first proper wakening of the day. As soon as you see sleep cues, settle your baby to sleep. He still needs a suckle of milk followed by a rocking, or shushing, a thumb or a dummy, but find something that works and help him get off for a sleep. Some babies continue to be happy to sleep in a sling, which is great. A crib, pushchair, car ride, lap – all these are perfectly fine, but your baby is signalling a need for sleep and you can help him get it. It will probably need about an hour minimum for your baby to restore properly, so consider how you can help him stay asleep for that length of time – maybe a walk or drive out to see friends; maybe a settled sleep in your arms while you read or rest; maybe gently putting your rocked-off baby into his crib. It really doesn't matter so long as his needs are met.

A second morning sleep may follow one and a half to two hours after he wakes from his first nap, and then, in the afternoon, it may well be three hours before you see sleep cues.

You might find that there is a late afternoon/early evening nap that you think is him going to bed for the night but is not. This is your time to gently watch and learn.

Coping with nights

During this transitional phase, trying to get your little one 'going through the night' is a miserable experience: he is too young. If you try to 'sleep train' him now, it will be months before he actually 'clicks' and by then your nerves will be in tatters.

It can be less stressful to accept that and look for coping strategies rather than to spend dismal evenings trying, fruitlessly, to squeeze your baby into an unachievable routine. Leaving a baby to cry it out is inappropriate and a waste of time. You cannot teach him to sleep through the night any more than you can teach him to read and write. He is too young.

If you are suckling your baby and are happy to, consider safe co-sleeping. Your bigger baby may stick his fingers in your ears and sleep like a starfish, but it is still more restful for you than getting out of bed every hour or two to resettle your growing human. This phase will pass. Keep free access to your boob and you won't be too disturbed.

If you are bottle-feeding infant formula milk, or are suckling your baby but not happy to safely co-sleep, you may need to accept that, for the next couple of months, your baby will need regular soothing back to sleep. This is tiring and frustrating if you don't understand why he is behaving like this. Once you know that he is just getting ready for the next evolutionary phase and that it will end soon, it is easier to bear.

Dummies, white noise or an uncovered thumb to suck may happily replace your rocking arms, but, if not, don't worry that if you don't 'get him into a routine' now he will be ruined for life!

Each time he wakes in the night, try to listen to his cries and, if it is moany or dreamy or a half-cry rather than a panic cry, don't rush to him but see if he will doze off again. Rushing to him might actually fully wake him from a half-sleep that would otherwise have naturally progressed back into another sleep cycle. If it is a proper *'Help! Come now!'* cry, go to him.

Your baby still needs night milk, so make sure that he gets at least one feed between midnight and morning. In any case, suckling him gets him back to sleep and also ensures that your deep-sleep hormones remain high and you are refreshed enough in the morning.

During daytime naps, if your baby is in his crib, don't rush in too hastily if you hear him waking: one of the main problems with baby alarms is that they alert parents to every sniff and mutter, disturbing their rest and, when the parents jump up, disturbing the baby too. Consider daring to turn it off – it offers no protection for your baby and may be jangling your nerves.

How your baby will move on

So, through months four and five, simply watch, make notes and ensure that naps are had. There is no need to rush your highly evolved baby through this phase.

As you get closer to the sixth month, your baby will show distinct rhythms in his day and will let you know more and more when he is tired and when he needs to head for his night-time sleep. No matter what you do – everything or nothing – he will develop into the next phase in time and you will be ready to adapt again!

Partner ponderings

The four-month-old baby brings mixed blessings. Sure, he smiles at you now when you get home from work and this warms your heart and makes your time away seem worthwhile. But he still fusses for his mum an awful lot more than you may think is normal at this age. This 'only mum will do' stage seems to go on forever and you may feel that you will never have a deep relationship with your child.

Trust that there is a protective rhythm to life and that evolution is still at work, ensuring that everything pans out just fine. Hours spent suckling in order to remain skin to skin with mum is no longer the order of the day. This older baby still needs plenty of time in arms and those arms could, increasingly often, be yours.

Don't rush your baby to separate from his mum, but simply make it more and more possible for you to take him. If you are not currently doing the bath times, think about making that your thing (see page 157). Or take your little one for a nice evening stroll before dinner. Or maybe just pop him in a knot sling and wander around the house for a while, chatting to him about your life and your day. If he cries for his mum, don't take it personally or get fractious. Simply wander back, confidently, to your partner and hand him back. Far from making him clingy, this will build trust and confidence. This is a process built over millions of years and there is nothing to be gained from rushing it.

Naps

Many mums find that, as the baby gets older and starts to need more settled naps, their partner can really help in guiding their child to discover his own self-soothing strategies. Until the sixth month, you cannot expect him to learn good self-soothing habits, but you can gently ease him in that direction as well as giving your partner some valuable time to herself.

When you are around and your young child shows the sleep cues described above, offer to help. He will still need his mum to suckle him or give him a bottle but then, whether or not he has actually dozed off, you can take him and help him to nap. This might mean gently walking him to his crib and placing him in it, or rocking him for the duration, or pushing him around the neighbourhood while he sleeps. The idea is not to teach your baby to get himself off to sleep (he will almost certainly be unable to do that) but to ensure that he gets his sleep and that it is long enough for him to be well rested. You will find what works for you and that may actually be a different strategy from your partner's. It's nice for a baby to have different parents able to soothe him in different ways, so don't get too hooked up on consistency.

If you manage to help your child nap one time and not the next, that is quite normal. Don't throw in the towel but simply accept that your little one is a human being and has good moments and bad moments. The moment does not define him or your relationship with him.

Bath-time routine

As with nap times, it is possible that you are around for at least some bath times and could use this time to have some unique space together.

If your baby likes baths, and if your partner is around, get her to pass your child to you while you bath yourself. Or simply bath him in the kitchen sink. As the weeks go on, your baby will enjoy simple bath games: plastic squeezy bottles to pour water over his feet gives a nice tickle and showing him how to pat his hands on the water to make little splashes builds water confidence and is simple fun.

For many partners, bath time brings a welcome end-of-day wind-down for them and their baby and can be the start of a longer routine as the child gets older.

Nights

While sleep training is off the table for a while yet, there are still things that you can do to make the nights easier. Take note of the natural rhythm your baby is developing. You will see that, as you approach the midnight hours (and probably earlier), your little one gives very distinct sleep cues. Just as at nap times, after he has had a suckle with his mother, offer to take him upstairs to his crib.

Turn the lights low; pop on some white noise; rock or simply cuddle your baby while you shush him; and, if he likes it, give him a dummy. When he is just drifting off, gently place him in his crib or cot. If he needs you to get him right off to sleep, do it. Sure, you're providing him with a soothing strategy rather than letting him develop his own, but that doesn't matter at this age. Sleep does. If the white noise works, leave it running, all night if necessary; you might find that it helps you sleep more deeply too.

During the night, if you don't have work the next day, take your turn in helping your child get back to sleep when he inevitably wakes up. He may not always need to suckle for milk (although he probably needs at least one suckle overnight), so you can help your partner by offering your baby an alternative soothing strategy so she doesn't always have to suckle. If you have work the next day it is probably more sensible for your partner to soothe the baby back to sleep each time he wakes. It isn't important for each night to be the same, so help when you can and concentrate on being thoroughly rested on the other nights. Babies benefit from a flexible approach and both you and your partner will discover your own unique techniques for baby-soothing.

If you keep all your senses alert during months four to six you will see big changes taking place. This need not be a worrying or exhausting stage. It can be a time of wonder and fun and increasing closeness to this youngest member of your tribe!

Questions and answers

Dribbling

My baby has started dribbling all the time. My mum tells me that he is teething but I can't see anything. Is there a problem?

No. It is a common myth that dribbling is a sign of teething. It isn't. Although babies dribble when teeth are coming through, that isn't the only cause of dribbling. Dribbling starts as babies begin to verbalise with coos and hums. The saliva moistens the tongue and lips, which makes vocalisation easier. It also increases as your baby moves towards weaning: saliva helps with chewing and food digestion as well as with clearing the mouth of food bits. The dribbling may increase when teeth are coming through but it starts well before teething. As your child grows, he will learn how to manage the dribble but, for now, gently dry his chin when you notice it is wet. You could use a tiny smear of petroleum jelly on the chin to act as a waterproof barrier. Generally a dribble rash is best simply kept dry and it will heal quickly.

Teething

My baby is cutting teeth and is obviously sore. How can I help?

The first teeth appear at widely different ages in different babies. Some cut the first one at around four months, others nearer their first birthday. Some babies are actually born with teeth. Many babies are very fractious when teeth are pushing up through the gums and breaking through the skin. The discomfort stops as soon as the tooth is through. A teething ring (cooled in the fridge – not the freezer) can give your baby something to chew on, which can distract and ease the discomfort. Some teething gels contain a little local anaesthetic which, when gently rubbed into the gums, gives temporary relief, but ensure that you get a gel designed for babies and read the instructions carefully. Homoeopathic treatments work no better than placebos and can be expensive, while amber necklaces are also completely unsupported by good scientific evidence and pose the risk of choking. They look pretty but are not safe for babies. There is no evidence that teething causes diarrhoea or a temperature but, because teeth come through over such a long period of time, and babies sometimes get runny poo or a temperature, parents make connections when those two things seem to come together. However, many parents notice a particularly fierce nappy rash in the week or so before a tooth erupts, which may be due to the increased saliva altering the poo and making it more irritating to the skin. Be rigorous in washing your baby at changing times with plain water, avoiding wet wipes. If your baby is unwell, don't assume it is 'just teething': see a doctor and offer a child-appropriate paracetamol liquid, given according to instructions, to bring the temperature down. Once a tooth has emerged, it needs cleaning. Use a soft toothbrush or a cloth over your finger and a smear of fluoride toothpaste twice a day and gently clean any teeth that have broken through.

Biting at the breast

How can I stop my baby biting me when he suckles?

The bottom two teeth generally come through first and these are covered by the tongue during suckling. If your baby forgets himself as he dozes at the boob and bites, you will instinctively yell and pull him off, of course. As you tend to your poor, tender nipple, your shocked baby will yell (he has probably never been shouted at before). At this point, most mums feel so guilty that they sweep the weeping baby back to the breast. This can give a mixed message to your child. Better to sort out your nipple for a few moments while your baby cries safely in your arms and then, when you come to offer the breast again, go slowly and use your tone of voice and facial expression to give a clear message: 'Watch what you are doing. That is *my* nipple, so be careful.' Your hesitation to take him back and unapologetic care for your nipple gives a clear message and will help to prevent another nip. Some people suggest pressing the biting baby's face into the breast to cause him to fight for breath and come off in panic. *Don't do this!*

Baby walkers and door bouncers

My baby wants to be on his feet all the time. Can I use a baby walker or door bouncer?

Many babies love to bounce up and down on their feet at the same time as getting a better view of the world. If your baby can hold himself upright for a short period of time with the sort of support offered by a walker, a sturdy, safe baby walker can be a great gadget. Ensure that your walker has a very broad base and meets legal safety requirements. Use it well away from any stairs and for short times only: as soon as your baby starts to fret, take him out. The same goes for door bouncers.

Weaning

My baby watches me eat and is really interested. I'm told this means that he is ready for solids. How do I start?

You don't! Your baby probably shows an interest in you driving, but you know he isn't ready to get the keys to your car yet. At four months, your baby's gut is simply not ready for food. If your baby grabs food off your plate, you will discover that, although he puts it in his mouth, it will come out again. Watching you eat is not a sign of readiness to wean, and neither is wanting more milk or waking at night. Introducing solids to make a baby sleep more has simply not been shown to work. So hang fire, relax in the knowledge that your baby can get everything he needs from milk and read Chapter 9 on weaning!

Vitamins

Should my baby have daily vitamin drops?

It depends. While the jury is out on giving babies multivitamins, supplementing with vitamin D is a different matter. If you took vitamin D as advised during pregnancy, your own milk will provide enough for your baby until about the six-month mark. After this, it is recommended that you give your baby vitamin D drops containing between 8.5 and 10 micrograms daily as babies simply do not get enough sunshine or vitamin D-rich foods. Infant formula has vitamin D added, so if your baby has more than 500ml (about a pint) of formula each day, he will get enough. Do not be tempted to introduce formula alongside your own milk simply to get vitamin D into your baby: the formula will give your baby many additional ingredients that he doesn't need and that could cause problems. Current advice is that everyone in the northern hemisphere should take a daily vitamin D supplement, so it's a good habit to get into. Look online for the correct dose for different ages.

9 Weaning: keeping it simple

Reaching back ...

The primitive group has been walking all day. The baby, now halfway through her first year, has jiggled happily on the back of her mother, looking around at her fascinating world. An ever-changing, living mobile of clouds, trees and animals.

Content to spend some time on the hip of an older child while her mother walks solo for a while, before long she fidgets and frets and finds herself back for a brief suckle before being slung back out of the way into her primitive cloth sidecar.

As the light softens and this nomadic group settles down for the night in the cooler shade of a sparse wood, lightly leafed trees provide just enough cover without the group being in danger from the forest-dwelling animals.

The growing baby, lying on her back and grasping playfully at her waving feet, delights in the attention of the other children while the leaders prepare food over an expertly made fire. Suddenly she is scooped up through the smoky air and landed on the soft flesh of her mother's thigh. She can sit now and she looks outwards towards the chatting group, joining in with the stories with her own efforts, blowing through her lips, tongue poking out, to create a pleasing buzz and burr.

Her mother pulls a softly cooked root out of the embers, tossing it up and down in the air to cool it down. The baby watches every action, eyes darting up and down as the hot lump flies. And now her mother rips hungrily into the hot vegetable, chewing bits off and enjoying the tasty pleasure of worked-for food.

The little girl, entranced, reaches up to her mother's mouth with her chubby fingers, grasping desperately at this interesting, smelly chunk, and the rest of the tribe grunt with laughter as she recoils from the heat. Her attentive mother chews a little longer and then, once the food is soft and cool, lowers her mouth to her child's until their lips meet. The baby reaches out enquiringly with her tongue and her mother pushes a little of the mush towards her waiting mouth. Surprised, the baby looks in shock at her mum, rolls this warm weird taste around for a moment or two and then swallows! Her delighted mother laughs and kisses her, offering another kiss-food, which her baby takes. This time, the lump hits the back of her throat a little too quickly and she coughs and splutters. The vegetable lump flies out of her mouth and her mother catches it. Before this young woman can eat it, her young daughter grabs it and takes it into her own mouth, exploring it excitedly before swallowing and grinning. The group, enjoying witnessing this young child's first taste of food, erupts with happy shouts.

A big moment. And then, for reassurance in the noise of the celebration, the baby dives towards her mother's chest for a familiar mouthful of warm milk.

What is weaning?

Weaning is the long, gradual process of introducing your baby to a full family diet. The end point of when a child has 'weaned' is generally considered to be when your child no longer suckles at the breast, but this doesn't seem to me a very good definition. After all, many older babies, toddlers and young children eat a full family diet and yet still suckle at the breast, or on a bottle.

Quite simply, weaning is complete when your child eats a full family diet, whether or not she continues to suckle. So, when you consider weaning, it may help to think of the suckling separately. Your child will almost certainly gradually reduce the amount of milk she takes, but how long she continues to nurse is between you and her.

When to start

Babies vary in all their developmental stages. Some walk at nine months and some at i8 months. Some cut their first tooth at four months and some not until they reach their first birthday. So it is with readiness to wean. However, the World Health Organization advice has been, for many years now, to exclusively milk-feed your baby on either human milk or infant formula milk for six months. Human or formula milk should continue to be part of the diet for the first year and can be for up to two years or beyond, as long as the mother wishes. Cow's milk is not appropriate as the main milk drink until the baby is one year old, but it is okay to mix small amounts of full-fat milk into weaning foods such as cereals.

Anthropological evidence on weaning is hard to come by, but what there is, combined with evidence from modern hunter-gatherer populations, suggests that babies start having some non-milk foods on average at between six and eight months.

Night-time waking and watching people eat and even grabbing food off a plate are not signs that your baby is ready for solids. Your baby will grab anything and put it in her mouth. Putting everything in the mouth is the way babies learn about objects, not a sign of hunger.

Your baby is ready to eat solids when she takes food, puts it in her mouth, mushes it around and then swallows it. And then wants to do it again (in other words, it wasn't a one-off!). This is very different from the parent-led approach of giving a baby some purée off a spoon. The baby squirts it out and the parent scoops it back up off her chin and tries again and again until the baby just happens to swallow. This will generally be at about the same time as she can sit well without support and regularly reaches out with a hand and takes a toy into her mouth and chews on it. She may or may not have teeth.

So expect your baby to make her first efforts at eating family foods at around six months and don't fret if your baby is a little earlier or later than this. Let her lead. And remember that, from six months, giving a daily vitamin D supplement is a sensible move (see page 161).

Baby-led or parent-led weaning

For the last five or six months, you have learned to accept that your baby is completely able to be in charge of her appetite. You have let her muddle her way onto your boob when she has shown a desire and then switched your attention to something else, safe in the knowledge that she would take just the right amount and right blend of milk as she needed at that moment over the amount of time she decided was also right.

So why is it that, when we get to weaning, we suddenly lose all faith in our baby and start taking control? Then we wonder why we end up with a fussy eater! If we try to get a little bit more food down to help baby sleep longer or to get our little one to finish what we have so lovingly prepared, we override the appetite part of the brain and she might grow up to find it difficult to know when she has reached the 'full' stage.

Baby-led weaning is just what it says – led by the baby, not you. This is different from the traditional method your own mother might have used of preparing purées of baby rice, vegetables and fruit, and offering them by spoon until the bowl was empty.

Many women find that a baby-led approach is less stressful and pressured, but most use a combination of some baby-led and some parent-led weaning. The principle remains the same – ensure that, whether or not you have a spoon in your hand, the baby decides whether to eat or not and how much she wants. When she is finished, she is really finished.

A healthy approach

We want our babies to share in our family mealtimes. So, before you start weaning, have a good long think. If your diet is a healthy one with plenty of fruit, vegetables, wholegrains, healthy fats, and, if you eat them, a little meat and fish, then that's great. If, like many of us, you eat a really good diet through much of the week and then, on a Friday, enjoy a bowl of macaroni cheese with some lemon drizzle cake to follow, you need to decide whether to: wean your child onto your diet, warts and all; wean your child onto your diet and make her eat separately when you're having a treat; or change your diet!

I would warn against creating a culture of reward foods. If cake is seen as simply another food to be had in moderation as part of your normal healthy diet, it gains no particular value. However, seeing it as 'naughty' or as a reward or as a pick-me-up when we are upset can lead to emotional eating. Furthermore, if fruit is offered because 'you can't have cake if you don't finish your main course', fruit gets seen as a punishment. So, if you are considering continuing with your own mixed diet, including some fast foods and chocolate, but plan to give your child only 'clean' foods, think about the messages you are giving.

If you want your child to grow up to eat with the family, start as you mean to go on. Gradually introduce your child to *all* your family foods.

First foods

In primitive times, food was pre-processed by an adult to make it softer and more manageable for a baby and some cultures still do this. A baby can't be expected to wolf down steak and roast potatoes. After months of a liquid diet, you need to go slowly, very slowly. But you can still use your own foods.

Rather than having a set, formalised baby mealtime, simply sit your baby on your lap when you are having a bite to eat and ensure that there is something on your plate that is soft and that she can hold, for example well-cooked potato, a piece of avocado, ripe banana, a piece of tofu or some soft bread and butter. If you are having a stew, it can be deconstructed for your baby so that there are nice pieces of soft carrot, swede, potato, etc. and hers can be in a separate bowl for her to reach into. If she can hold it in her hand she can control the pace. She may enjoy squeezing cubes of cheese before they reach her mouth, or the sensation of letting a tube of soft pasta slip gently in and out of her lips before it finally heads in for swallowing. She might worry at a piece of chapati, destroying it with dribble into a soggy pap before discarding it with a grin. Food should be a pleasure, so let her play.

It's important to bear in mind that, as well as vitamins and minerals, babies need calories for energy, so look for calorie-dense foods such as cheese, banana, mashed pulses, potato and sweet potato. If she fills up with tasty broccoli and then can't manage her milk, she will be down on calories and fats. This is why it is not useful to give bowls full of baby rice: there are fewer calories and nutrients in a few tablespoons of baby rice than in the milk meal you have just replaced. First foods are about new flavours and textures, not replacing the milk.

In the first few weeks, expect to see your baby try a few bits and pieces here and there. Some things will be spat out, some enjoyed enormously. Don't try to force your baby to like certain foods. And don't worry that she will only pick an unhealthy diet if you don't insist she always picks fruit off your plate. You are in charge of the food in the house and so, as long as a wide variety of foods is available, your baby will choose a more and more varied diet. If all you offer is chips, she will only eat chips! (On the subject of chips, these are a favourite early weaning food – they're easy to hold, soft to chew, and tasty. Just don't add salt and vinegar!)

Relax and enjoy sharing food with your child. It may be that you only eat one meal a day with her or it may be that she has a little every time you do. Let her guide you and ensure that everything she gets into her mouth is pretty soft and cooled. As the weeks go on, she will probably be ahead of you and will grab and devour a tangy olive or a cheese triangle before you realise it has happened. I remember carrying my second son in a baby carrier when he was about seven months old. I was walking by the coast on a hot day enjoying an ice cream when, all of a sudden, a hand flew over my shoulder and grabbed the top of my ice cream! One astonished mum and one very happy boy. Until the brain-freeze hit!

As your child explores her first foods, you may be anxiously poised to whip her out of her high chair the moment she gags on something and it comes back up. While it's important to know what to do if your child does actually choke on something, gagging is part of your baby's inbuilt safety mechanism. Stay calm if your baby gags and don't make a fuss. See page 170 for more on gagging and choking.

Foods to avoid

If you wait until your baby is six months old, you needn't worry about the impact of wheat and gluten on her delicate gut. If you have started before the sixth month, hold off. Also, until the six-month mark, avoid eggs, fish, shellfish, nut butters, seeds and unpasteurised cheeses. This precaution is to avoid triggering allergies. Honey is not suitable in the first year, due to possible toxins, and whole nuts should be avoided until your child is about five years old, to avoid choking. If there is an allergy in the family, speak to your GP before introducing that food to your child.

Be sensible about salt and sugar. It isn't healthy for anyone to add salt to cooking *and* at the table, and no one benefits from lots of sugary drinks and cakes. But it's fine to add a little salt to cooking vegetables or to a savoury dish, and cakes and tarts are a welcome part of everyone's diet, just not for daily consumption.

Drinks

When your baby wakes from a nap, she may want a suckle. Even if it is lunchtime, let her nurse. No one can enjoy their food with a dry mouth and a hard thirst. You are not trying to replace the milk feed – that will come soon enough. During her mealtime with you, have some water in an open cup or a spouted beaker and hold it carefully for her, tipping it just enough so that the water hits her lips. She will slurp and lap if she is thirsty. Then, after the food, she may suckle again.

Bit by bit, over the coming months, she will take progressively more and more solid food and water, and less and less milk. You should not feel the need to control the pace of this reduction in nursing. She will move at a comfortable pace for her.

If you are giving milk from a bottle, offer enough to 'wet her whistle' when she wakes up and then the rest after the solid food. Remember that she can't control the flow so easily with a teat and so may glug down a big milk feed and then have no appetite for solids. This doesn't matter very much in the early days – little tasters of foods are what you are aiming for – but continuing to front-load a weaning baby with a lot of formula may inhibit her desire for foods. Ensure that, until your baby is taking plenty of foods spread through the day, she has her bottles of milk (about a pint through the day).

Don't be tempted to give fruit juices as drinks. You may think they are healthy, but they are actually just drinkable sugars which will fill your child up without offering many nutrients. Moreover, although her teeth aren't showing, they are there, hidden in the gums, just below the surface and needing protection from tooth-rotting sugary drinks.

Increasing the choice

Once you start, and realise that your baby will help guide this process, you will probably stop worrying about how to move forward. She will push out foods she can't manage or doesn't like, and enjoy those she can. At about seven months old my grandson had a passion for chunks of my husband's home-made bread. He liked to have a small pot of hummus so he could dip in his bread and then eat it. His pleasure in this treat was obvious. One day, I tried him with a pot of onion-flavoured hummus and he wasted no time in letting me know what a mistake that was – his appalled face and long-distance spitting told me everything!

As the sixth month moves to the seventh and eighth, introduce meat and boneless fish. Oh, the British delight for a fish finger sandwich! Why deprive your child of comfort food that you enjoy for the ultra-healthy option of yet more mango?

As your baby develops the pincer grip (bringing a thumb and forefinger together), she will love little things to pick up, such as cooked peas and sweetcorn. Sometimes babies love the challenge of getting really tricky things such as one single cooked lentil. They still love to dive their fingers into something wet like a soup (thicken it a little with baby rice) or dhal and slurping it off into their mouths. Thicker treats like mousse can be squelched in the hand before eating and, if it is summer, an outside slurpy picnic that ends up all over her face is hardly a problem.

Experiment together, show your enjoyment of all foods, from cabbage to cream, and your baby will follow.

Gagging and choking

Babies have a cough and gag reflex just like you. Likewise, they can also choke, although if you are sensible this is rare. If your baby is taking food and putting it in her own mouth, if it isn't right for her she will push it out again. If it goes too far back and it isn't right, she will gag and cough it out. Only if she inhales food and it goes into her windpipe will she actually choke.

Gagging on food is very normal for babies as they explore the sensation of swallowing food. Whenever your baby is having foods you must be right there with her – never leave her alone to eat. With small foods such as grapes, cut them in half or smaller so that they are unlikely to block the windpipe. If she gags, don't panic or she will see your face and she will also panic. Stay calm, or pretend to be calm if necessary, and happily reassure her. Gagging is a safety mechanism.

Actual choking is very unlikely to happen because all humans have inbuilt protective gag and cough reflexes, but it is important to know what to do if it does.

Quickly do the following:

- Take her into your arms, sit down and place her tummy down on your lap so that her head is lower than her bottom.
- Keeping away from the soft underside of her chin, support her head on your lap with your thumb on one side of her jaw and a couple of fingers on the other (this keeps the airway open).
- Using the heel of your free hand, give up to five firm slaps between her shoulder blades. Stop after each slap briefly to see if the food has come out. NEVER poke your fingers in unless you can see the food and hook it out – you might just push it further in.

If this doesn't work:

- Turn your baby over on your lap and slide your arm underneath her body (your arm will now lie on your lap and your baby will lie on your arm).
- Use your supporting hand to cup her head.
- Find your baby's breastbone and place two fingers of your spare hand on the lower bit of it.
- Give five sharp chest pushes with your fingers so that her chest goes down by about a third. Check after each push quickly to see if the food has come out and, as with the back slaps, don't poke about in her mouth unless you are certain that you can see and hook out the food.

If this hasn't worked, go back to back slaps and do five more, then five chest pushes and so on.

IF AFTER THREE ROUNDS OF BACK SLAPS AND THREE ROUNDS OF CHEST PUSHES NOTHING HAS HAPPENED, CALL 999, leave the phone on speaker and carry on with the slaps and pushes until help arrives.

If you have had to do the emergency back slapping and chest pushes and it has worked, still get your baby checked out at the hospital to make sure no bits of food have gone down into her lungs and that she is completely okay.

Cutting out milk

Left to their own devices, babies gradually reduce the amount of milk they take over the time they are weaning. Even if they don't cut down much on the number of feeds, some babies start to refuse the breast at various points through the day and end up having a few really good nursings, often first thing in the morning, to settle for each nap and then at bedtime. Some babies continue to dive on and off the boob throughout the day for cursory moments, 'touching base' for snuggles, relaxation and reassurance. Either is fine. If you wish to do the former, you will find that if, instead of offering the breast for those brief moments, you do something else with your child that provides closeness and relaxation (share some moments with a favourite toy or go for a wander and a chat in the garden), your little one will quickly move on to something else. She will still have her good milky snuggles when she needs them but gradually drop the frequent pop-ons. If you enjoy the frequent sucklings, carry on and ignore unhelpful comments. They are *your* boobs!

Many mothers worry about having to move their baby over to a bottle of dairy-based formula milk as they reduce the amount of their own milk their baby takes. No need. All mammals wean off their mother's milk and don't replace it with the milk of another mammal. It is very common for the breast milk-fed baby to wean in her own time off the boob and then never drink milk again. Sure, they may enjoy milk on cereal, and eat cheese or yoghurt, but a glass of milk? No thanks.

If your baby is one of those who is simply not interested in drinking milk other than yours, ensure that she gets to suckle regularly as well as getting offered plenty of calcium-rich foods such as nut butters, pulses, tofu, sardines and baked beans. These are better forms of calcium to offer, as they help absorb iron into the body, whereas dairy products such as yoghurt and cheese can inhibit the absorption of iron – and iron-deficiency anaemia is a common problem in children. You can add dairy or vegetable milks to her cereals and, as with all babies from six months, give a daily supplement that includes vitamin D. Then stop worrying. Having cow's milk is cultural and not essential.

Overall, remember that, just as in the early months, your baby is on an evolutionary developmental journey for which she is perfectly equipped. Don't rush, nag, fret or force and she will be fine.

Weaning can be a delightful time if you just dawdle along, sharing your lovely food with your little one.

Partner ponderings

Weaning can be an exciting and fun time for all the family. It marks a moving on from real babyhood into a new stage. Your baby is ready to join you more socially around the meal table. You may find you love this stage. Finally you can have the sharing cuddles and giggles over food that your partner has enjoyed in the first six months.

So get involved, offer your baby the foods that you enjoy, following the guidance above, and have fun. Maybe take her to visit your friends and family, let them feed your baby their foods, and treat it as a time for your baby to learn about different experiences of flavours. From a mother's point of view, there is a real thrill in seeing your precious baby at a distance, joining the wider world, momentarily oblivious to her presence.

Questions and answers
Poo

My baby used to have lots of yellow poo but now she has a hard brown poo once a week. Should I be worried?

It depends. Once solids are introduced, even a tiny amount, baby poo changes. You can wave goodbye to the soft, yoghurty-smelling poo and say hello to proper stinky brown poo! It will form into more solid lumps and your baby will start to obviously strain to pass it. She may go from

---

pooing every time you suckle her to only having a poo once a day, or less often. This is normal. If, however, your baby seems uncomfortable and can't poo despite her efforts, she may be constipated. The best cure is to increase the amount of human milk she gets (through suckling or from a bottle or a cup) as breast milk is a natural laxative. If you are formula-feeding, turn to Chapter 5 (page 110) for advice on constipation in your little one. Make sure that there is water available at every mealtime and give her plenty of time to roll about or crawl on the floor, as activity is great for the healthy working of the bowel. If your baby hasn't pooed for several days, despite increasing fluids and activity, and is obviously uncomfortable, see your GP.

Pee

My baby is not so wet now that I am weaning. Is this something to worry about?

It is important to ensure that your baby gets enough fluids alongside weaning foods. Allow her milk drinks to reduce at a rate that she dictates, rather than you, and always offer water at mealtimes. As she takes less and less milk, you will need to offer water right through the day. If her poo is hard and her pee is dark, she is not having enough fluids. Thirst is a big trigger and, if you are not offering enough fluids, expect her to get her drinks any way she can – some babies will suck a flannel at bath time! Use a spouted beaker or open cup. If your baby is over six months, don't worry about the water being sterilised – tap water is fine (boil and cool it if your baby is under six months).

Tummy bugs

My baby has caught her first ever tummy bug. What should I do?

While a baby only has human milk, it is extremely rare for her to get a tummy bug. Once she starts to have foods other than human milk, her risk of getting a tummy bug goes up. If there is a tummy bug going around, or if she has already caught it, stop all solids and go back to exclusively suckling your child or giving her nothing but expressed breast milk from a cup or bottle (ensure the expressed milk is fresh, not frozen). This is the quickest way to sort out vomiting and diarrhoea in a baby. If you are feeding your baby formula milk, stop all solids and only give milk and water. Do not water down the formula at all or add anything else to the milk feed.

If your baby has strong pee, hot, dry skin or dark, sunken eyes, do the above and also see you own doctor.

If she has a temperature over 39°C (or 38°C if your baby is under three months), is deteriorating, has bloody or mucousy poo or has green vomit, go to the hospital accident and emergency department to be seen urgently.

Diabetic mums

I am diabetic. Are there any additional things I should do when weaning?

Having diabetes may put your baby at an increased risk of developing diabetes. There are some pretty straightforward things that can help you manage your own blood sugar as well as reduce the likelihood of your baby developing diabetes. First, if at all possible, exclusively suckle your baby, or ensure that she has nothing except your own expressed milk, for a minimum of four months. There is good evidence to show that exposure to dairy milk in infant formula increases the risk of your baby developing diabetes and that, the earlier the exposure, the greater the risk. Nursing your baby will help you to stabilise your blood sugars too, although it is important to keep up your regular checks and let your diabetes specialist know that you are a nursing mum. Start the weaning process at the normal age and go really slowly. This will help her gut adapt gently as well as helping your blood sugar to adjust slowly. Wean her onto your diet, which will be naturally lower in processed carbohydrates and sugars, so automatically healthier. The evidence that diabetic mums should wean earlier is not yet proven and so the current recommendation to wean at about six months remains in place.

Fussy eating

My first child is a terribly fussy eater. How can I avoid this problem with my younger child?

It is very common for a baby who will eat pretty much everything to become fussy at the age of about three. Suddenly they will eat everything as long as it is white! White bread and butter, bananas and macaroni cheese. Anything green or red is greeted with huge suspicion. Parents panic at this emergence of fussiness and go overboard with rewards and other interventions that further increase the child's belief that there is something worrying about the food. Three-year-olds are venturing further and further into the world and it serves them very well from an evolutionary point of view if they become very nervous of eating things with a bit of colour – it might be a poisonous berry …

So relax with your three-year-old and let her self-serve from a range of foods. Your toddler will get a balanced diet over the course of a week.

As for your baby? Follow the advice above and allow self-governing to continue into toddlerhood. If you put a lasagne, some salad, some bread and some peas on the table and let everyone help themselves (giving gentle help to the tinies), everyone will choose different portions of each food. Watching what children choose and passing judgement breeds anxiety and can create the very problem you are trying to avoid. Mealtimes are for sharing stories from our day, not causing self-consciousness.

10 Sleeping: strategies to suit your own parenting style

Reaching back ...

Darkness falls over the tribe. After many days of walking, they reached their destination soon after the sun reached the top of the sky. The young mother was relieved to be back at this lakeside spot, which she remembered from earlier years. Here they could make camp, and stop. Stop and settle for a while and enjoy rest and companionship.

Over the afternoon, sturdy shelters, built from animal hides, strong tree boughs and branches, started to form. Shelters from the cool breeze, and a welcome refuge to share with friends and family.

As her mate went off with a group of younger men and children to fish for supper, the mother and her closest companions put the finishing touches to the shelters and built a fire for cooking and light for the night. Tonight would see no moon, the only light in the sky the vast sparkling splash of stars like so many twinkling ants, moving together, split every now and then by a flash of light, speeding across her vision, making her heart race.

As the companions built and set the fire, the children played together, the babies welcomed into the throng. When they were tired, they fell asleep where they were, under the shade of a hefty branch, flung with a coarse cloth. A large pile of snuffling, snoring chubby cheeks and thighs.

Now, bellies full of tender fish, watching from the shelters as the fire glimmers, the tribe settles for rest. Families snuggle together for warmth, younger children and babies never more than a reach away. A group of chattering children whispering and giggling as they recount imaginary stories of wolves and shadows, delighting in the mutual shock and fright as the story is punctured by the loud cracks of branches popping on the nearby flames.

The men of the tribe lie on their fronts, one hand under the chin and the other resting on a spear, ready to pounce and protect the group if the need arises. The women wrap themselves close to their mates and babies and hush the children until peace descends and each, in turn, begins to drift off.

The baby lies on her back, cradled in her mother's curled arm, kicking her legs in the air and babbling. Her need to suckle is now reduced to grabbed moments of warm milk throughout the day whenever her busy mother stands still long enough to drop her breast into her smiling mouth. Earlier, she had a fistful of tender vegetable which her father had blown on to cool it down.

Through the long, dark night children fidget and wake, shouting suddenly with worrying dreams before falling back to sleep with the help of a pat from a nearby friend. And the adults wake whenever there is a sound, check quickly for safety and then return to doze contentedly until the next waking.

The young mother sleeps deeply for a couple of hours and then wakes, stumbles quietly outside the shelter, and enjoys the fresh night air. She takes a pee and then carefully heads back to her half-awake mate and child. Happily, she snuggles up close, her baby grabs the opportunity for a warm suckle before dozing off to sleep, leaving her and her mate to enjoy some intimate moments. She missed the deep pleasure of this close touch during the early months after the birth, and now that her young child nurses for shorter periods of time, she is ready again for a more adult night-time encounter!

What is a normal sleep pattern?

Sleep habits vary from culture to culture, family to family and person to person. It appears that, until pretty recent history, and still today in some nomadic tribes, the night sleep was split into at least two parts with a significant time in the middle spent awake and busy. In many countries today, sleep is split across the whole day and night, using a siesta to make up the sleep not taken during the night. And all of us sleep in cycles, lightening out of sleep a number of times. Some of us remember the wakenings and some of us do not. Once we stop setting the bar so jolly high at 'sleep through the night', our broken nights do not seem so awful.

So the normal sleep pattern may well just be whatever we decide it is, for us, in our house.

While our primitive ancestors probably slept together in groups throughout their lives, our lives are very different. We cannot share the night-time workload with a large group; we have different demands on our daytime energies and do not have the luxury of nodding off after lunch to catch up on our sleep.

Interestingly, when you get talking with friends, you will find that many older children creep into each other's beds at night for companionship and warmth, and, let's be honest, most of us like to sleep with another human being every night. You can certainly choose to follow the primitive model and have a 'family bed', but you may simply find the notion impossible to entertain and need a more modern way of organising your night.

Sleeping through the night

When parents talk about getting their baby to 'sleep through the night', what they actually mean is 'When will our baby stop waking us through the night?' If your baby was waking every hour or two but rolled over and went back to sleep again, you'd be none the wiser, unless, of course, your baby monitor is set so that the quietest burp sounds to your sleeping brain like a door slamming. When I wake during the night, I do not go around the house banging on every bedroom door, shaking the sleeping occupants awake and demanding to be entertained. I do the things I know help me to nod off again and, if these don't work, I get up and do something quiet for a short while and then go back to bed to settle again.

Our babies have not evolved to have self-soothing strategies and so rely, mostly, on the presence of others to help them nod off. Again, and again, and again.

Self-soothing

But, I hear, 'He *can* get off to sleep okay without me rocking him off. At nap times and at bedtime I put him in his crib awake and he dozes off. So he *can* self-soothe.'

Think about this a little more carefully. Maybe at nap time you offer a brief suckle or a little bread and butter with a warm drink. Then maybe you say 'Time for a nap' before walking him up the stairs; turning down the light; popping his cuddly blanket into the crib; turning on the baby monitor; rocking him for a minute or so until he is calm and relaxed and then, finally, placing him into his crib. Then you say 'See you later, alligator!' and leave. After his daytime naps, which are maybe one cycle long, he wakes up and you get him up. (See page 153, Chapter 8 for a reminder of how sleep cycles work.)

At night, when your baby wakes, he doesn't get the brief suckle or a little bread and butter with a warm drink, 'Time for a nap', walking up the stairs, turning down the light, his cuddly blanket popped into his crib, turning on the baby monitor, a brief rocking until he is calm and relaxed ... You get the picture? You are soothing him. This is his routine and it is absent every time he wakes, as we all do, at various points through the night.

Until he is around six months old, he is incapable of learning how to go from being awake to being asleep, then awake again, and asleep again by himself. You can try, but it is mostly a long and miserable process because you are trying to teach him something he is not yet ready to learn. So, if your baby is not yet six months old, go back and read Chapter 8.

If your little one is a skilled thumb-sucker, you might strike lucky and find that he can soothe himself back to sleep repeatedly overnight with a well-sucked digit. Most parents find that, in spite of all the books telling them that babies sleep through the night from whatever age (name your number), their reality is very different. Everyone else's baby is right; their baby is wrong! He is broken and he needs mending.

To train or not to train

If you have been keeping an eye on your baby's sleep cues and rhythms over the last two months or so, as suggested in Chapter 8, you will have noticed that, during the morning, he gives sleep cues at around one and a half to two hours after his first proper wakening of the day, and then again about one and a half to two hours after the end of his first nap. In the afternoon, he can stay awake for about two and a half to three hours before he shows sleepy needs and then, if you manage to get him to sleep, he only naps for 30 to 45 minutes, whereas his morning naps are an hour or so.

At night you may notice that he goes down a little earlier now, say at about nine o'clock, and then you need to resettle him around the midnight hour. After that, his nights will be hit and miss with anything from one waking to hourly shout-outs.

You will also have discovered that he sleeps more deeply than in those catnapping early days and is pretty grouchy if allowed to skip a nap.

Maybe you have also discovered that, if you put him down sleepy but awake, his cries are not always full-on crying but are more frustrated grumbling. If you leave him with his grumbling, sometimes he will nod off and sometimes the crying will change to a full, upset cry, requiring your attendance to soothe him. Many parents never experience the grumbling to nodding-off thing; their baby is always reliant on external soothing.

How your baby behaves at this stage is independent of whether you have breastfed or bottle-fed, co-slept or cot-slept, parented your baby mostly in arms or been able to leave your baby out of arms for long periods. Like so much of what we have talked about so far, this is a developmental stage and your baby is the expert at being himself, no matter what you try. Once you get to the six-month mark, you can sit down with your partner and have a good think about your next move.

Consider the following: would you prefer to let things follow their own course or instigate some type of 'sleep training'?

If you fall into the first group, consider whether you prefer to safely co-sleep, have your baby sleep in his crib in your room, or have him sleep in his own room.

If you fall into the second group, you need to understand that there is only one way to help your baby to discover his own way to move from being awake and alone, to a dozy state, to a nodding-off state, to being asleep, to waking up alone, to drifting back off again alone and so on. That is to let your baby be awake and alone to discover his strategies, to wake up again and have to do it all over again. Every 'sleep training' strategy amounts to exactly the same thing and the only difference is how much time he is left alone to work things out before a grown-up goes in to reassure and then leave him to his own devices again. From the 'no-cry' strategies like 'camping out' through to 'controlled crying' and finally to 'crying it out', your baby needs to ultimately be alone and awake and have the time and space to discover his own self-soothing strategy. So be sure, before you start, whether and what you are happy to try.

What to expect

The results of sleep studies of young children and the outcomes for those parents who 'sleep train' their babies and those who follow a 'wait and see' policy are really rather interesting. In the sleep training group, there is no doubt that babies stop bothering their parents overnight. It doesn't seem to matter overmuch which strategy the parents decide to try – after a period of time (how long it takes to 'sleep train' a baby depends on the baby and the chosen method), the nights are quiet. But, and it is a very big but, every time the baby has a cough or cold, visits granny, has an overly exciting day or cuts a tooth, he drops his new sleep habit and reverts to waking his parents, who have to do the training all over again. And again. And again. Sure, it is quicker the second, third and fourth time, but they do have to retrain over and over.

Both groups of children start to become pretty reliable in terms of not waking other people through the night at about the same age – about five years – irrespective of whether their parents have repeatedly 'sleep trained' or co-slept or walked to and from the nursery every hour or two to rock their child.

This matches my own experience of my children and those of the hundreds of clients I have seen over the years.

So, over and above everything else, decide what path you want to take and then manage your expectations right down! Be as flexible or rigid as suits your home situation and personal parenting styles and don't feel the need to share your decision with well-meaning but judgemental friends and family. If you choose to go with the flow and fear that your mother will take delight in regaling you with stories about how you were sleeping 'through the night' before you were even born, feel free to lie about your plans. Parenting is tough enough in the modern world without having to deal with other people's atrocious memories.

If you have decided to 'sleep train' your older baby and the rest of your friendship group plan to merrily co-sleep until the GCSE results plop onto the doormat, do not feel shamed into confessing your choice unless you actually want to. This is your business and each choice seems to lead to the same outcome in any case.

Different approaches to sleep training

There is only one way to give your baby the opportunity to work out his own self-soothing strategy, and that is to give him that opportunity. The difference between the various approaches is down to how long a baby is left to discover what works in the absence of another person. A minute, half an hour, a night?

So let's have a look at three approaches. While reading, please remember that each approach works for some families and not for others. If it looks as though it would suit you, give it a try.

Camping out

In this scenario a parent is present but unavailable for comment (a bit like a politician!).

- After the agreed bedtime routine, the baby is put into his cot. The parent sits at the edge of the cot and quietly strokes the baby off to sleep. When the baby is asleep the parent leaves the room.
- When the baby can manage this step, the stroking is removed and the parent simply sits and reads until the baby is asleep, and then leaves the room.
- When this step is successful, the chair is moved away a couple of feet and the parent sits and reads until the baby falls asleep.
- The chair is gradually moved further and further away until it is outside the door and the job is done!
- Every time the baby wakes overnight, the process is repeated.
- If the baby is crying in step two onwards, he can be quietly stroked and soothed, but not off to sleep – just enough to calm him. If he is very upset, he can be lifted and soothed but not off to sleep – he should be gently popped back in his crib when his upset has eased.
- Eye contact and talking should be avoided.

Pros

The message given to the baby is that everything is okay and this 'getting off to sleep' business is really rather dull and needs no great party tricks from a parent. This is called congruency and is very important whatever strategy you may choose. Think of the midwife in the labour room: while a woman becomes more and more noisy and animated, her partner may join in with the ever-increasing anxiety, pleading with the midwife to 'Do something!', but the midwife stays completely calm and writes her notes or rubs the woman's back. The message she gives is: 'This is completely normal and nothing to be scared of. I am so relaxed about this that I am going to sit and write.' If the midwife joined in with the rising noise and looked equally fraught, the partner and labouring woman would think, 'Oh no! If the midwife is looking anxious there really *must* be a problem!', and the anxiety would escalate. So it is with babies and children – if your body language says 'Nothing to fear here!' they can switch off and calm down.

Cons

While some babies will be soothed by the presence of a quiet parent softly stroking them, just as many babies get completely hysterical and the parent finds it impossible not to get engaged and end up suckling or frantically rocking or doing all the other things that you know will get the baby off to sleep but were trying to cut out. Furthermore, many parents find that the process takes so long and they get so unbelievably tired that they 'give in' and declare the process a failure before a week is up.

Shush, pat

This method is not dissimilar to 'camping out', but there is more engagement throughout.

- After the agreed bedtime routine, the baby is put into his cot and the parent leaves the room with an air that says, 'You're okay. I'm not in the slightest doubt that you can nail this getting off to sleep palaver!'
- As soon as the baby cries (not a grumbling, annoyed 'Excuse me! Where the heck do you think you've gone?' protest, but an upset cry), the parent goes into the room and picks the baby up. The parent pats the baby's back and simply says 'Sshh, sshh, sshh' until the baby 'lightens' in their arms. The purpose is to reassure, prevent prolonged upset and soothe, *not* to get the baby to sleep. As soon as the baby settles, he goes back into his cot.
- The second he starts crying again (proper upset crying, not annoyed protesting), the process is repeated.
- The process is repeated at every waking during the night.
- The number of visits to soothe should become fewer and fewer until the baby can be put down and will lie awake and able to get himself off to sleep without any 'shushing and patting'.

Pros

This is considered a 'no cry' method and babies are reassured that they have a parent available at any time to soothe them if it all gets a bit much. This suits both parents who cannot tolerate the idea of their baby being upset and those babies who do not need complete peace and quiet to get off to sleep.

Cons

As with 'camping out', some babies get progressively more and more riled at having a parent available but not doing very much. Parents complain that their baby starts to cry before they have even reached the mattress and so they may spend the entire first night stood patting and shushing. The process may require more commitment and patience than the tired parent possesses. If your baby is energised and disturbed by the slightest stimulation, this approach may not work at all.

Controlled crying

The purpose of this method is to allow the baby the space and opportunity to be alone for safe periods of time so that he can discover a self-soothing strategy without distraction from a parent. It also gradually removes all other soothing strategies.

- After the agreed bedtime routine, the baby is put into his cot and the parent leaves the room with a relaxed air.
- As soon as the baby starts to cry (proper upset cries, not annoyed protesting noises), a clock is set to five minutes. If the crying is still going after five minutes, the parent goes in and pats the baby in his cot (or he is lifted and patted and shushed – you choose) until he has stopped crying and is eased a little. He is put back into his cot and the parent leaves the room even if he starts crying again immediately.
- As soon as crying starts up again, the clock is set for seven or eight or 10 minutes (you decide) and the process repeated.
- The length of time the baby is left is gradually increased at a rate that suits you, up to a maximum of no more than 30 minutes (or less if you can only bear, say, 15 or 20 minutes).
- Once the maximum is reached, that length is repeated until the baby is asleep (so: five minutes, eight, 10, 15, 20, 30, 30, 30, 30, for example).
- The process is repeated, from the beginning, at each waking through the night.
- The following night, or a week later, you can choose to start with a longer period of waiting.

Pros

Many parents find that this method is more successful if they have a baby who finds having a parent in the room too distracting from the process of nodding off. It also allows for more flexibility so that parents can do what they can tolerate. They can reassure themselves that their baby is fine.

Cons

Waiting for even five minutes of crying can feel like torture and many parents simply cannot do it. Often they find that they can tolerate doing it a few months down the line, even if the first time was too tough all round. Some parents find that they struggle to work out whether the sound they are hearing is protest crying, 'just humming myself off to sleep' noises or really upset crying – they go in to the room only to discover their baby is actually on the point of nodding off and is simply crying-humming, but now he has been disturbed he kicks off, so that the whole rigmarole starts again!

Ultimately, whether you try any of these (or all of them in turn) or not is completely your business. All of them are tricky and upsetting for everyone and each of them will work given enough time and diligence. The first usually takes longest and the third generally is fastest. You will not make this particular omelette without breaking a whole heap of eggs, so do it if you and your partner feel it is right for your household, not because you have been bullied and shamed into it by well-meaning friends and relatives.

How long will it take?

The time it takes for a particular baby to discover the ability to self-soothe is very variable. Pick a time when your baby is well and you have good support around. If you are at all unsure about whether or not your baby is completely well, ask your GP.

Talk to your neighbours to reassure them that you are available for your baby but that you are struggling with sleep right now and, over the next few weeks, there may be some crying. Any family with children will understand completely.

Agree with your partner how to support each other – maybe one does the routine and the other provides food and support. Maybe you act as a tag team. Maybe one goes away for a few nights and the other does the deed. Use a baby monitor to call for your swap if this has been agreed.

Some parents find that the 'camping out' method delivers peaceful nights within a week or two and some still struggle with it well over a month down the line. Some parents find that 'controlled crying' works within a couple of days and others need a couple of weeks. Try not to compare with friends or with an older child.

Keeping a diary can really help you to see progress when you are in the middle of it all and feeling tired. You may be surprised at how fast things are actually changing, or notice that you are defeating yourselves by soothing your baby off to sleep every other night and slowing the process down. Be kind to each other: these things are difficult and there is no place for blame and recriminations when a plan is not going as smoothly as you had anticipated.

Family beds

If you decide that sleep training is not for you, and you have agreed this with your partner, you may decide on a family bed. Many parents who choose this way of managing nights discover that, as the children get older, they gravitate away from the parental bed and into a shared children's bed. Many people I speak to recall that, although they have no memories of being allowed into their parents' bed, they have vivid and happy memories of sneaking into a sibling's bed in the middle of the night.

Almost all of us remember certain times when we were invited to bed share: when we were poorly or for a big family weekend breakfast in bed. Bed sharing, either as a regular, planned event, or on an ad hoc basis, has been with us forever and should cause no judgement or alarm.

Take sensible precautions:

- Don't let an older child sleep next to a baby under the age of one.
- Don't bed share if you are a smoker.
- Don't bed share if you are drunk.
- Don't push the bed up against a wall.
- Don't allow pets to share your bed if there are young babies and children in it.
- Ensure that this is a joint decision!

This last point is really very important. The security and happiness of your relationship with your partner was of paramount importance to your child, no matter what his age. Insisting on a family bed if your partner finds the idea intolerable is unreasonable. If one partner wants to sleep train and the other doesn't, you really need to agree on as good a compromise as you can manage. This might mean that the keen-to-train partner agrees to do the sleep training while the other disappears for a few nights after suckles and snuggles and 'night nights'. It might mean agreeing to a family bed for a few months more on the promise that a gentle sleep training approach is taken after that.

Although many mothers can continue to tolerate quite disrupted nights for a long time, their partner's sleep quality is not hormonally protected in the same way and so exhaustion becomes a constant bane of their life. You should be prepared to consider each other's needs and support each other as best you possibly can, even if this means giving way sometimes.

Consistency

No one is ever totally consistent in life. Things change and we change our minds. We may cope with a bad night one day and not another. We may handle a baby in our bed one week but find it utterly unthinkable the following week. This is simply life as we know it. Accept your humanity along with the reality that, if you change your sleep training approach, results will take longer. If you are happy for your baby to snuggle next to you one night but not another, as a parent you have the absolute right to change your mind but you will have to put up with cross protests from your little one. It is not one of the deadly sins to be inconsistent, so give yourselves a break!

Sex

Ah! Remember sex? It's what led to this book being bought in the first place! At some point, we all want to welcome those intimate moments back into our lives. For about 60% of women, their doctor's suggestion that they try having sex by their six-week check-up can only be met with hysterical laughter. For many women, it is at least six months before they feel physically able to want and enjoy sex. At the other end of the scale, I am the midwife who walked in on a couple having sex on the postnatal ward!

We are all different. Reassure each other and be gentle. Episiotomies, Caesarean scars, exhaustion and a baby in our bed can all put the kibosh on any hope of intimacy, but all these things do pass and life is quite long enough for more sex than anyone can possibly get through.

If you have opted to bed share, you may simply get used to stealing moments while your little one is asleep and blissfully unaware of the passion being enjoyed nearby.

Combinations and compromise

It might be that you neither want a family bed nor care for sleep training. Then decide where and how you can best manage the nights. Talk to your partner and see what their views are. Be prepared to compromise where necessary so that both of you feel heard and able to face nights from here on.

If you want your child to sleep in his own room from six months but are happy to continue to get up to go to him every time he wakes, that is a perfectly reasonable decision. If your partner is happy to do the night-time soothing whenever possible (maybe non-working nights?), so much the better.

If you want to have your child sleep in your room and are happy to soothe him to sleep for naps and at bedtime but want him to self-soothe overnight, have a good think together about how this can best be achieved and then support each other in implementing your plan. Your child might be more flexible than you think.

If you agree that your older baby is to sleep in his own room but you will put a mattress in there so that a parent can go in there to sleep when he wakes up, decide how that will be worked out between the two of you.

Often, however, parents want different things and a compromise needs to be found. This may not be as easy as you think if you are determined not to sleep train and your partner is adamant that night-time disturbances must stop. Or vice versa. It might be that you agree that you will always do the night soothings and not moan about your dreadful nights, or that your baby is expected to self-soothe on weeknights and then gets to co-sleep with you both at weekends. People may well throw their hands up in horror and tell you that your child will be confused, but if you can manage to sort this plan out, your child will simply grow up knowing that this is how his house 'works'.

Away from home

Sleeping in a different house or a different bed upsets the very best of sleepers: adult, child and baby alike. Well-learned routines fly out of the window, sleep is beset by fidgetings and we wake with a jolt, wondering for some minutes where on earth we are. This is a universal human experience and your baby is a very soundly working human being.

However long your child is away from his usual bed, expect some unsettled behaviour both during the holiday and on your return. You can help at least a little by sticking to any bedtime routine you may have. Ensure that the white noise generator is packed and teddy is close to hand on journeys and take familiar cot blankets too.

Try to allow a little leniency where it seems appropriate: if you want to go out to see the sights in the dark evening and have no babysitter, take your little one along, wrapped snugly in his pushchair, and accept that he will be pretty grumpy tomorrow and need a quieter day.

You are the parents and you can quite easily re-establish the bedtime and night-time routines and rules again when you need to if you can stop fretting about the permanent psychological trauma you have undoubtedly caused by a single act of inconsistency. Enjoy your holiday and accept that there will be an inevitable period of readjustment when you get back home.

If you find that packing up and travelling with a baby or young child is not worth the hassle, just don't bother: a week with a sandpit, a paddling pool and good company is enough of a break for many parents and your little one really doesn't need to visit the pyramids just yet.

Partner ponderings

Lack of sleep affects everyone in a household. Even if you are currently the sole occupant of the spare room and sleeping like a log, there is a fair chance that you are noticing that your partner is more tired than usual or she is wondering when you two will ever be back in the same bed again.

Many women are currently interested in the 'attachment parenting' approach and are keen to keep their babies with them day and night, until the child chooses for himself when to sleep in his own bed and wave goodbye to suckling. It can make you wonder whether your views are of any importance at all in this parenting lark or whether you simply have to go along for the ride.

The truth is that you play an essential role in helping your partner gently separate from your baby. You are the best person to give your baby a safe bridge from his mother to the outside world. Having developed a strong and deep attachment to mum, the little one now needs to make other close attachments, and this helps foster even better confidence in the world.

If you cannot be very involved in weaning, you certainly can be in the area of helping to establish healthy family sleep habits.

How and where your older baby spends his night needs to be agreed by both of you. Your needs are as important as everyone else's in the household, so ensure you are clear and reasonable about what those needs are. It is reasonable to ask for a negotiation about your place in the adult bed and also perfectly fair for you to have your say about what is reasonable in the way of overnight baby care if it is impacting on your ability to stay awake in the day.

Find a good time to talk rather than trying to have a conversation over the head of an over-tired baby at two o'clock in the morning. And remember that your partner really is deeply, hormonally tied to your child and that this is how it should be. Your job is to provide another pair of arms that your little one learns is just as safe and trustworthy as his mother's.

Read this chapter together. Talk about your expectations and worries as well as hers and make a joint decision on how you'd like to handle nights from here on. Generally, I find that mothers often find it difficult to know whether their views are really their views or simply those of others, and guilt can cloud their judgement. You may be able to tease out whether she is actually more than happy to continue to co-sleep for now but feels she 'should' be getting him going through the night. If this is the case and you feel happy with baby in your bed, then that is good enough.

The trickier scenario is if you decide to 'sleep train' your baby but your partner finds the sound of her upset baby too hard to bear. She is not being soppy or weak. She has not created this situation by being overly involved with your child or by suckling him for too many months. This is evolution working. A mother cannot be rational when her baby howls. It hurts deep in her belly, and yet she knows that the entanglement she feels with her child needs lessening just a little so that she can regain her sense of self.

If you can arrange to put your chosen plan of action into place when you have some days off, this is ideal. It can really be helpful if you confidently reassure your partner that you will do the majority of the instigation of the plan. It is great for your child to learn that someone other than his mother can safely see him into the land of nod and it will help the transition towards having a night off for both of you with grandma putting him down for the night. Your input will build confidence in your partner, in your baby and in you.

Try not to worry that your baby will associate you with the misery of learning to self-soothe: his mother has held him while he has screamed with colic and thrown up all over the carpet, but no one would suggest that that will leave a nasty association between him and his mother. Rather, you are building a relationship of trust and warmth and also helping your child have safe experiences of frustration and learning from someone who loves him just as deeply as his mum.

Questions and answers

Naps

How long should a nap last and how many should my baby have?

It depends on your baby's age. A baby of six months can reasonably be expected to have one or two morning naps of at least an hour and an afternoon nap of 30 to 45 minutes. Less than this may leave you with a really crotchety child. A one-year-old may only need one good morning sleep of an hour and a half and an afternoon nap of half an hour. A three-year-old may thrive on a post-lunchtime siesta of an hour and an occasional doze on the sofa in the mid-afternoon. Many four-year-olds still value a lunchtime sleep of about an hour. If your child is giving you sleep cues, take the hint and put him down for a nap. If he seems tired but is not giving sleep cues, you can still put him down for a nap – you are the grown-up, after all, and you may well know better than him that he needs a kip.

My baby is happy to nap anywhere. Should I insist he naps in his cot?

If your baby sleeps well anywhere and is properly rested, leaving him nice to know, thank your lucky stars. Many babies need the peace, dark and familiarity of their own cot. If you can introduce a travel cot, then as long as you pack it in the boot if you are visiting friends for the day, naps need not be missed. If your older baby really needs a nap and can't sleep elsewhere, you will have to choose between changing your plans and putting up with a tired baby.

I like to meet friends for lunch once a week. Is it okay to skip a nap on those days?

Sleep is extremely important for young babies and children. They need sleep to grow and develop as well as to give their hard-working parents a much-needed break. Wherever possible, incorporate your little one's nap into your plans. Maybe rotate the lunch venue so that your baby doesn't miss his nap every week. If you can't and you prefer not to miss your lunch, then accept the inevitable grouchy afternoon you will have to endure from your tired tiny and make extra time for a long, relaxing bedtime routine later.

Bedtimes

What is a sensible bedtime?

Whatever you decide, between your baby's sleep cues and your lifestyle, but don't sacrifice your child's sleep for your social life except on exceptional occasions. Most babies gradually bring back their natural bedtime bit by bit. A six-month-old baby often needs a nine o'clock bedtime with a brief suckle at midnight; a baby near to his first birthday is often ready for pyjamas by seven or eight o'clock and can sometimes 'go through the night'. Sleep helps relax a child and makes it more likely that he will nap the following day and sleep well again the following night. If you want your child to have good sleep hygiene, he can't do it without your help and support, so protect his sleep.

My partner often works late and misses bedtime. Can I keep our baby up late so my partner gets time with him?

Many parents try this only to discover that their partner gets an hour after work with a cranky baby and the mother has to deal with a miserable moaner the next day. Your child is really not in this world to entertain you or your partner, so you might have to accept having the bedtime routine to yourself except when your partner has days off then it can be their lovely wind-down time while you take some time out for yourself.

Crying it out

I have read that letting a baby cry harms him. My mum says this is rubbish. Who is right?

This is a very tricky question to answer. When a person gets upset and stressed, certain hormones flood the body. If these hormones stay high enough for long enough, it seems to cause long-term damage. However, stress hormones can also facilitate learning and emotional growth if they are not experienced for too long or in too high an amount. Getting the balance right is hard and, no doubt, in years to come, scientists will be able to guide us more accurately. Certainly, 'sleep training' is unsuitable for babies under six months and for parents who do not wish to try it. Over six months, babies do cry in different ways for different reasons and we do not need to respond instantly at the slightest grizzle, as we will have done in the first three to four months. Allowing your baby some gentle experiences of being safely alone, of dealing with brief frustrations and of being unhappy with our partner for a change can build a confidence in his own resilience and a trust in others. Leaving an older baby to cry alone for more than half an hour is probably allowing those stress hormones to climb too high for too long, so avoid doing this. A gentle, managed approach to sleep training, as detailed above, does not appear to do any harm. Neither does *not* sleep training, so think about what suits you and your family, make a well-thought-out choice and then surround yourself with those who can support rather than undermine you.

Co-sleeping with siblings

Is it okay for my older baby to co-sleep with his big sister?

Having a kids' bed solves many problems in many families. In our house, our four boys each had their own room but chose from early on to all sleep in the same room and often in the same bunk. They learned to co-operate, resolve conflicts, story-tell, compromise, sleep in ridiculous positions and laugh so loudly that their exasperated parents stomped upstairs yet again to read them the riot act! If each child knows that they have their own space to escape to (even if it is just the other side of a shared room), sibling room-shares can free up your bed and provide overnight warmth and snuggles for the children. However, your baby really does need to be an older baby. Although it is hard to make definite rules, a one-year-old and an older sibling safely co-sleeping in your bed is fine, but if siblings are bed sharing away from your bed, wait until the youngest is at least two years old. Generally, then, the decision is made for you: you go to your youngest's bed in the morning only to find it empty and the older child's bed rather shockingly full of arms, legs and cuddly toys. Before that point, put the younger child's cot in his sibling's room if the older child is happy with the idea, and see how it goes.

11 Moving and talking: joining the wider world

Reaching back ...

The young primitive family is enjoying a time of brief rest in their waterside settlement. It is a wonderful time of reflection on the past half a year and a joy to see their youngest tribe member make her first wobbly efforts to join the big people.

The baby girl has been moving more and more over the past months. From lifting her head off her mother's chest to search for a breast, to pressing away with her hands to get a good look at the noisy companions around her, to rolling over, to her surprise as much as everyone else's, a few months ago when she was playing with her waving feet in the warm shade provided by a chunky toddler. Once she could enjoy being on her tummy, she spent every moment she was on the ground heaving her belly clear off the dust until her shaky arms were stick straight and she could push back onto her knees. Rocking backwards and forwards, she would burble to anyone who cared to listen before collapsing back down, to the giggles of her playmates.

And a few weeks ago, late in the afternoon, while her family was chatting around her, she tentatively lifted an arm, shifted the opposite knee and moved one little bit forward. Her delighted father clapped and his little girl grinned and made another tremendous effort before easing back down onto her tummy.

Now here we are. This youngest of humans is moving. Her ability has improved rapidly with her diligent practice. Her muscles are sturdy and lean from many months of pressing against her human carriers and primed through the constant nutrient supply of her mother's milk. She is now able to explore her world in a new way and she makes the most of it. Fighting free of arms as soon as she has suckled and nuzzled, reaching towards open space, her mother, glad to have her aching arms relieved, places her down with the other children, busy as they are drawing pictures with sticks.

These children, more of a see-you height than her parents, hold a special allure and our little mover heads towards them, crawling through the artwork and bringing howls of upset from the artists in residence. Plonking herself back onto her bottom, our lithe baby grabs a stick and waves it about, blowing bubbles at it and making 'da da da' sounds which puncture the air like the sounds of stones hitting a rock. Her mother looks up suddenly, so surprised to hear these sounds.

After months of increasing babbling, her daughter's new focus on moving her limbs had brought an unexpected peace from her once noisy lips and she had quite missed the chatter. Putting down her work and sitting back on a log, our young woman gazes quietly at her baby as she waves and chats before turning her head and, on seeing her beloved mother, discards her stick, flips to her knees and starts to crawl, double speed, back to her. Stopping on the way, transfixed by a bug that just has to be pincered up by her dusty fingers into her mouth, she is surprised by its gritty tang and her mother's cry and, looking up, sees her shocked face of disgust. Alarmed, she quickly spits the wriggly creature back out onto the filthy ground and crawls on, faster still, back to the ever-ready lap.

When do babies move and talk?

We are looking at these two things together because the way they develop, in fits and starts, alongside each other often puzzles parents.

Some children talk and crawl at a pretty average age: first babbles at around four to five months, repetitive sounds at about six to seven months and first recognisable words by their first birthday. The average baby rolls both ways at around six months and then crawls at about eight to 10 months. Walking starts at around 12 to 14 months.

Those are the averages and the variation either side is huge. But something that all parents I speak to notice but no one seems to tell you is that, as one set of skills takes off, another goes on the back burner for a while. The very early talker who can deliver a monologue worthy of a soapbox orator may find it impossible to move her backside off the ground to crawl until she is well past her first birthday, and then, once she discovers the joys of exploring the furthest reaches of your pan cupboard, she forgets how to bend your ear with constant chatter. The baby who is raiding every corner of the house with her precocious crawling at five months old may find it far too troublesome to utter a recognisable word until the birthday candles for her second birthday are being lit. And then when talking takes off, she suddenly can't quite remember how to move so fast.

My fourth son made me despair when he crawled at four months old. If I had been a first-time mum I would have hailed this achievement as a sign of genius but, with three other sons to run around after, I simply knew it meant yet another child to haul out of the cat basket! Needless to say, this unusually early mover didn't utter a sentence that I could understand until he was four. Until then he spoke fluent 'scribble'.

They just can't do it all. The late walker may grow up to be a long-distance runner and the late talker may become a notable orator. Or not. It is fascinating to watch but foolish to predict.

Touching base

We feel thrilled when our baby reaches towards the ground, begging to be put down to explore. That's it, we think, no more constant carrying. My arms are my own again. Just as we start to shake our arms to feel the fresh air around them, who's heading back? A quick nuzzly cuddle, and then off she goes again for a few paces. And then back again. And so on. Oh no! We have created a nervous, clingy crybaby. All our lovely close mothering and time in arms has made that rod for our backs that we have been repeatedly warned about.

Breathe. Your baby has learned to leave the safety of your arms and explore her world. How sensible would it be if she could crawl and crawl and crawl without ever looking back? If she could willingly pootle off to a stranger on the other side of the room without checking to make sure her mother was still there to protect her?

Evolution has built in, over millions of years, a little protective mechanism. Your crawler will repeatedly 'touch base' with you. Over the weeks and months she will gradually pay out more rope, but it is essential that her rope is securely attached to her rock. How else could she feel safe and secure? Unhook her rope by pushing her away and she will panic and cling to her rock even more tightly. Let her lengthen her rope at her own pace, knowing that she is strongly anchored in case she should get into trouble, and her confidence and skill will increase at a pace.

Stranger anxiety

As well as 'touching base' repeatedly, she will now also develop significant stranger anxiety – more pronounced than you've experienced in the previous months. This is completely normal and, of course, very protective, so don't try to overcome it by forcing your child into situations she is unable to cope with. Stay calm and just let your little human be a little human.

Dealing with the unhelpful comments of other people is tiresome. The constant fretting that 'she has you wound round her little finger' and 'she has to learn to let go' can get into your head.

It is tempting to push her off into a group of other children at the toddler group to encourage independence, or, despite her protests, to leave her in a crèche while you shop so that she can 'get used to it'. But she isn't ready to be left like that yet and a large group of toddlers would terrify anyone, let alone a new-to-this-world crawler.

People who understand babies will pass your child back to you the second she reaches for you, knowing that this is a passing phase and, before you know it, she will turn her affections elsewhere and you will be longing to be back as number one in her life.

Accepting that your child is not ready to put too much distance between her and you just yet does not mean that you need to match her anxiety. *You* know she is safe with Great Aunty Vera; *she* doesn't. So when your baby shows stranger anxiety, let her come back to you but ensure that your face, tone and body language give a confident message. If your unspoken message is 'You may be worried about Great Aunty Vera, but I'm not and I know that, in time, you will just love her experienced cuddles and sloppy, lipsticky kisses!' then your child will learn that there is nothing to fear and she is safe to explore the uniqueness of her great aunt again before too long. If your face says 'Oh, no! My poor baby is upset! This is too terrible for me to bear. Come to me, poor child, and be protected from this terrible world!', don't be too surprised if your baby grows up to be terrified of her own shadow, let alone poor Great Aunt Vera.

Protection from bugs

Your baby heads off across the floor. You swept and mopped it just this morning and then, just to be sure, you swept it again. You have put some interesting toys on the carpet to fascinate and delight. And now you watch, shocked, as your child crawls straight past all the gaudy playthings and heads for the tiniest lump of fluff that somehow has missed your careful attempts at annihilation. Before you can reach her she has clamped her lips shut, chewed it around like dusty chewing gum and sent it packing down her throat. A quick cough brings it momentarily back up for another chew before it heads back down, never to be seen again.

Unless you decide to sterilise and seal every centimetre of your house, your baby is going to get a fair amount of filth into her mouth over the next couple of years. She will try out bits of old food that have got lost, way out of your reach under the sofa, and, as soon as she makes it into the garden, she will excite her tastebuds with everything from grass to snails – you will know she has a mouth full of snails by the sound of castanets emanating from behind her dinky teeth! I speak as one who knows.

Her need to 'touch base' ensures that you are never more than a moment away and will be able to stop too much damage: your inbuilt mum-alarm, switched on with the birth of your placenta, sounds more loudly and frequently the further your baby travels. However, she will still 'eat a peck of dirt' and you will panic.

Remember that, from her fourth month, her immune system works nicely, testing itself out on the various neighbourhood bugs and making antibodies to obliterate them. So your little mover's shiny new system will do a pretty good job of protecting her; but there is another weapon in her armoury. Your milk. Just at the time when your baby starts to put all manner of unmentionables in her mouth, the protective antibodies in your human milk rise back up to the level they were at in your colostrum. You remember how everyone told you to make sure that, if nothing else, you should ensure your baby had your first milk to help protect her from bugs? Well, here is evolution at work again. Your baby crawls off a short way, explores the microbiology of her domain and then scuttles back to you, and, if you are still suckling, pulls up your T-shirt and has a quick gulp of antibody-rich milk before heading back to the cat fur in the laundry basket that just must be looked at.

Not many babies completely self-wean off the breast before they crawl. Even if they only want a bedtime snuzzle, they recharge their bug-busting capacity with a warm slosh of your milk.

So keep your house normally clean, wash your baby's hands before mealtimes if she has been mud-wrestling, keep a careful eye on her at all times and then stop worrying. Life is too short to sterilise all the carpets and, even if you did, your crawling kamikaze pilot will only head for the kitchen tiles that have not yet been mopped.

Baby-proofing the house

Your baby is a human and, as such, is hardwired to explore her environment. Your house, unless you already have a child, is probably full of lurking dangers for crawling and toddling babies: stairs, table corners, stone steps, knives ...

It is tricky to get the balance between ensuring that your baby is free to explore relatively unencumbered and overprotecting her to the point that she becomes scared of her own shadow. Parents take different approaches to baby-proofing, and you do need to think about your house and make a decision about how you handle safety in the home.

No baby-proofing

Some parents don't alter their house at all, and decide that their child must simply learn what to touch and what not to touch.

Pros

Parents can keep their things around them and not spend a small fortune on child locks, stair gates and anti-slam devices.

Cons

The child must be watched all the time and be kindly removed over and over again from the fascinating cable attached to the reading lamp. Many parents quickly become frustrated that their child does not understand 'No!' But if you choose not to baby-proof, you will need to repeat this endlessly repetitive process for every item you wish her to ignore. If you think that you can cut it without becoming angry with your young explorer, forget about anything other than monitoring your child closely for 12 hours a day and crack on.

Maximum baby-proofing

Some parents box away anything precious, install stair gates in numerous places and put locks on every cupboard. The child then has freedom to roam everywhere without having to be continually monitored at an arm's length.

Pros

The crawler gets a lot of freedom, and so do you.

Cons

The cost of all the baby-proofing paraphernalia. Parents can get a false sense of security that their little one is safe everywhere. The baby can get frustrated by her boundaries – getting bored with the sitting room but not being able to get past the gate into the hall, or rattling a drawer but not being able to see inside.

If you can afford all the protective gadgets and want to use this approach, manage your child's frustration by ensuring that she has plenty of opportunities to explore around the house with you and also to learn about stairs and shutting doors when you are present.

Do not assume, because you think you've thought of everything, that you haven't forgotten something. Little ones see the world from a different angle, so even though your house is a showroom of child safety, you must still keep a careful eye on her.

The middle ground

Some parents hide or box what they really can't bear to lose, put a stair gate up at the top and bottom of the stairs and lock away sharp things, medicines and cleaning products.

Pros

The child has plenty of freedom to explore an interesting environment and parents do not have to watch as much as if there were no child-proofing.

Cons

The need to accept that unlocked cupboards will be raided and parents need to keep their wits about them more than they expect. If you choose this middle approach, try to create some 'free' cupboards with wooden spoons, pots and pans and rattly (non-glass) jars. Then your baby can manage her frustration at being locked out of one cupboard by getting right into another.

I chose not to install stair gates and had to accept that, until my boys were reliable at coming down stairs on their tummies, feet first every single time, I had to be right there, talking them through it. I quite liked doing this, so it was fine. I am, however, utterly neurotic about doors and so insisted on anti-slam devices on every door in the house. The hatred I developed of the ka-thunk, ka-thunk noise they made every time they were activated was overridden by my relief that my sweet, rumbustious boys would get through their early years with 10 digits apiece!

Many other parents will have different worries, priorities and available time to watch and teach. Think ahead, decide on what approach best suits your house, know where your child is at all times and be ready to deal with the unexpected.

Congruency

Congruency means that everything matches: our voice, our tone, our facial expressions, our body position. Being congruent is at the very heart of discipline and conversation. Lack of it leads to anxiety and misunderstanding. You are going to need to be expert at congruency in order to raise a happy, self-disciplined child so get into practice now!

Most conscientious parents want to breed a relationship where negotiation and reasoning are encouraged and their child understands the reason for any particular rule. They do not want to be the 'shouty parent'. When a child transgresses, they adopt a gentle, pleasant voice: 'Sarah, please leave the cat alone. She doesn't like it. Sarah, Mummy has said stop upsetting the cat. Sarah, Mummy is getting a bit cross now: I have told you that puss doesn't like having her fur pulled. It hurts her and she might scratch you. Sarah, are you listening?' And so on. Eventually, just before the cat takes a chunk out of Sarah's tuggy hand, her mum screams, '*Noooo!*' Sarah jumps through the roof in surprise, pulls back her hand and then looks at her mum with utter shock. The cat has run off, the hand is saved, mum's nerves are rattled.

Your baby watches your face all the time. She loves your voice and your smiles. She mirrors your expressions and responds to what you say with gurgles and coos. You think she understands your words. But she doesn't.

Imagine you have suddenly found yourself in a foreign country and can't speak the language. You sit on a bus and listen and watch. You can tell, can't you, that the elderly couple is recounting a bit of gossip even though you don't understand a word. They speak in a hush, eyes wide, mouths in a mischievous grin ...

Another couple, two young teens, are arguing loudly, hands waving, brows furrowed. But you know they are having a friendly row about football by their closeness to each other, their occasional miming of a header and a grunt here and there of grudging agreement.

Had you only heard the words, you might have been confused. That elderly couple says, 'The mum was out when I went around and I could hear a lot of noise upstairs. I wondered what was going on but didn't dare go up to see!' Now maybe the story is about a disturbed burglary, or a wild animal that had escaped and was rampaging around the house, or a storm breaking a window. Who knows? Put the faces and tone in and suddenly you understand that this is a bit of much-enjoyed salacious gossip and you want to know who was doing what and with whom!

Those teens? The words are: 'You idiot! How could you even think that? You're utterly wrong. That should never have been allowed!' Crikey. Someone is going to be in tears any minute. Something terrible has happened and someone is in big trouble. Get the whole picture and you feel quite calm and happy to let this argument continue.

Your baby cannot understand the words, so she is an expert in all the other stuff. And so, actually, are you. You think your first language is English. But it isn't. It is non-verbal language. And, if there is a mismatch between the two, you will always rely on your primary language to get the right story. This is the basis of misunderstandings. When your friend says, 'Nice dress, Sue!' but her tone is sarcastic and her head is to one side, her eyebrows cocked, you retort, 'That's not very kind!' No matter how much your friend insists that she wasn't being sarcastic, you just know she was and your hurt feelings will linger. Your partner says, 'Any more of that nonsense and you're sleeping in the shed tonight', the quirky smile and the wink tell you that this is a joke and you can relax.

Back to the cat ...

If the tone mum uses sounds the same as 'Sarah, I'm thinking of painting the front room purple. Purple is a lovely vibrant colour. What d'you think, Sarah?' you can see why her daughter might carry on taking handfuls of fur out of the poor beleaguered cat. As soon as mum becomes congruent, shows her genuine internal alarm in her tone and her face, Sarah stops immediately.

So, if you are worried about your child going near a cable, sound and look worried. If you don't like to see a cat teased, make that clear as you gently remove your child from the animal.

Likewise, if you want your baby to feel okay about going down for a nap, when you lean over her to say, 'Sleep tight, sweetie. See you later', make sure your tone and face say, 'You are completely safe; you are okay to be alone; I know you can settle and sleep happily.' If your face leaks like crazy – 'Oh heck, I know she's going to cry and I can't bear it; maybe it's mean of me to expect her to nap; maybe she's scared of the dark; I'm scared of the dark' – expect your baby to panic before you reach the door.

Be congruent. It saves you hours every day and builds confidence and trust.

Emotional literacy

Babies and children have a multitude of emotions to learn to read at the same time as trying to decipher their own. If all they hear is a monotone of pleasant burblings, they cannot know what you are trying to communicate and can struggle to name their own feelings.

They might even become very fearful of their own frustration and anger; after all, 'If this big feeling I have is one that my parents never show, I must be the only person in the world with it and it must be a terrible thing.'

Sometimes we try to show only our good feelings; 'I'm fine. Don't worry about me,' said with a broad smile when we have just had a paper cut. Sometimes we try to cheer a baby away from difficult feelings: 'You're fine! The dog won't hurt you. He's just playing. No need to cry.' By negating our own feelings and brushing over those of our child, we can stop them understanding our emotions and trusting their own.

Try to name your feelings, congruently, at the same time as those you see on your child's face and you will help your child build emotional literacy that will stand her in good stead in all her relationships.

Exclaiming 'Ouch! I've given myself a paper cut! That *really* hurts!' with a tone of voice that matches your pain shows a child that we all experience hurt, even from supposedly tiny things; that we survive; that sucking a paper cut helps to soothe; and that people with even little paper cuts need sympathy.

Saying 'Goodness, that dog has a big bark! You look scared and surprised. Barks can make us jumpy!' while showing in your tone of voice and facial expression that you understand her fear, that you are a bit scared too, that you will stay with her while her fear subsides and then you can both stroke the dog helps her accept that fear is normal and it passes.

Helping language skills

Children develop language slowly and with a lot of repetition. It is charming to listen to much of the time and pretty frustrating at others. In order to really fly with language, babies need exposure to lots of it.

If you chatter away all day, giving a running commentary as you go – 'I'll pop the laundry in this basket and then I'm going to phone the garage to see if my car is ready ...' – bit by bit your child will build up a varied and appropriate vocabulary.

As your child gets a bit older, she may repeat things you say:

Mum: It's a lovely day.

Child: Lovely day.

Mum: Mmm.

Child: Lovely day!

Mum: Yes. Lovely day!

Child: Lovely day!!

Mum takes large glug of extra-caffeinated coffee and sighs.

Your child needs to be given more:

Mum: It's a lovely day.

Child: Lovely day.

Mum: Yes. The sun is shining.

Child: Shining!

Mum: The sky is blue.

Child: Sky blue!

Now you have the beginnings of a conversation.

If you like having the radio on, try talk radio rather than mostly music. Tell your baby what she is doing: 'You have hidden your face under your bib! Is this peep-o? Oh, you've popped out again with a smiley face!' It's tempting to think that you must bring your language down to the one or two words that she has so that she can understand. But she needs lots and lots of words. Bit by bit she will make sense of it all and learn to speak confidently and fluently.

Save the short sentences for when you need to make a rule understood: 'No poking puss!' Congruently.

Some parents use 'baby words' such as moo-cow and choo-choo train. As sweet as this may seem, it seems more sensible to say, 'See the cow. It says moo!' to save your little one having to learn the name for things twice.

Sign language

The latest fashion is for baby-signing. The assumption is that babies will be less frustrated when they are learning to talk if they can have signs to use too for when their words are unclear. I can see the sense in this. However, don't feel that you need to spend your hard-earned cash on classes. Or that, if your child is the only one who doesn't learn to sign, she will be behind her peers.

We all use signs. Think about how you say, 'D'you fancy a cuppa?', bringing an imaginary cup to your lips at the same time. Or, 'Call me!' while holding a non-existent phone to your ear.

This is how humans communicate. Words have always been just a part of the whole conversation. Babies have always learned to talk without their parents bankrupting themselves and having to learn a whole heap of signs that are useless the first time their baby spends an afternoon at non-signing grandma's.

> In short, if you have the cash to spend, fancy some adult company and want to learn something you can share with your baby, sign up to sign. Otherwise, chat merrily away to your little one, sign in the normal, human way and spend any saved pennies on a shared treat.

Gendered language

Boys will be boys and girls are sugar and spice, apparently. Numerous studies have shown that, once we have been told what gender a baby is, we alter the tone of our voice and our choice of words accordingly.

I saw this at first hand with my first son. Sitting in his pram as I pushed him around town one day, his blond curls falling around his round face and sky-blue eyes, a woman stopped me. In a soft, high voice she said, 'What a beautiful baby! Aren't you sweet. Are you shopping with your mummy? Aren't you a good girl! What's her name?'

'Ted.'

'Short for Edwina?'

'Short for Edward!'

Oops! Apologies ensued and then, with a voice an octave lower and quite firm, she turned back to the pram: 'Oh yes! Of course! I can see now, you are a sturdy little fellow. You'll be out kicking that football soon!'

You may think this doesn't happen any more, but it does. All the time. Stickers in the backs of cars declare that on board is a 'Cheeky Little Monkey' (for those of the male variety) or 'Daddy's Little Princess' (for those of a female type). I regularly hear girl babies described as 'bossy' before their first birthday while similar boys are often described as 'knowing their own mind'. An emotional girl can be dubbed a 'drama queen' while her equally lachrymose brother is a 'crybaby' or 'mummy's boy'. A girl who likes the colour pink is a 'girly girl', no matter how many tree-climbing scabs she has on her knees, and a boy who cannot live without blue is a 'rufty tufty boy', irrespective of the number of dolls he has in his bed.

Does this matter? Well, it seems to me that to paint one gender one way and the other a different way reduces choice and flexibility of thinking. No one sees adults in such a one-dimensional way. We accept that men can be sweet and gentle and have a passion for pink ties while still being utterly and completely male. A woman can be bold and direct and spend her free time with her head under a car bonnet while retaining her femininity. We are complex and fascinating and so are our delightful, inventive, grubby, courageous, emotional, annoying, irresistible children.

Our choice of words can limit our children or set them free.

Verbal idiosyncrasies

As babies begin to copy our words they make mistakes. Sometimes they hear a string of words as a single word. Every day, as I took my son downstairs from his nap, I would say, 'We've got to go down for lunch now.' As his words emerged I was puzzled by the word he used for stairs – 'goddagadon!' – until I remembered my regular phrase.

Sometimes a word gets flipped: 'micus' instead of 'music' was a favourite for many years in our house.

Grammar rules get used in the wrong places: 'I show; I showed. I go; I goed. I swim; I swimmed.'

Some toddlers struggle with certain letters: our next-door neighbour's toddler just could not manage her Ks and so her sister was 'Tatie' and, for many weeks one summer, she would be brought over to see the new 'Tittens!'

These idiosyncrasies are ironed out in time and you will really miss them, so don't worry. No need to stifle your child's creative learning by constantly correcting her. Enjoy these charming words while they last and, if you really like them, they may become family words that end up going down the generations.

Partner ponderings

Your child is on the move! Watch your plants, nail down your belongings and prepare for some serious fun.

Horseplay/rough-housing/rough and tumble

As they get moving, children enjoy the feeling of their body in the world even more. Mothers have an instinctive urge to protect their child from even the smallest hurt. This is natural. Most partners feel able to introduce their baby to a bolder way of life – aeroplaning through the air, rolling on the bed for an outrageously giggly tickle-fest, held high in the air before being flipped upside down to see the world in a whole new way. Horseplay.

Horseplay helps babies, toddlers and children to learn trust, to gain body confidence and, some studies say, to develop flexible thinking. Make sure that your baby has not recently filled up on macaroni cheese and carrots before you hold your little one high above your face with her open, laughing mouth or you may get more than you bargained for. But let your child feel her body move in space, catch her mid-crawl for a wrestle, let her lie on top of you on the floor and clamber over you.

Expect your partner to need lots of reassurance. The mum alarm tends to go off, very loudly, at the smallest thing and it is just so difficult to ignore. This isn't her being melodramatic or ridiculous. The anxiety is real. And yet your baby really benefits from the sort of physical play that partners enjoy so much. Some women find it easier to leave the room, some shut their eyes but prefer to stay close. Some mums are actually fine with aeroplane babies.

As your child gets older, you can be guided by her as to how robust your rough and tumble can be. Horseplay is a great way to teach even small children about trust, kindness and the importance of consent.

Language

For many babies, their first joined-up syllables are da-da-da-da. Soon followed by ma-ma-ma-ma. Hence our words for mum and dad and the close variations of these in other languages. It is often said that da-da was given to dads by way of a selfless gift of reassurance that the baby's paternity was in no doubt!

You will have different words and tones from your partner; a different rhythm to your voice. This is a benefit to your child, who needs the experience of different voices in her life. She will learn what differences there are between your happy voice and her mother's happy voice. How to tell when you are tired, which seems a little different from the exhausted sound of her mother. As with your partner, talk to your baby about your feelings and how your day has been. Give her the emotion word to match your face so that she learns to read you. Tell her things that you know she can't possibly understand – she will just love to hear the different hum of your unique vocal cords.

Read her stories from an early age and sing her songs as you bath her. Babble back at her and blow raspberries for her to copy. Wallow in the ridiculous, and embrace nonsense. If both parents shower their baby with a love of language, she will grow up to be eloquent and expressive and delight you both.

Questions and answers
Delayed development

My baby seems to be much later than her friends at walking and talking. When should I worry?

The normal range for walking and talking really is vast and is not associated with IQ. If your child is an early walker, she may talk late, and vice versa. Some children are late walkers and talkers. Some are actually average but all their friends are early and mum worries about her child in comparison. In the UK, health visitors still offer developmental checks at certain stages but if you're worried about your baby's development at any time outside these checks, make an appointment to see your health visitor. It will be reassuring just to voice your concerns and, if there really is a problem, fast intervention is crucial.

Baby language

My partner uses baby talk. I prefer to use adult language. Who is right?

There isn't a right or wrong, but if both parents use baby words, the baby then has to relearn at a later stage (and they do). If it irritates you, ask if this part of their unique relationship can be saved for when you are out of earshot so it doesn't grate on your nerves. Most people soften their tone and language around babies and this is quite natural. Baby talk is an extension of that and, although annoying for some, as long as the baby gets plenty of exposure to the more widely accepted words, all will be well.

Sterilising

Now my child is crawling, do I need to sterilise and clean more?

How dirty is your house? If there is mouldy food on the floor and a cat litter tray in the corner of the living room, you'd better get busy cleaning to prevent your crawler getting sick. If your house is a bit dusty and the carpet tends to gather fluff, this is your child's environment and she will build up immunity, just like you, by daily exposure to normal levels of bugs. It also seems to help babies' immunity to be allowed to stroke pets, so don't fret if your little one plants her face into the puppy's fur on a regular basis. Take sensible precautions around animal poo – dog and cat poo can contain some nasty bugs and worms which can cause infections and lasting eye damage. Worm pets regularly and keep your baby away from the litter tray at all times.

For bottles and teats, carry on as normal, sterilising all bottles used for milk until she is a year old. Other utensils need simply be well cleaned along with the rest of the family's.

Protecting the formula-fed crawler

How can I protect my baby against bugs if I don't give my own milk?

Your baby will get immunity from bugs over time, just like you do. Exposure to bugs stimulates the immune system to make antibodies to fight a future infection. Some infections, however, can be too rough for small babies and children and, for these, there are immunisations. Vaccinations are provided, free, to all babies in the UK and have been tested for many years to ensure their safety. Can they sometimes cause problems? Yes they can, but the problems seen with vaccinations – a temperature, a sore arm, an unhappy baby – are signs that the immune system is working! A healthy immune system spots an invader and responds vigorously. Any injection or medicine can cause an allergy in some people, but this is rare with vaccinations. If your child does have a nasty allergic reaction to a vaccine, your doctor will discuss with you whether or not she should have the next one.

There is no getting away from the fact that the formula-fed baby visits the doctor more often than the breast milk-fed baby in her first year, so it is essential that you continue to take sensible precautions with preparing feeds until your baby is a year old and keep her well clear of people with tummy bugs. The formula-fed baby is far more susceptible to catching these and being really poorly with them. Having said all this, constant cleaning and sterilising of work surfaces and floors is as unnecessary for your baby as it is for the breast milk-fed baby.

Disobedience

I have told my crawling baby repeatedly to come away from the plug sockets but she keeps going back. What should I do?

Either get socket covers or continue to remove your child when she goes to them. It is not enough to tell her. You need to pick her up, say 'No touching sockets' and distract her. It will take a thousand times before she starts to lose interest and this is just normal baby behaviour. She can't be *naughty*. You are much smarter than she is, so use your imagination to turn her attention to something far more interesting than a square of plastic on a wall.

12 Growing up: the end of the first year

Reaching back ...

So here we are. The earth has journeyed once around the sun, the leaves have blossomed, bloomed, faded and fallen and our primitive baby has reached her first birthday and stands, wobbly, under her birthday moon, clutching her mother's hand in her own chubby-fingered grip. From first wail to first step, her parents, knowing no different, have simply protected and nourished while their daughter has led them along, laying out in front of them the astonishing survival tricks that evolution has hardwired into her, and their, DNA.

Challenges and setbacks have been met by a dogged determination to see the next dawn, and mistakes have been an opportunity to learn and adapt.

This family's life is, in many ways, brutal. It will almost certainly be, by our standards, short. But we know that they, their children and their children's children survived. We stand beneath the same moon and stars, gazing up at the inky sky, scattered with patterns we have learned from childhood. In the whisper of the wind we can, if we try, hear their voices. Our ancestors can reach out to us across time and hold our hand as we tread tentatively into this new world of parenting: 'Trust yourselves; trust your child; you will survive.'

Returning to the world of work

With only about one in 10 UK mothers staying at home full time to bring up their children, most mums will face the challenge of finding suitable alternative childcare before their child starts full-time school. This is a daunting prospect for most parents and is not made any easier by sometimes having to compromise, due to financial constraints, on the type of childcare you'd ideally choose.

These pulls on a mother have always been there. It is tempting to think that our primitive ancestors were able to devote themselves solely to their children for many years, but there is interesting evidence that women sometimes weaned their babies off the breast rather early in order to return to work in the field when times were hard. Furthermore, it seems as if there was a broadly egalitarian approach to childcare, with men taking an equal, active role. Parenting may have been a more communal affair. Older babies may have been looked after by older siblings or a young adult in a kindergarten-type set-up.

In more recent times, our own grandmothers may have shared childcare with other women at times and many women would have loved the opportunity to hand over their children for a day or two so that they could go and re-enter the world of grown-ups!

If you have made a decision to stay at home full time and be with your children, be sure to let people know that you 'work full time in the home' rather than describing yourself as 'not working any more'. Your work may not be financially recognised by the state, but you are working hard, long hours nonetheless.

If you have planned to go back to some form of paid work, there is plenty to think about in terms of childcare. Aside from affordability, you will need to think about what sort of environment you want for your child. As tempting as it is to think that your older baby or young child will enjoy the company of 15 other children, being in a group of relative strangers you have not chosen for yourself, at a time in life when emotions run pretty close to the surface, can be very stressful and tiring.

Think first about your partner. Is there any flexibility in your work schedules and income needs that can enable you to share childcare?

More and more companies encourage working from home and it may prove more economical to pay someone to provide support in the home while you or your partner work in the home office. Then you would be 'there' without needing to drive your child somewhere else for care, with all the inevitable pressures that can bring. Can you both drop to part-time work? Can one of you work a couple of nights a week and bring in the same income as if you worked four days? Can either of you change roles within the workplace to give you greater flexibility?

As parents demand greater flexibility and creativity in the workplace, change gradually appears. Sometimes the impossible becomes, actually, quite possible.

If both jobs must remain unchanged and neither of you can be at home, you either need to employ a nanny or your child must be cared for outside the home.

If family can offer childcare, consider it carefully: they will be able to offer a home-from-home environment with people who deeply love your child. Grandparents have traditionally always helped with childcare, not so much in the formalised way as happens when a mum returns to work but, nonetheless, children have historically always enjoyed close relationships with grandparents. With the advent of more people moving to look for work, children can miss out on the unique relationship that an 'almost but not quite parent' can offer. So if the opportunity arises to create this for your child, consider grabbing it with both hands.

If this isn't possible, look into local childminders. They will also be able to offer a home environment, often with a mixture of ages, which gives a family feel alongside a natural routine to the day.

If neither of these two options is available, consider local nurseries. You are not trying to hothouse your child to create a genius: you simply want somewhere for your child to spend his days when you are at work that will provide as home-like an atmosphere as possible. He needs small groups of children of different ages, with a very high adult-to-child ratio and lots of opportunities to enjoy normal home stuff like going shopping, cooking, hanging out in the garden and throwing the occasional (or not so occasional) tantrum, safe in the knowledge that he is among people who will treat him with warmth and kindness and give him a big cuddle when the red mist has faded. He does not need lots of expensive toys; he just needs someone around to let him be in the world as he is.

When the day comes to drop him off at childcare, try to show in your face, body language and tone of voice that you are not worried about leaving him, that you are completely confident that he will be fine and that you look forward to hearing his news at the end of the day. If he cries, seeing panic in your face will simply confirm his worst fears. Seeing calm and confidence reflected back will reassure him that he is safe.

There is a fair chance that the routine outside your home will be different from the one he has been used to. There is often a worry that this might confuse or disorient a young child. But humans are renowned for their great adaptability and flexibility. Your child will simply learn that different routines and rules apply in different settings. After all, once he starts school, the set-up will also be very different from his home life. So don't change your home routine to match that of your childcare, or demand that the carers stick to your child's home routine. Relax and let your child have the experience of difference and change. Let him discover the delight that can come from seeing things from another angle, and the weirdness that we all feel when we find out that not everyone in the world lives in the same way as us.

Getting used to a bottle

It is an almost universal belief that a baby must be 'used to' a bottle by the time he goes into day care so that his carers can feed him milk. Many breastfeeding women spend their last few months at home with their baby fretting so much about trying to convince him to take a bottle that it spoils their suckling times. When I ask parents why they believe their child must have milk, or any other fluid for that matter, from a bottle, they are generally at a loss for words. For your baby, your boob never has been about getting milk. It has been his 'sucky thing' that just happens to give a warm drink too, if he chooses. Half the time, your little one is not actually bothering to take milk but is loving the snuggles and company, passing the time of day before setting off again to hunt for adventure. A bottle of milk isn't the same thing at all, so you should not expect him to take it when it is offered.

However, when your baby is thirsty, truly thirsty, he will take fluids from whatever you choose to use and most breastfed babies like a spouted beaker. Some like an open-topped feeding cup, some a regular cup – my youngest preferred a cup with a straw! Few get what the fuss is about with a bottle. Likewise, you cannot expect your baby to understand why he should drink the cold, thick milk of another mammal. The sweet, thin, coconut milk-like flavour of human milk is completely different from cow's milk or formula milk. He will probably prefer plain water.

It is very common for the breastfed baby to suckle before his mum leaves for work in the morning and then refuse all drinks (except, maybe, a little water with food) and then thoroughly enjoy a prolonged coming-home suckle on the sofa at the end of the day. Many mums find this time is perfect for winding down with their feet up, letting the endorphins that come with suckling a child flow through them like warm syrup.

So give yourself a break in the lead-up to your return to work and, on the big day itself, hand your tiddler over with a receptacle of fluid and leave it up to your baby and his carer to sort things out. You'll have enough to be getting on with, dealing with your own tears!

Giving up milk

The baby who is used only to his mum's milk will, in all likelihood, wean onto solid foods and eventually stop suckling, never to drink milk again. That is completely normal, despite what you are led to believe by healthcare professionals.

The boob-suckled baby may well enjoy full cream doorstep milk on cereal, as well as cheese, yoghurt and butter (or non-dairy equivalents). But a drink of milk? Unlikely and unnecessary. A varied diet plus an appropriate multivitamin should be enough to stop you fretting about the lack of milk. So try to relax.

If your baby is used to having formula milk, he can start having doorstep milk as a drink from his first birthday and you can happily stop buying formula. Milk is no more necessary in his diet than in that of his breastfed friends, so if he doesn't like it, don't give it. Nor does he need to keep having his drinks from a bottle: with all the problems associated with prolonged exposure to milk from a bottle, it is advised that you switch to a beaker by the first birthday. In any case, never give a bottle of milk for a baby to have in his cot, as the constant suckling overnight can cause damage to his teeth.

Transitional objects

The blanket, the teddy, the muslin cloth, the dummy ... a transitional object belongs solely to the child and is (or should be) under his control. The things that disgust you about it – its filthy look, its frayed tattiness, its rancid smell – are the very things that make it special to its owner.

If you fear that it might get lost at nursery or on holiday, it is better to keep it at home and provide a different snuggler for away days. Coming home from school, rushing upstairs to find my blanket, climbing into 'my' chair and settling down to zone out completely in front of the TV is a remembered pleasure that is almost impossible to explain to anyone who has not had a transitional object.

Whatever your child chooses as his transitional object, treat it with deep respect, wash it rarely and *never* throw it away! Whether or not to ditch the dummy, to chuck the cuddly or bin the blanket should be completely up to its owner.

Ditching the dummy

Dummy use goes in and out of fashion and, thanks partly to evidence linking night-time dummy use in the bottle-fed baby to a decrease in SIDS, dummies are currently popular. They provide comfort when parents are not close to hand and can ease a baby from wide awake but tired mode into the happy land of nod. When it comes to arguments about thumb – and dummy – sucking, many parents feel that a dummy is better: you can wash it, you can take it away and, because it is soft, it won't distort teeth. However, many healthcare professionals see things rather differently: thumbs naturally come out of the mouth for play and crawling, a thumb is less likely to cause nasal speech, a thumb is less likely to cause middle ear infections. The evidence for some of these claims is a little uncertain but cannot be ruled out completely.

It is always sensible, if your baby has a dummy rather than a thumb as his main comforter, to start to remove it from his mouth when he is occupied with toys or is on the move (as would happen naturally with a thumb). Babies who are busy rarely mind at all: if it is out of sight it is out of mind and this will enable the normal babbling that accompanies exploration to take place unimpeded.

Treat the dummy like any other transitional object – save it for dozy, sleepy and stressful times rather than something to be hung onto 24/7. You might find that your baby transitions to his thumb or a snuggly blanket for naps and bedtime, but do give the dummy at these times if he wants it – it is his special comforter and, as with thumb-sucking, if its use is limited to appropriate times and places, it can be enjoyed until he naturally gives it up by himself.

The emergence of independence and tantrums

With movement comes independence and with independence come challenges for you all.

As your child gets closer to his first birthday you will start to see the emergence of will and, inevitably, therefore, the first hints of tantrums. Just like all emotional blowouts at all ages, tantrums generally occur when a child feels emotionally overwhelmed. This tends to occur in the younger child when his independence or will is frustrated. Tiredness, hunger and poorliness can increase the likeliness of occurrence but, even when your child is well rested and well fed, there are still many times in an average day when you have to take control away from him and his frustration overflows into a volcanic eruption.

Although we cannot get rid of all tantrums – they are, after all, a developmental stage that serves a purpose – we can greatly reduce their number with smart parenting.

Start by ensuring your child is as well rested and as regularly fed as possible. Then really try to see the world through his eyes. Everything he wants to see and touch is so high up, everything he wants to do is so fiddly and awkward, everything he wants to eat is measured or withheld.

Be bold and creative and, as your child reaches his first birthday, start to open up opportunities for him to have independence and you will hugely cut down on tantrum triggers.

- Continue to let your child be in control of his portion sizes by letting him take foods from shared bowls to put on his own plate.
- Keep toys in open baskets at his level.
- Let him wear easy pull-on shoes or wellington boots rather than buckles or lace-ups.
- If he refuses his coat in zero temperatures, simply pop it in your backpack as you head out for that winter walk so he can have it when the reality of the weather hits home.
- Patiently let him haul himself upstairs rather than carrying him and accept that the 20 minutes of bath time have been lost today.

No matter how many ideas you come up with, you will sometimes have to frustrate his will and he will be unable to cope.

Tantrums are just horrid. Coping with one is exhausting for you as well as for him, so try these strategies:

- Wherever possible, if you have time, distract him. An aeroplane in the sky, looking for squirrels in the garden, a phone call to Nanna. It really doesn't matter. There is no benefit in letting a tantrum take off just to let him experience it: there will, trust me, be plenty of other opportunities!
- If you cannot distract him and he is going to boil over, pop him somewhere safe (little ones are quite safe on the floor or in a cot) so that he cannot hurt himself. Now calmly read a book or watch TV while being nearby. The message you are trying to give is 'You're fine, sweetie. I know you won't come to harm. I'm so confident that you will survive this that I am going to read my book.'

- If you are in a shop or somewhere public, quickly pick him up and get somewhere you can feel calm and unwatched. Then put him safely by you on the ground, sit close and read or just talk gently to him: 'It's okay. You're safe. This will go.' If having you talk just inflames him even more, then be quiet.
- If you cannot put him anywhere safe and he might hurt himself or you, hold him on your lap. Turn him away from you so that he can't headbutt you, hold his arms in a cuddle and stay completely calm until the storm subsides. Then cuddle some more while you reassure him that he is quite safe.

Once a tantrum has run its course, carry on exactly as before it struck. A tantrum should change nothing. If there is still time to go and feed the ducks, do it; if you said 'No' to an ice cream, it is still 'No'. Tantrums are powerful enough as they are; do not imbue them with any more power.

Don't talk about your child's tantrum with anyone while in his earshot – he will feel confused and embarrassed enough about his emotional outburst without having it replayed for the judgement of others.

As your child moves into his second year and then into his third year, he may well become even more emotional. Try to stay calm – your child is not turning into a monster; he is simply going through a difficult developmental stage that requires him to strive for independence of thought and deed. It is confusing and scary for him (a bit like adolescence) and he needs you to provide as much stability and support as you can possibly muster. This is a big ask from you and your partner and sometimes you will find it impossible to remain level-headed. Be kind to yourself and accept that a bad day is just a bad day.

If you are having a really awful day, either head out to visit a very good friend who understands that your tantrumming child does not define you, or clear your diary and stay at home. As tempting as it is to fill the days with wall-to-wall activities rather than face being stuck at home with an ill-tempered tot, toddlers often get too tired and over-stimulated, and the effort of endless socialising with other over-tired, over-stimulated toddlers really is the last straw and a meltdown is almost inevitable. Toddlers often really benefit from some gentle at-home time spent idly knocking around in the garden or helping to hoover the stairs.

While you might think that the goal in dealing with this stage is that your child stops throwing tantrums, this isn't quite what pans out. Think about it: we all have emotional blowouts at times. We get overwhelmed and can't see the wood for the trees; we get so tired and stressed that we can't think straight; we can't make ourselves understood and the frustration builds up and overflows.

The difference between our toddler and us is that we have some coping strategies. For a starter, we know that this emotional tornado will eventually dissipate and we will still be standing; we may feel it coming on and take ourselves off to avoid a public outburst; we might sense crashing blood sugar and grab some carbs to help us calm down; we can apologise and explain afterwards and regain a little composure. Put simply, we grow up.

Children whose parents don't reward or punish tantrums, but simply support their child with firm boundaries and plenty of emotional warmth, give them the space and time to discover their own strategies for handling those very human moments when the red mist descends and reason flies out of the window.

Discipline

We all want a well-disciplined child. Quite what we mean by well-disciplined is, of course, a matter for debate. There are, however, some things to bear in mind that can help steer your parenting no matter what you think defines a well-behaved child.

First, the word itself is a clue – discipline. Far from being about a system of rewards and punishments designed to create compliance with a set of rules, discipline is about seeing our child as our disciple and our role is showing him how to exist well enough in the world. We are polite, nice to know and work thoughtfully with other people, not to gain a reward or to avoid a punishment but because that is simply the way that the world works best.

The fashion for naughty steps and time out does not teach the child anything except how to sit and seethe until the time is up. Asking a toddler to sit on a naughty step really is no different from putting them to stand in a corner. It is a way of venting our spleen and giving our child an experience of shame. It does not help learning.

Likewise, rewarding good behaviour says: 'My word, I did *not* expect that! How amazing!' We want to expect good behaviour from our child. It may take a lot of time to get to the point when our child always hangs up his coat, but we do expect him to get there. Reward something you expect to happen and you should not plan on the behaviour being repeated over and over again.

Your child can only know what you expect from him if you tell him: 'Muddy shoes go by the back door.' If your child stamps mud all over your clean carpet, it makes sense to him to say: 'You have walked over the carpet with muddy shoes. That is a horrid mess to clean up and makes me feel pretty grumpy! Muddy shoes go by the back door.' And then walk him through the process of taking his shoes off, putting them by the back door and, finally, cleaning up the carpet together rather than doing it all for him while he sits on the naughty step.

This approach of describing the problem (muddy shoes on a carpet), saying how it makes you feel (grumpy because of the mess), stating what the rule is (muddy shoes live by the back door) and how to sort things out (put the shoes by the back door and clean the carpet) shows your child kindly and realistically how the world works and supports him to learn how to put things right. No long-winded explanations or threats – just quickly getting things back on track so that everyone can move on. You can use this simple step-wise approach in all manner of situations. Just be sure that the consequence makes sense of the problem: a thrown plate of food needs to be cleaned up; a refusal to get ready for bed eats into story time; a bitten hand gets a shocked yell from mum and needs a proper sorry hug ...

Never hit, smack, shake or hurt your child in any way at all. If your child hurts you, do not return the hurt but say, firmly: 'You hit me! That hurt and upset me. We do *not* hurt people. Hurts need a hug and a kiss.'

Being congruent

Congruent is the word we use for when everything matches up (see page 205). When you find that, despite your very best efforts, your little one does not do as you have asked, check that you are being congruent. If, when your child continues to jump on the sofa despite your requests – 'Stop jumping on the sofa ... I'm getting angry now ... please get off the sofa ... I'm going to count to 10 ...' – there is a fair chance that your face or, more likely, your tone of voice does not match your feelings.

If you believe he *should* come off the sofa but are actually thinking 'I remember jumping on the sofa. Such fun. I'm being mean. I should be more relaxed but I really don't want a messy sofa. But he does look funny ...', expect your child to grin at you and carry on.

If you are annoyed that your child is jumping on the sofa, save yourself a whole lot of time and your child from the frustration of not getting a clear message and tell him straight: 'Hey! You're jumping on the sofa. Stop now and get off!' Deliver this with exactly the right emotion – if you are annoyed, be annoyed; if you are really cross, make that clear with your tone and expression. If you are dealing with a child under one, you will need to say this as you pick him up and pop him on the floor. When he is off the sofa, you are done. No nagging, no punishments, no seething. You have made yourself clear and the sofa is now free from jumping tots.

Congruence in parenting will save you hours. Hours are valuable. Be congruent.

Partner ponderings

Bringing up children is really very hard work. Sure, it is fun and interesting, joyous and exhilarating. But it is also relentless, dispiriting and exhausting. You and your partner will really need to pull together.

Many parents make the mistake of thinking that pulling together means being the same, but this is simply not true. From your child's point of view, having different people in his life with different styles and different buttons to press helps teach him valuable life lessons such as not assuming that all people need the same approach: some people are a pushover when it comes to getting a treat and some require a little more work! He will learn that if he is difficult with one parent he may get a degree of leniency, but he had better not try the same trick with another parent. That one parent likes to snuggle with him watching TV under a sofablanket with some biscuits while the other prefers a little more personal space.

The important thing is that you back each other up to provide a united front and can agree on simple house rules. No hurting people should be at the top of everyone's house rules. But then think of the things that will bring harmony in your home. For example: no shoes worn in the house, sit down to eat, and so on.

Consider making a regular job list.

Mothers who work outside the home still, so studies tell us, end up doing far more of the childcare and housework. She may ask you for help – as if the housework is actually her responsibility and she is just delegating some of it to you. You kindly do as asked and then, when you do not do the job again tomorrow (because she has not asked you again), tempers fly. From your perspective, of course you'd help – she only has to ask!

Once it is acknowledged that, despite the obvious changes to household dynamics that a baby brings, housework and childcare are a joint issue, you can set about ensuring that each of you gets some time off by negotiating how the everyday household and childcare jobs can be shared out. This doesn't necessarily mean that each of you does the same number of jobs. After all, one of you may be at home for more hours of the week than the other. But talk about it. Where are the pinch points? What job does one find really hard but the other less so?

Be flexible and creative and try hard to see things through the other's eyes. I know this sounds obvious, but couples get worn down. Really tired. Add into this a degree of frustration with an active, emotionally immature toddler and even the most rational of couples flares up.

Try to schedule regular time to reconnect and discuss how you can support one another. Avoid blame and recriminations or trying to prove that your way is the best way. Accept and value your different styles as important for helping your child's developing relationship with the wider world.

You are on a journey together, with a pretty blurry map and a destination that is, as yet, uncertain. It is difficult and scary, so be kind to one another.

Most babies, as they reach their first birthday, will settle for enough hours before midnight to make getting a babysitter worthwhile occasionally. Many mothers find the idea of leaving their baby with anyone else, even for a couple of hours, really hard. But relationships need space to flourish and creating time for yourselves is vital. Your child gets wonderful care and attention for many, many hours every week. A regular night off can recharge batteries before they become so flat that they are incapable of even the tiniest spark. Find someone you both really trust and then trust that person. Go. Out. Somewhere. The first time we got a babysitter in, we skipped the 10 minutes to our local pub like naughty teenagers. Once there, we managed just half a pint each before feeling so edgy that we ran back home again. Poor babysitter. Not a lucrative night for her!

Practice makes perfect, so keep booking that sitter.

And so to the end?

Bake a cake, festoon it with candles, invite everyone round to watch the ceremony and then celebrate.

Stand and marvel. Look at your highly evolved child. How utterly amazing is he? Over the last 12 months you have seen millions of years of the human struggle for survival play out, day by day, in your very own home.

From those first shuddering reflexes that sent his hands waving and mouth searching, causing his mother to instinctively draw him into her arms, to those Bambi totters, legs splayed and wobbly, face beaming widely as he took his first steps into the world we share.

We humans, hand in hand, surviving.

If we can follow our baby's instinctive cues, adapting to him in his early unadaptable months and then gently supporting him as he grows towards independence and flexibility, we will find that we can parent more confidently. If we can continue to watch and wonder rather than agonise and wrestle, trying in vain to mould this baby into someone who, if we succeeded, we would no longer love and recognise, we will free ourselves to revel in this fascinating and unique opportunity to watch evolution unfold before our very eyes.

Useful resources

Birth and early days

www.aims.org.uk: Association for Improvements in the Maternity Services.

www.birthchoiceuk.com: Explains your place of birth options and gives information to help you make the choices.

www.birthrights.org.uk: Promotes dignity and human rights in childbirth.

www.birthtraumaassociation.org.uk: Provides support following a traumatic birth.

www.caesarean.org.uk: Research-based information and support on all aspects of Caesareans and vaginal birth following Caesarean section.

doula.org.uk: The non-profit association of doulas in the UK.

www.henleybirthcare.com: Freelance specialist midwife and doula services promoting and supporting Rachel's approach to parenting.

www.homebirth.org.uk: Research-based information and support on all aspects of home birth.

www.mind.org.uk: Support and information for those suffering from perinatal depression (search 'perinatal depression').

www.moneyadviceservice.org.uk: Free and impartial financial advice (search 'benefits in pregnancy').

www.multiplebirths.org.uk: Support and information for parents with twins or multiple births.

www.nhs.uk: Comprehensive and evidence-based information on pregnancy, birth and beyond (search 'pregnancy' and 'baby').

www.tamba.org.uk: Twins and Multiple Births Association – support and information for parents with twins or multiple births.

www.twinsuk.co.uk: Support and information for parents with twins or multiple births.

www.which.co.uk: Online tool for exploring UK birth options and finding the right place to give birth (search 'birth choice').

New babies

abm.me.uk: Association of Breastfeeding Mothers – support and advice.

www.babycentre.co.uk: Resources for parents.

www.bliss.org.uk: Support for those with sick or premature babies.

www.breastfeedingnetwork.org.uk: National network for supporting mums with breastfeeding. Gives details of local support groups.

www.cafamily.org.uk: Support, advice and information for parents with disabled children.

www.clapa.com: Cleft Lip and Palate Association – support for families with babies affected by clefts.

www.cry-sis.org.uk: Helpline and support for those with a crying baby.

www.facebook.com/HM4HBUK: A Facebook community for connecting women in the UK, who wish to donate or receive human milk, for use where others are struggling to lactate.

www.familylives.org.uk: Provides a helpline number offering help and support 24/7 in all aspects of family life.

www.frg.org.uk: Family Rights Group – support for parents and other family members whose children are involved with or need social care services.

www.gingerbread.org.uk: Help and advice on the issues that matter to lone parents.

www.laleche.org.uk: Support and information for parents of a breastfeeding baby.

www.nationalbreastfeedinghelpline.org.uk: Independent, confidential, mother-centred, non-judgemental breastfeeding support and information.

www.nhs.uk: NHS advice on the safe use of infant formula milk (search 'bottle-feeding advice').

www.tongue-tie.org.uk: Where to find a local practitioner to divide a tongue-tie.

www.uk-sands.org: Stillbirth and Neonatal Death Charity – UK charity providing support for bereaved parents and their families.

www.unicef.org.uk/babyfriendly: Evidence-based information and resources for parents and professionals on infant feeding.

Weaning

www.allergyuk.org: Advice on weaning where there is a family history of allergy (search 'weaning').

www.coeliac.org.uk: Support and advice on weaning babies with a risk of developing coeliac disease (search 'babies').

Sleeping

www.isisonline.org.uk: Infant Sleep Information Source – information for parents and carers.

Language and development

www.afasic.org.uk: Support and information for parents with a child with verbal communication difficulties.

www.autism.org.uk: Support and information for families living with autism.

www.blindchildrenuk.org: Support and resources for families with a visually impaired child.

www.childautism.org.uk: Support, advice and services for children with autism.

dyspraxiafoundation.org.uk: Support for families living with dyspraxia.

www.foundationyears.org.uk: Information and resources for the early years.

www.gov.uk: Where to find your local Sure Start centre (search 'Sure Start').

www.healthvisitors.com: Information and resources for the early years.

www.ndcs.org.uk: National Deaf Children's Society – support for families with a hearing-impaired child.

www.scope.org.uk: Support and advice for those living with disability.

www.talkingpoint.org.uk: Information on children's communication.